The Spitfire Manual

The Spitfire Manual

Edited by Dilip Sarkar
MBE FRHistS

First published 2010

Amberley Publishing Plc
Cirencester Road, Chalford,
Stroud, Gloucestershire, GL6 8PE

www.amberley-books.com

British Library Cataloguing in Publication Data.
A catalogue record for this book is available from the British Library.

ISBN 978-1-84868-436-2

Typesetting and Origination by Amberley Publishing.
Printed in Great Britain.

CONTENTS

INTRODUCTION: SPITFIRE!

Spitfire! The very word is evocative, the perfect description of a fighter aircraft. The shape and sound of the Spitfire is equally perfect, particularly those marques powered by the legendary Rolls-Royce Merlin engine. Look at a Spitfire today and its sleek elliptical shape would not be out of place on a modern designer's computer screen - seventy years after it was actually created at a comparatively simple drawing board. That Supermarine designer Reginald Joseph Mitchell's Spitfire, ever the air show star, should still excite and the deeds of those who went to war in her continue to inspire, can only be a special tribute to everyone connected with this wonderful aircraft.

So what was it about the Spitfire that made it so great? What is it about a vintage aircraft that continues to fascinate us so nearly a century on? What is it about the Merlin's roar that brings a tear to the eye, a lump in the throat? To understand this phenomenon we need to travel back in time, to a desperately dark period in world history.

When the guns fell silent in 1918, the end had supposedly come to the 'Great War to end all wars'. Tragically that utopian scenario was not to be, as in 1933 Adolf Hitler and the Nazis came to power in Germany, bent upon bludgeoning their way to create a new world order dominated by the Fatherland. Although Germany's army and navy were heavily restricted by the terms of the Versailles Peace Treaty in 1919, Hitler set about developing new weapons and re-arming. Indeed, Germany was forbidden to have an air force, so military aircraft were developed under the guise of being civilian craft, and personnel for the new Luftwaffe were secretly trained in Russia. Britain and France, however, had disarmed after 1919, the latter hiding behind the so-called Maginot Line and hoping that Hitler's ambitions focused around no more than righting what many saw as harsh injustices imposed upon Germany by the Allies at Versailles.

In terms of aircraft development between the wars, Britain and France held the belief that 'the bomber will always get through'. There was little or no interest in fighter development. Indeed, in 1921, Marshal of the RAF

Sir Hugh Trenchard said:

> It is not necessary for an air force, in order to defeat the enemy nation, to defeat its armed forces first. Air power can dispense with that immediate step, can press over the enemy navies and armies, and penetrate the air defences and attack direct the centre of production, transportation and communication from which the enemy war effort is maintained. It is on the destruction of the enemy industries and, above all, in the lowering of morale of enemy nationals caused by bombing that the ultimate victory lies... The aeroplane is the most offensive weapon that has ever been invented. It is a shockingly bad weapon for defence.

In fact, Trenchard thought so little of defensive (fighter) aeroplanes that he considered it 'only necessary to have some defence to keep up the morale of your own people'.

The misconception regarding the value of bombing was articulated by no less a statesman than British Prime Minister Stanley Baldwin in 1932:

> I think it is well for the man in the street to realise that there is no power on earth that will save him from being bombed. Whatever people may tell him, the bomber will always get through. The only defence is offence, which means that you have to kill more women and children than the enemy if you want to save yourselves. I just mention that so that people may realise what is waiting for them when the next war comes.

On 1 September 1930, Air Vice-Marshal Hugh Dowding, a veteran Great War fighter pilot, was appointed Air Member for Supply & Research (later Research & Development). 'Stuffy' Dowding did not share the belief that 'the bomber will always get through' or indeed that spending on the bomber force was necessarily the priority. On the contrary, he considered that although the fighter force should not be expanded at the bomber's expense, a powerful bomber force would be useless unless the fighter force was strong enough to ensure that the commander did not lose a decisive battle before the bomber force commander had time to fight one. Trenchard, Dowding believed, had 'forgotten that security of base is an essential prerequisite'. It would prove fortunate indeed for Britain that Dowding held this view and, moreover, was prepared to fight anyone who opposed his efforts to prepare a sound defence for these islands.

At the time of Dowding's appointment the RAF's fighter squadrons remained equipped with biplanes. Constructed largely of wood and fabric, and lightly armed with just two machine-guns, their performance remained comparable to those primitive machines that had fought in the Great War. Any progress in aviation design was in the civilian, not military, sector. In 1912, Jacques Schneider, of the French armaments family, had created the Schneider Trophy, to be awarded to the victor of an international seaplane race. The experience gained by aircraft designers during the course of this competition, which was a matter of fierce national pride, was later put to good use in the creation of modern warplanes. The leading British Schneider Trophy designer was Reginald Joseph Mitchell.

Although Dowding had been against government funding of Mitchell's Supermarine built S.6B 1931 winning entrant, he did appreciate that Mitchell's designs held enormous promise for fighter aircraft. In 1930 the Air Ministry issued the specification for a modern day and night fighter, capable of being flown by the average squadron pilot, to replace the RAF's existing and obsolete biplanes. The requirement was for higher speed and an enclosed cockpit in conjunction with eight-gun armament. It was in line with this specification that the Rolls-Royce engined Hawker and Supermarine fighter projects progressed, leading to Specifications F.36/34 and F.37/34 being drafted around the designs that would respectively become the Hurricane and Spitfire.

The racing seaplanes that Mitchell had designed as Schneider Trophy entrants were monoplanes, sleek and fast looking much like flying bullets. Mitchell had first designed a prototype fighter under the Air Ministry Specification F7/30, but the result was an ugly gull-winged monoplane – very unlike the streamlined S.6B - that he knew was not up to Germany's challenge. Returning to the drawing board, Mitchell created the Spitfire.

In 1933, at the age of thirty-eight, Mitchell had actually been diagnosed with rectal cancer, requiring surgery. After the operation he was told that there was every chance of the cancer returning, and with it the inevitability of an untimely death. Who would have blamed Mitchell if he had retired to spend more time with his wife and son? Thankfully our hero did not; had he done so, there would have been no Spitfire, that iconic and charismatic fighter that contributed so much to final victory.

The Spitfire was a revolutionary design, whereas Sydney Camm's Hawker Hurricane was not. Spitfire production called for new manufacturing skills and techniques, and was a complex process. The fuselage was of three sections, a tubular case for the engine, a monocoque centre section and a detachable tail section. The wing's main spar comprised girders of different lengths, the thickest part being at the wing root where most strength was needed. The wing leading edges were covered in heavy gauge aluminium, the trailing edges in a lighter covering. Such construction provided an unparalleled combination of strength and lightness. The Spitfire was powered by Sir Henry Royce's Merlin engine, Royce having provided engines for Mitchell's Schneider Trophy entrants. Once more it would prove to be a winning combination.

On 5 March 1936, a small group of men gathered at Eastleigh airfield, near the Supermarine works, which was on the banks of the Itchen Estuary at Woolston, near Southampton. The occasion was an event which could be considered one of the most important flights since the Wright brothers flew at Kittyhawk: the first test flight of the prototype

Spitfire, K5054. Vickers' Chief Test Pilot, 'Mutt' Summers, made a short but successful flight, after which he told excited onlookers that he did not want any of the aircraft's controls altered in any way. Spitfire legend interprets this as meaning that the aircraft was perfect from the off, but such a statement is quite ridiculous even for an aircraft as outstanding as Mitchell's Spitfire. What Summers really meant, of course, was that he did not want any of the controls interfered with before his next flight. Nevertheless, from that very first flight the Spitfire legend was born.

It is worthy of note, however, that Camm's Hurricane first flew in November 1935, and was immediately ordered by the Air Ministry. Although a monoplane the Hurricane relied upon tried and tested design and production, meaning that it was not difficult to produce; in fact it would reach the squadrons in January 1938, eight months before the Spitfire. A month before the Air Ministry ordered the Hurricane, however, the Germans commissioned a new single-seat monoplane fighter: the Messerschmitt 109. Ominously, from the outset, the 109 was 30 mph faster than the Hurricane.

Shortly after the Spitfire's maiden flight it was demonstrated to a group of Air Ministry officials at Martlesham Heath. Suitably impressed the Air Ministry ordered 300 Spitfires, but this was against an order for 600 Hurricanes. Why did the Air Ministry order twice as many of an inferior design, an aircraft already slower than its German counterpart? The answer lay in the problems arising from the Spitfire's complicated construction, which was time consuming at this early stage. It is perhaps, however, fortunate that so many Hurricanes were ordered at this juncture, because at least RAF Fighter Command would find itself equipped with monoplanes, as opposed to its existing biplanes, when called upon in Britain's greatest hour of need - even if the majority were not the superior Spitfire.

With the Spitfire in production, Mitchell finally succumbed to cancer, aged forty-two, on 11 June 1937, over two years before WW2 broke out and three years before the Battle of Britain. The Spitfire's creator therefore died without ever knowing of the immeasurable contribution made by his fighter during the global conflagration of 1939-45. Moreover, due to an oversight in the current system it has not been possible to confer any posthumous honour in respect of this massive achievement. Reginald Joseph Mitchell therefore remains amongst Britain's most noteworthy but unsung heroes.

On 1 January 1938, 111 Squadron at Northolt took delivery of the first Hurricanes. On 4 August, Supermarine Test Pilot Jeffrey Quill delivered the first production Spitfire to 19 Squadron at Duxford. Slowly, over the next year, virtually all Fighter Command's squadrons would exchange their Gladiator and Gauntlet biplanes for the new, fast, monoplanes, which was just as well: had the squadrons gone to war in biplanes the Me 109 would have swept Gladiators, Gauntlets from the skies with little ado.

Just a month after 19 Squadron received its first Spitfire, Europe was on the brink of war. In September 1938, Hitler demanded that the German-speaking Sudetenland of Czechoslovakia be incorporated into the Third Reich. Hitler expected, and was prepared for, a confrontation over the issue, but Britain and France betrayed the Czechs and failed to make a stand. Confident that the leaders of Britain and France were too weak to oppose him, in March 1939 Hitler occupied the remainder of Czechoslovakia, land to which Germany had absolutely no claim whatsoever. It was now all too clear that war with Germany was inevitable, and that the British Prime Minister, Neville Chamberlain, had failed in his attempts to appease Hitler. What Chamberlain had achieved, however, was a breathing space, time in which the RAF was able to re-equip with modern fighters for the crucial battle ahead - the importance of which must never be overlooked.

In the Far East too another territorially ambitious and jingoistic nation, Japan, looked to expand its territories. In 1936, Japan was condemned by the League of Nations for invading Manchuria; Japan simply resigned its membership and instead became a party to the Anti-Comintern pact with Germany and Italy. On 23 August 1939, the Soviets signed a surprise Non-Aggression Pact with Hitler, a secret clause of which divided up a conquered Poland between Russia and Germany. Six months earlier, in the wake of having sold out Czechoslovakia to Hitler, Britain and France both pledged themselves to the defence of Poland, which, in fact, neither was geographically situated to do. On 1 September 1939, German troops invaded Poland, unleashing Blitzkrieg – Lightning War – and against which the Poles, with their obsolete aircraft and mounted cavalry, were powerless. Britain and France delivered Hitler an ultimatum: withdraw from Poland or face the consequences. Needless to say Hitler ignored this. On Sunday 3 September 1939, Britain and France declared war on Nazi Germany. The storm had broken at last and the Spitfire's finest hour was at hand.

As Britain and France were unable to offer Poland actual military assistance, the two powers prepared and braced themselves for war in the west. The British Expeditionary Force (BEF), comprising largely of territorials and reservists, was dispatched to France, there to await events. Poland fell in three weeks and the world held its breath, awaiting Hitler's next move which, everyone knew, would be an attack on the West. Naturally against this backdrop Spitfire production increased throughout the rest of 1939, as the nation braced itself.

The original Mk I Spitfires were powered by the Merlin II engine and fitted with a two bladed, fixed pitch, propeller made of mahogany. Improvements were rapidly made by way of the Merlin III engine and fitting of a metal de Havilland twin speed propeller. This meant that, as opposed to the fixed pitch propeller, the pilot had two settings: coarse and fine pitch, the 'pitch' being akin to changing gear in a car. In June 1940, however, this device was replaced by the de Havilland Constant Speed Unit, enabling the pilot to change the propeller's 'bite' throughout a large selection of settings to suit different flying conditions and needs. Needless to say, however, the 109, which was technically superior in many ways, was already fitted with such a device.

At this time, Spitfires were still produced at Supermarine's Woolston factory. In early 1940 a school leaver by the name of Terry White joined the workforce there as a 'handy lad'. Years later, Terry remembered those days, when he was 'utterly bewildered by the noise and, it appeared to me, confusion of what was a very, very busy factory'. Spitfires built at Woolston emerged from the paint shop resplendent with green and brown camouflaged upper surfaces and half white, half black undersides. The national colours were over sprayed as red, white and blue roundels (known to the Germans as 'Peacock's Eyes') and vertical flashes, the propeller and spinner black, the blades having bright yellow tips. Out on the airfield at Eastleigh, new Spitfires awaited their test flights, successful completion of which meant that the fighter was ready to he taken on charge by the RAF. The standard test flight was formulated at Eastleigh by test pilots Jeffrey Quill and George Pickering after production of the first Mk Is. Other than alterations to cater for changes in Spitfire design, the formula remained unchanged throughout the ten years of Spitfire production. The test was thorough indeed, and there was no doubt that if a machine passed thirty minutes at the hands of an expert test pilot it was definitely ready for operational service. The courage, hard work and dedication of the test pilots must neither go unrecognised: to them went the task of making the first flight in every Spitfire, so if anything was unsafe it would be the test pilot who found out; the consequences could be fatal, and all too often were. Jeffrey Quill:

> It usually took a few short flights of not more than five minutes duration each at the start of a production test to clear the engine and propeller settings. This would be followed by a flight of at least twenty minutes to check performance at full throttle settings. For simplicity we usually entered in our log books a total of thirty minutes per aircraft under the general heading of 'Production Test'. No doubt we did ourselves out of a lot of logged airborne time as a result of this clerical laziness, but one's mind was not focused on posterity in 1940!

In those far off days it must have been the dream of most young men to fly Spitfires, to be a fighter pilot, one affectation of which was wearing the top tunic button undone. But it was not just pilots to whom the Spitfire appealed; Bob Morris:

> I joined the RAF before the war started and was more interested in the technical rather than the flying side. I studied aeronautical engineering at the RAF Technical School, Halton. In May 1940 I passed out as an Airman 1st Class, looked at the list pinned on the board and discovered that I had

been posted to 66 Squadron at Coltishall in 12 Group. I knew not where Coltishall was, or what aircraft 66 Squadron had.

As it happened, Coltishall was in Norfolk, and my first glimpse of 66 Squadron was from the bus which travelled along the airfield for a short distance; what an absolute thrill to see Spitfires. Here was a young man's dream!

Pilot Officer Hubert 'Dizzy' Allen was a pilot with 'Clickety-Click', and had joined 66 Squadron at Duxford the month before Bob Morris arrived:

I didn't know where Duxford was and nor was I aware of what aircraft 66 Squadron had - they could have had Hurricanes, which did not appeal to me in any way. On the other hand they might be Spitfires, which appealed to me very much. I had seen the Spitfire in flight, had seen many photographs of it, to me it was the very pink of perfection (and after due experience proved to me that it was indeed perfection). When I arrived at Duxford's hangars I could see nothing but Spitfires littering the airfield - not a Hurricane in sight. Wherever Heaven is, St Peter opened the doors when I arrived at Duxford!

In May 1940, Pilot Officer David Crook, an Auxiliary Air Force pilot, completed his Service Flying Training and joined 609 'West Riding' Squadron at Turnhouse in Scotland. An indication of the uncertainty of the times is provided by this simple statistic: of the fifteen pilots who trained together with Crook, just a few months later five had been awarded the Distinguished Flying Cross, but eight, alas, were dead. In his superb first-hand account *Spitfire Pilot*, published in 1942, Crook wrote:

The next day I did my first trip in a Spitfire. I had waited for this moment for nearly two years, and when it came it was just as exciting as I always expected.

Having mastered the cockpit drill, I got in and taxied out on the aerodrome, sat there for one moment to check that everything was OK, and then opened up with a great smooth roar, the Spitfire leapt forward like a bullet and tore madly across the aerodrome, and before I had realized quite what had happened I was in the air. I felt though the machine was completely out of control and running away with me. However, I collected my scattered wits, raised the undercarriage, and put the airscrew into coarse pitch, and then looked round for the aerodrome, which to my astonishment I saw was already miles behind.

After a few minutes cruising round I realized that this fearsome beast was perhaps not quite as formidable as I had thought in that breathless minute, so I decided to try a landing. This came off reasonably satisfactorily, and I took off again, feeling much surer of myself. So I climbed up to a good height and played in the clouds in this superb new toy and did a few gentle dives to 400 mph, which gave me a tremendous thrill. Altogether I was almost light-headed with exhilaration when I landed at the end of an hour's flight, and I felt that I could ask nothing more of life.

Actually, once you have done a few hours flying in a Spitfire and become, accustomed to the great power and speed, then it is an extraordinarily easy machine to fly and is absolutely marvellous for aerobatics. Practically everybody who has flown a Spitfire thinks it is the most marvellous aircraft ever built, and I am no exception to the general rule. I grew to like it more than any other aircraft I had flown. It is so small and compact and neat, yet possessed of devastating fire power.

Having already successfully invaded Denmark, that month also saw Hitler's long awaited offensive against the West begin at last. Chamberlain was replaced as Prime Minister by the bellicose former First Sea Lord, Winston Churchill, who offered Britons nothing but 'blood, sweat and tears' in the Armageddon ahead.

With unprecedented fury, Hitler's Wehrmacht crashed into Belgium, Holland, Luxembourg and France. Two days later Liege fell and the, panzers crossed the Meuse at Dinant and Sedan; the following day the Dutch surrendered. The BEF immediately pivoted forward some 60 miles into Belgium, across unprepared ground, to meet the Germans at what was believed to be the main thrust, i.e. into northern France via Holland and Belgium as in the Great War. In fact German armour was actually undertaking the supposedly impossible and safely negotiating the Ardennes forest, much further to the south. Once through, Panzergruppe von Kliest bypassed the Maginot Line and punched upwards, the panzers racing for the coast. By 20 May the Germans had, incredibly, reached Laon, Cambrai, Arras, Amiens and even Abbeville. Soon Lord Gort, the British Commander-in-Chief, had no option but to retire upon Dunkirk, from which French port the BEF was evacuated; the British soldiers were shocked and exhausted, their heavy weapons and vehicles left strewn across the continental battlefields. On 3 June the port of Dunkirk fell, the evacuation concluding with the rescue of over 300,000 British, French and Belgian soldiers.

During the Battle of France, the Commander-in-Chief of RAF Fighter Command, none other than the far-sighted Air Chief Marshal Sir Hugh Dowding, had committed only Hurricane squadrons to the fray. Dowding's priority was the 'defence of base', and therefore 'Stuffy' preserved his Spitfire squadrons for the assault on Britain itself. Spitfires, however, were used in the air operation covering the Dunkirk evacuation, known as DYNAMO, and over the French coast engaged the Me 109 for the first time. Amongst the Spitfire squadrons rushed to operate from bases close to the south coast was Duxford's 19 Squadron; Pilot Officer Michael Lyne:

> To us the Mess at Hornchurch had a new atmosphere, people clearing rooms of kit belonging to casualties and the Station Commander closing the bar and sending us to bed early. On 26 May we were called upon to patrol over the evacuation beaches, heading off to the east and seeing columns of black smoke from Dunkirk's blazing oil storage tanks. We patrolled for some time uneventfully when suddenly we sighted some forty enemy aircraft ahead, heading for Calais where the Rifle Brigade was holding out. Squadron Leader Geoffrey Stephenson lined up our twelve Spitfires in sections of three to attack these Ju 87 Stukas; he was a former Central Flying School A1 instructor, a precise flier and rigidly obedient to the book, which stipulated an overtaking speed of just 30 mph. What said book had not foreseen was that we would attack Ju 87s doing only 130 mph. Stephenson led his Section, with Pilot Officer Watson No 2 and myself No 3, up behind the Stukas, which appeared very relaxed as they probably thought we were their fighter escort. The enemy fighter leader, however, had been very clever and led his 109s off towards England, so that when they turned towards Calais he would be higher than and protecting the Stukas' rear.
>
> Meanwhile Stephenson realised that we were closing too fast. I remember his call '19 Squadron prepare to attack!', then to Watson and me 'Red Section, throttling back, throttling back'. We were virtually formating, now, on the last section of Ju 87s, an incredibly dangerous speed in the presence of enemy fighters, and behind us staggered along the remainder of 19 Squadron at a similarly ridiculous speed. Stephenson then told us to select a target each and fire, so far as I know we got the last three, we could hardly have done otherwise. By the time our final section attacked the 109s were engaging and I came under fire for the first time, mysterious little corkscrews of smoke passing my starboard wing. Then I heard a slow thump, thump, thump, and realised that I was being attacked by a 109 with tracer and cannon. I broke away sharpish and lost him.
>
> Alas my friend Watson was never seen again, and Stephenson was shot down and captured.

Michael was in action again that afternoon:

> I found myself alone with a pair of 109s circling above me left-handed whilst I went right-handed. The leader dropped his nose and fired, hitting me in the engine, knee, radio and rear fuselage. I was in a spin and streaming glycol. He must have thought I was gone for good, so did I. But for a short time the Merlin kept going as I straightened out and dived into cloud, setting compass course shortly before the cockpit filled with white smoke, blotting out everything. In a few seconds the engine seized and I became an efficient glider, breaking cloud and seeing Deal some way off. I crossed the surf with

> 200 feet of height to spare and crash-landed on the beach. That adventure ended my flying until February 1941.

It was an inauspicious start. The enemy fighter pilots, however, had the advantage given that many had already seen combat in Spain during the mid-1930s before annihilating the Polish air force and all comers during the Fall of France. The air battle was not completely one-sided, however, as indicated by Flight Lieutenant Brian Lane's report concerning a combat with Me 110s 4,000 feet two miles north-east of Dunkirk occurring on 1 June:

> I immediately attacked in line astern and the E/A (enemy aircraft) turned towards the coast. A dogfight ensued just over the beach. I continued to attack E/A and observed one engine stop and the starboard one emitted large quantities of vapour, presumably coolant. E/A dived towards the ground but had not pulled out at 50 feet. I turned and attacked another E/A head-on. E/A passed below me to avoid collision and I lost sight of him. Burst appeared to enter nose of E/A. During the combat I observed one E/A dive straight into the sea and another crashed on the shore, bursting into flames.

Wing Commander George Unwin:

> The tacticians who wrote the book believed that in the event of war it would be fighter versus bomber only. What they could not foresee was Hitler's modern ground tactics that took his armies to the Channel ports in an unprecedented period of time, thus providing bases for his fighters and putting England within their limited range. Over Dunkirk we found that our tight formations were all very well for the Hendon Air Pageant but useless in combat. What happened to Geoffrey Stephenson was a prime example: without modern combat experience he flew exactly by the book – and was effectively shot down by it.

Amongst the successful Spitfire pilots over Dunkirk was Douglas Bader, who, having lost both legs in a blameworthy pre-war flying accident had argued his way back into the cockpit. By the conclusion of DYNAMO, the indomitable 'Dogsbody' had fighter tactics 'sussed': 'He who has the height advantage controls the battle; he who has the sun achieves surprise, and he who goes in close shoots them down'.

At home the need for fighters, to make good losses of 25% suffered in France and over Dunkirk, was urgent. Churchill predicted that 'the Battle of Britain is about to begin', proclaiming that Britons would 'fight on the beaches, we shall fight on the landing grounds, we shall fight in the fields and in the streets, we shall fight in the hills; we shall never surrender'. Whilst Herr Hitler saw the sights of Paris, like any foreign tourist, Churchill's clear message was one of absolute defiance against Nazi tyranny – in this 'total war' the Spitfire would become both sword and symbol. Certainly the Spitfire was already the star of this most desperate hour. Churchill appointed the Fleet Street magnate Lord Beaverbrook as Minister for Aircraft Production, and the 'Beaver', a genius of propaganda, devised the 'Spitfire Fund', to which, surely, every home in Britain contributed. The figure of £5,000 was set for the production costs of a Spitfire, excluding engine and armament, and so if an individual or organization donated that sum to the Air Ministry it was considered that they had paid for a Spitfire – which would proudly bear, in bright yellow paint, their chosen name. Beaverbrook came up with the tremendous slogan 'Saucepans to Spitfires', imploring households to donate their aluminium cookware. So it was that housewives in Britain enthusiastically responded to this call, donating in the process mountains of saucepans to the Air Ministry – not one of which was of sufficiently high grade metal to actually be used in aircraft production, but that was inconsequential: the country felt involved in producing the Spitfire, the one weapon above all others that would be their saviour from the terrifying prospect of sustained aerial bombardment.

For the Germans, the proposed invasion of England was an unexpected bonus. Like the Spitfire and Hurricane, however, the 109 was designed as a short-range interceptor and not as a long-range offensive or escort fighter. Quite simply it had not the fuel capacity for operations over England, twenty minutes over London was the maximum a pilot could expect at combat settings. Although the 109s were in a geographic position to undertake sweeps and bomber escort missions, fuel calculations were extremely critical and distracting. The 109 did, however, have three technical advantages over the RAF fighters. Firstly, armament comprised not only two 7.9 mm machine-guns but also two hard-hitting 20 mm cannon (as opposed to the eight .303 machine-guns of the Hurricane and Spitfire). Secondly, the 109's Daimler-Benz engine was fuel injected, meaning that it was not starved of fuel during a dive, unlike the gravity affected float carburetors of the British fighters. Fuel injection ensured that the 109 could escape in a dive, and this became the Germans' standard evasive tactic. Thirdly, the 109's canopy was completely jettisoned by the pilot in the event of needing to abandon the aircraft; both Hurricane and Spitfire had canopies which slid back along rails, which could be damaged in combat and jammed. Recent research suggests that there was a much higher incidence of survival amongst 109 pilots forced to bail out when compared to Spitfire and Hurricane pilots. The other technical differences between the Spitfire and 109 were really inconsequential: the Spitfire was a little faster below 15,000 feet but slightly slower above 20,000; the Spitfire could always turn tighter than the 109, but the 109 was superior in both climb and dive.

As the Germans peered across the Channel at England's coastline, just twenty-two enticing miles away, they were sublimely confident of victory in this new contest to defeat Fighter Command and achieve aerial supremacy over England as a prelude to a seaborne invasion. Reichsmarschall Hermann Göring boasted 'My Luftwaffe is invincible... And so now we turn to England. How long will this one last - two, three weeks?' Dowding, however, saw the situation much differently: 'My strength has now been reduced to the equivalent of 36 squadrons... we should be able to carry on the war single-handedly for some time, if not indefinitely'.

The Battle of Britain began on 10 July with skirmishes over Channel bound convoys, progressing through various distinct phases as Göring frequently changed strategy. Just when Fighter Command's Sector Stations in south-east England were on the verge of becoming non-operational, after days of bombing, the enemy attacked London in the hope that this unique target would lure Fighter Command to respond en masse – and be destroyed in a knock-out blow. Dowding and the commander of 11 Group, Air Vice-Marshal Park, cleverly preserved their forces, responding to threats with penny-packet formations, thus denying the arrogant Reichsmarschall of the victory he now so desperately demanded. The ever-escalating battle raged until reaching its crescendo on 15 September, shortly after which Hitler postponed the invasion of England indefinitely.

During the Battle of Britain, however, it had become abundantly clear that the Hurricane was no match for the Me 109, whereas the Spitfire was, and so a partnership was created whereby Hurricanes were used to attack the slower bombers, protected by Spitfires which kept the 109s at bay. The Germans soon developed a respect for Mitchell's Spitfire; Leutnant Heinz Knocke of 1/JG 52, wrote:

> The Supermarine Spitfire, because of its maneuverability and technical performance, has given the German formations plenty of trouble. 'Achtung Spitfire!' German pilots have learned to pay particular attention when they hear this warning shouted in their earphones. We consider shooting down a Spitfire to be an outstanding achievement, which it most certainly is.

Group Captain Peter Townsend (a Hurricane pilot in the Battle of Britain):

> The 109 pilots held our Hurricanes in contempt. The Luftwaffe airmen often mistook Hurricanes for Spitfires. There was the crew of the Heinkel which landed in the sea on Wick airfield and swore that a Spitfire had downed them, when it was in fact a Hurricane. During the Battle of France, Theo Osterkamp seemed to see Spitfires everywhere, but there were no Spitfires in France, only Hurricanes. Even General Kesselring said 'Only the Spitfires

bothered us'. The Luftwaffe, it seemed, suffered from 'Spitfire Snobbery'.

Flight Lieutenant Ken Wilkinson:

> If you were a fighter pilot you were a cocky so-and-so, but if you were a Spitfire pilot then you were cockier still, a definite cut above the rest.

Wing Commander George Unwin:

> At the time I felt nothing out of the ordinary. I had been trained for the job and luckily had a lot of experience on Spitfires. I was always most disappointed if the Squadron got into a scrap when I was off duty, and this applied to all of the pilots I knew. It was only after the event that I began to realise how serious defeat would have been - but then, without being big headed, we never ever considered being beaten, that was impossible in our eyes and was simply our outlook. As we lost aircraft and pilots, replacements were always forthcoming. Of course the new pilots lacked experience, but so did the German replacements and it was clear by the end of 1940 that these pilots had not the stomach for a scrap with a Spitfire.

Group Captain Peter Townsend:

> Our battle was a small one, but on its outcome depended the fate of the western world. At the time, however, no such thoughts bothered us, although obviously we knew that we had to win. More than that, we were somehow certain that we could not lose. I think it had something to do with England. Miles up in the sky, we fighter pilots could see more of England than other defender's had ever seen before. Beneath us stretched our beloved country, with its green hills and valleys, lush pastures and villages clustering round some ancient church. Yes, it was a help to have England there below. She was behind us, too. When, at the end of the day, we touched down and slipped out for a beer at the local, people were warm and wonderfully encouraging. They were for us, the fighter boys, who had once been the bad boys, who supposedly drank too much and drove too fast. Now people realised that, on the job, we were professionals. They rooted for us as if we were the home team, and we knew that we had to win, if only for them.

By the end of 1940 all of 11 Group's squadrons were exclusively Spitfire equipped. Wartime demands soon indicated that the small Supermarine factory at Woolston was unable to produce Spitfires in the quantity now required, however. The new site chosen for a 'shadow factory,' was at Castle Bromwich, near Birmingham, where it was intended to apply the mass production techniques of the motor industry to building Spitfires. Lord Nuffield himself, pioneer of the inexpensive and mass produced automobile, was chosen to oversee the project.

The Castle Bromwich Aircraft Factory (CBAF) produced the first Spitfire Mk IIs in June 1940, and these started reaching the squadrons in July. Unlike the Spitfire Mk I, all production Mk IIs incorporated an engine-driven hydraulic system for undercarriage operation, and constant-speed propellers. The Mk II also enjoyed the benefits of the Rolls-Royce Merlin XII engine, increasing the Spitfire's ceiling by 2,000 feet. This new engine also ran on 100, as opposed to 85, octane petrol, and was fitted with a Coffman cartridge starter. Naturally there were teething problems at CBAF, as at first the motor industry production line technique lacked the flexibility to keep up with the ever changing list of modifications required by the RAF. With great determination on behalf of all involved, these various problems were overcome and production of the Mk II steadily increased: 23 in July 1940, 37 in August and 56 in September. The dedication of the CBAF workforce during the years of Spitfire production is now legendary, and it is no small measure of commitment that 57.9% of the 20,334 Spitfires ultimately built were made in Birmingham.

During the autumn of 1940, there were changes to the command structure of Fighter Command (see *Bader's Duxford Fighters: The Big Wing Controversy*, also by Dilip Sarkar). Sholto Douglas replaced Dowding as Commander-in-Chief, and the ambitious Leigh-Mallory took Park's place as commander of 11 Group. Douglas and Leigh-Mallory were keen to drive forward an offensive strategy, to 'reach out' and take the war across the Channel to France. On 20 December 1940, two 66 Squadron Spitfires strafed the coastal airfield at Le Touquet. On 9 January 1941, five RAF fighter squadrons swept the skies above north-east France. Sensibly the Germans did not react, so the following day 11 RAF fighter squadrons escorted six 114 Squadron Blenheims to Foret de Guines. The operation was known as 'Circus No 1', the idea being that the Germans could not ignore the presence of bombers so would have to scramble fighters, which would be met by numerically superior force of (at that time mainly but not yet exclusively) Spitfires. As a portent of things to come during the so-called 'Non-Stop Offensive' of 1941, the RAF lost two fighters, the Germans none.

Improvements were constantly being made to the Spitfire. The advantages of the 109's 20 mm cannon were evident early on, and Fighter Command rapidly made efforts to give the Spitfire such a weapon. The Mk IIB was subsequently developed, armed with two 20 mm cannon and four machine-guns. The cannons, however, weighed 96 lbs each, and the Merlin XII of the Spitfire Mk II was not powerful enough to cope with this. So it was that the Merlin 45 was developed, which powered the Spitfire Mk V. This new Spitfire weighed 6,622 lbs, had a top speed of 359 mph at 25,000 feet, an altitude it could reach in eight minutes, and could attain 35,000 feet in fifteen. Biggin Hill's 92 Squadron received the first Mk Vs, which began reaching Fighter Command's remaining squadrons, in numbers, during May 1941.

Flight Lieutenant Ron Rayner, of 41 Squadron, recalled flying Spitfires on operations across the Channel when a sergeant pilot in 1941:

> I suppose it was a bit noisy, but with the flying helmet strapped down tight, the ears were almost sealed by the ear pieces' rubber rings, which helped. Anyway, after a combat started, from then on until back at Merston the R/T was chatting away constantly. Of course these Spitfires had no cockpit heating at all, and so we had to take steps to protect against the cold. My mother knitted me some woolen stockings which I used to pull up over my legs at high altitude. Flying a Spitfire was also a very physical business, especially when in formation which required constant jiggling about of the control column. Regarding range, this depended on use of the throttle, and of course combat used up more petrol; when attacked you would automatically go into a steep climbing turn, pushing the throttle forward for maximum boost as you did so. Crossing the water with one engine was always a concern, so of course we monitored our fuel gauges very carefully. After an operational flight I suppose we were tired, but we were young and fit and just glad not to be in the infantry!

Warrant Officer David Denchfield was also a sergeant pilot flying Spitfires in 1941:

> Until the day I was shot down over France and captured (5 February 1941), I thought the war an exciting affair which I would not have missed for all the tea in China. The war had released me from a hum-drum office job and realised my ambition to fly His Majesty's Spitfire and I got paid to do it! We seldom thought or spoke of any downside, although we knew that our occupation held little long term future, but we were young and unimaginative and thought 'it won't happen to me.

Squadron Leader Jack Stokoe:

> The offensive operations of 1941 were just as vital as the Battle of Britain, and certainly more nerve-wracking as we were operating at range, over enemy territory.

In a reversal of the Battle of Britain scenario, in 1941 it was the Spitfire pilots who now had to cross the Channel and fight over enemy occupied territory. Air Sea Rescue remained embryonic, and downed pilots were often, if they were lucky, rescued by passing Vessels. Jack Stokoe continues:

> On 20 April 1941, we were patrolling off Clacton, about ten to twenty miles out over the North Sea, having been vectored there by Control due to a report of 'bandits' in the area. Suddenly we were in a combat situation and I

was firing at an enemy aircraft. Then - a blank! I was still airborne but minus my Spitfire, which had disappeared entirely, probably as the result of one or more direct hits from cannon shells behind the armour plated seat. I had not opened my hood or disconnected my oxygen supply or intercom, or unstrapped the seat harness, but I seemed not surprised or unduly worried that I was apparently flying with no visible means of support. Nor did I have any sensation of falling! My helmet was missing, as were my gloves and a flying boot. When I got round to looking, my parachute seemed rather the worse for wear, however I pulled the ripcord, the chute opened and I landed in a very cold and somewhat wild sea.

Jack inflated his dinghy, which then burst. Managing to maintain a small amount of air in a pocket, the hapless pilot desperately clung onto this buoyancy. Soon suffering from the effects of the cold water, Jack was relieved to see a ship, from which ropes were thrown. Grabbing one, the exhausted pilot was hauled aboard and subsequently returned to shore and admitted to Harwich Hospital. On 6 May 1941, Jack Stokoe was back in action.

Bob Morton was a sergeant pilot with 616 Squadron, at Westhampnett, in the Tangmere Sector, and makes some interesting observations regarding the fighting in 1941:

Although we maintained strict radio silence on the way across the Channel, the enemy fighters generally got wind of our approach and were waiting near their ceiling by the time we crossed the French coast. This meant that they could gain a greater speed than us through a long dive, overhaul us rapidly from behind, get in one long burst and break away. To avoid this, one Spitfire pilot in each section had to fly with his chin on his shoulder, watching his tail. Naturally this did not make for good formation flying.

By now we had copied the Germans and were flying sections of four aircraft, known as the 'Finger Four'. Although in action each section split into two pairs, after a time almost every pilot found himself alone. At this point the 109s, having broken up the Spitfire formation, would re-climb, ready to attack loners.

In these scraps we were disadvantaged in several ways, not least regarding combat claims. To claim and aircraft destroyed, a pilot had to see the aircraft concerned strike the ground, the enemy pilot bale out, or the aircraft burst into flames. The first was almost impossible, as most of our fighting was down above 10,000 feet, and no-one would be fool enough to keep his eyes on an aircraft he had shot at, or follow it down. The second took time to occur, and in any case other enemy aircraft would probably be shooting at the Spitfire pilot because the Germans always worked in pairs. As for the third, although in the film Battle of Britain, every German machine hit exploded, I never saw such a thing happen. Finally, if we were shot down over Enemy Occupied Territory, unless you were very lucky and received help from civilians, you would see out the war incarcerated in a German prison camp.

The new chiefs of Fighter Command were convinced that the more fighters were put in the air the better results would be, but this was based upon what, recent research has shown (see *Bader's Duxford Fighters: The Big Wing Controversy*), was a flawed theory. During the Battle of Britain, contrary to Dowding's system, which revolved around fighters intercepting the enemy in squadron strength and as individual units, five of Leigh-Mallory's 12 Group squadrons, operating from Duxford and under the aerial leadership of Acting Squadron Leader Douglas Bader, flew as a massed formation. The 'Big Wing's' combat claims were high and accepted with little cross-reference, much higher, in fact, than those by neighbouring 11 Group, which was adhering to the System. On this basis tactical thinking changed, but we now know that the 'Big Wings' combat claims were actually hugely inflated. This was because with so many fighters in action simultaneously, several pilots could attack the same enemy aircraft independently but oblivious to the fact that, in that split second, other RAF fighter pilots were attacking the same target. The result was that one enemy aircraft destroyed could ultimately be credited to a number of pilots, therefore becoming not a single aircraft destroying but sometimes, on the score sheet, several more. The Big Wing's combat claims have since been proved to be highly exaggerated, meaning that, in fact, it was 11 Group, after all, which destroyed more enemy machines and in so doing confirmed the excellence of Dowding's thinking. In 1941, however, the Big Wing theory was believed to hold true by Sholto Douglas and Leigh-Mallory, and they therefore planned operations over France by fighters in wing strength, the intention being to engage and destroy smaller formations of enemy fighters in an ongoing war of attrition.

The changeover to operations in wing strength, of up to three squadrons (36 fighters) led to the creation of a new appointment: 'Wing Leader'. Each Sector Station boasted a wing, so each sector was appointed its own Wing Commander (Flying). Air Vice-Marshal Johnnie Johnson, who should need no introduction as the RAF's official top scoring fighter pilot of WW2:

> The Wing Leader's job was every fighter pilot's dream, as the Wing Commander (Flying) responsible for his wing's performance in the air. The logistics were left to the Station Commander, usually a Group Captain, and the wing's three squadron commanders.

On 7 December 1940, Leigh-Mallory drew up a list of potential Wing Leaders Amongst them were 'Sailor' Malan, who ultimately went to Biggin Hill, Harry Broadhurst got Hornchurch, Victor Beamish North Weald, Johnnie Peel Kenley, the indomitable Douglas Bader, went to lead

Tangmere's Spitfires. On 1 March 1941, Sergeant (now sir) Alan Smith was sitting at readiness in 616 Squadron's dispersal at Westhampnett:

> I heard the roar of a Spitfire as it dived low, climbed, did a half-roll and lowered its undercarriage whilst inverted, rolled out, side-slipped and made a perfect landing. Out of the cockpit climbed none other than Wing Commander Douglas Bader, who walked with his distinctive gait over to us at dispersal. Our new Wing Commander (Flying) introduced himself and announced that he would be leading the Tangmere Wing at the head of our 616 Squadron. He seemed to already know Flying Officer Hugh 'Cocky' Dundas and Pilot Officer Johnnie Johnson, and said 'You'll be Red 3, Cocky, and you, Johnnie, will be Red 4'. Looking around he caught my eye and said 'Who are you?' 'Sergeant Smith, sir!' I replied.
>
> 'Right. You will fly as my Red 2 and God help you if you don't watch my tail!' I couldn't believe my ears; it was like God asking me to keep an eye on heaven for him! Flying with Douglas, Cocky and Johnnie was to become the greatest experience of my life, and I considered myself quite the most fortunate sergeant pilot in the RAF!

During that 'season', it was Flying Officer Dundas who persuaded Wing Commander Bader to copy the German schwarm formation. This was duly imitated and became the 'Finger Four', soon adopted as Standard Operating Procedure throughout Fighter Command. Although this undoubtedly saved the lives of countless RAF fighter pilots the cross-Channel operations were proving costly, particularly in respect of experienced leaders. There were no targets of strategic importance in Northern France, and the mixed bomber and fighter operations were merely the only means of continuing the fight against the enemy during the day; leaders such as Finucane, Lock, Tuck and even Bader himself, as we shall see, all ended up either dead or incarcerated and were a poor exchange for the results achieved. On 14 August 1941, Flight Lieutenant Archie Winskill was shot down near Calais:

> It was the first sweep flown by the Tangmere Wing since Wing Commander Bader was lost on 9 August. I baled out and was fortunate to receive help from the French, which ultimately enabled me to escape over the Pyrenees and return home via Spain. Whilst hiding on a farm in the Pas-de-Calais, I was visited by a British agent, Sidney Bowen, from an escape organisation based in Marseille;` he asked me why more Spitfires were crashing in France than 109s. I had no answer for him.

After the German invasion of Russia on 22 June 1941, the politicians, anxious to relieve the pressure on Soviet Russia, put Fighter Command under pressure to increase the tempo of its operations over France. At that time, the Germans had two fighter groups on the Kanalfront, namely JG 26 and JG 2, but it was never necessary for the strength of these units to be supplemented by Eastern Front fighters. In fact, Fighter Command was losing the day-fighter war by a loss ratio of 2:1 in the enemy's favour.

Johnnie Johnson:

> The Germans had a slight edge over us in those early years. The 109E was superior to the Spitfire Mk IA and B, because of 20 mm cannon and fuel injection. I also thought that the Me 109F was slightly superior in performance to the Spitfire Mk V. Of course then the FW 190 appeared and saw everyone off.

The FW 190 had first appeared in small numbers during September 1941, the new shape in the sky causing great confusion amongst RAF Intelligence Officers who were bemused by Spitfire pilots' reports of a squat, snub-nosed, radial engine German fighter which out performed them in every respect. At first the possibility of it being a new and awesome enemy fighter was dismissed, and the puzzling fighters were written off as being Curtis Hawks, some of which had been captured by the Germans. The RAF pilots knew that this was not so, however, as the Hawk is considerably inferior to the Spitfire in every respect. Eventually intelligence from the continent confirmed that this was indeed a potent new enemy fighter.

The FW 190 was powered by a 1,700 hp BMW 801D-2 14 cylinder radial engine which gave a maximum speed of 312 mph at 15,000 feet; with a one-minute override boost it could exceed 400 mph! The 190's operational ceiling was 35,000 feet, and it could reach 26,000 feet in twelve minutes. Furthermore, it was extremely maneuverable. By comparison the Spitfire Mk VB, with which Fighter Command's squadrons were most commonly equipped at this time, could achieve 371 mph at 20,000 feet, but could not operate much above 25,000 feet, by which height the speed dropped to 359 mph and took fifteen minutes to reach. The German pilots were impressed with their new mount's rate of roll and acceleration, but, significantly, the 190 was unable to out-turn a Spitfire Mk V. For the first time, however, Spitfire pilots began losing confidence in their machine, and morale sank.

The 190 threat caused so much consternation, in fact, that plans were hatched to capture an airworthy example for evaluation. A commando raid was to cross the Channel and steal a 190, which would be flown back to England by Jeffrey Quill. Fortunately this hazardous undertaking became unnecessary when on 22 June 1942, Oberleutnant Armin Faber (of Stab III/JG 2) became so disorientated after combat with the Exeter Wing off Start Point that he mistook the Bristol for the English Channel and mistakenly landed at RAF Pembrey in South Wales. The quick thinking Duty Pilot, Sergeant Jeffries, rapidly stuck a flare pistol under Faber's nose, until which point the German was blissfully unaware of his catastrophic mistake. Faber's 190 was quickly evaluated and compared to the Spitfire Mk V. The essential information gained was rapidly fed into the Spitfire development programme and eventually the Spitfire Mk IX emerged, putting the Spitfire back on top.

Johnnie Johnson:

> When I commanded 610 Squadron we had Spitfire Mk Vs and were cut to pieces by the FW 190. On one particular occasion we went over to Cherbourg but got chased out, and on the way home I lost four chaps. We could see the 190s coming in, and we were breaking round and that sort of thing, but those bloody things were far superior and of course you couldn't spend all day turning in mid-Channel, you have to make a dash for it sometime. So the Spitfire Mk IX gave us the chance of getting stuck into the bastards again. The IX was a very good combination of engine and air frame. In my opinion the Mk IX was the best ever Spitfire. When we got the Mk IX we had the upper hand back, which did for the 190s! We could turn inside him and hack him down, which we did. Those cannon shells were as thick as your wrist and when you sent them crashing through his armour plate the 190 pilot didn't like it one bit!

Interestingly, by this time the Spitfire pilots' war had changed again. Hitler was now fighting on two fronts, which in the long term would prove a fatal mistake. Then, on 7 December 1941, in what was an undeclared act of war, the Japanese attacked the American fleet at Pearl Harbour. The Americans immediately declared war on Japan, and when Germany declared war on the United States, 'Uncle Sam' found itself no longer pursuing a policy of Isolationism from events in Europe but fighting shoulder-to-shoulder with Britain. The 'Yanks' lost no time in sending Brigadier General Ira Eaker and his staff to England where they prepared for the arrival of American Eighth Air Force combat units. Eaker wholeheartedly believed in the use of aerial strategic bombardment as a war winning use of air power, but believed that best results would be achieved by daylight attacks. From bitter experience the RAF thought otherwise, and bombed the Third Reich by night. Eaker was determined to stick to his guns, however. Although the Americans initially suffered heavy losses, with no shortage of men or materials Eaker pressed on with his 'Round-the-Clock Bombing'. On 17 April 1942, General Eaker flew in the lead B-17 attacking the railway marshalling yards of Rouen-Sotteville, which was a success. During these early raids, whilst the Americans felt their way and gained experience, the bombers' depth of penetration was confined to the range of escorting fighters, which meant targets close to the French coast. This new requirement for fighters to have offensive range changed everything, in terms of both new fighters being designed and Spitfire development.

As we have seen, the genius R. J. Mitchell created the Spitfire as a defensive fighter, to win such a battle as indeed visited Britain during the summer of 1940. A defensive fighter needs but short range, as the enemy is bringing the war to his territory. Successfully escorting long-range strategic bombers in a defensive fighter is therefore, virtually impossible.

Johnnie Johnson:

> That efforts were not quickly made to significantly and properly increase the range of our Spitfires was a disgrace, and that was down to the Chief of the Air Staff, Portal, who wrongly believed that to do so would impede the Spitfire's performance as a defensive fighter. Had we more appropriate and increased range in 1943, we could have prevented many American bomber losses. I well remember those sad days in 1943 when the Americans got chewed up at Schweinfurt and Regensburg. We escorted them as far as we could but then had to turn around to get home and re-fuel. Then we were off again to meet them on their way back. In the meantime the German fighters had set about them like packs of dogs, and their once proud formations came home battered, bleeding, and with many gaps.

Various means were explored with a view to increasing the Spitfire's range, all of which involved the fitting of auxiliary fuel tanks which, in the main, could be jettisoned when empty or in the event of a 'bounce'. The airframe itself could not accept permanent additional fuel tanks, the fuselage already being cramped and the wings too thin. 'Drop tanks' were, therefore, the only answer, but as the Americans flew deeper and deeper into enemy territory, Spitfire pilots were continually frustrated at having to leave their charges just when the jagdflieger pounced. It is, however, to the credit of this defensive fighter that it was possible to extend the range at all, indicating the versatility of Mitchell's flexible but robust design.

The answer to the problem of range, however, was at hand in the shape of the North American P-51. The 'Mustang' had first flown in October 1940, and did so due to a British requirement for an offensive fighter. The original Allison engine provided only mediocre performance, and the Mustang was found particularly wanting at high altitude. Consequently the first Mustangs received by the RAF in April 1942 could only be assigned to army co-operation roles. The British soon replaced the inadequate American Allison engine with the mighty Merlin, and the results were awesome. Comparison trials indicated that the Mustang had parted company with mediocrity and was now superior to all comers in every respect. The P-51A had a range of 2,200 miles, the P-51B 2,301 miles. Both figures are staggering when compared to the Mk IX's range, which, even with a 30 gallon drop tank, was around 980 miles. By early 1944, Mustangs were with the bombers all the way to Germany and back; in

August that year a Mustang even flew over Berlin. So it was that Mustang became the long-range offensive fighter that the Allies had needed so badly from 1942 onwards.

Johnnie adds a final informed comment on the subject of range and offence:

> The problem was that throughout WW2, Fighter Command was not really aggressive enough, never really fought as a proper offensive force. We became a tactical air force, which was of short range and therefore within the Spitfire's capability. In any case we only had one wing of Mustangs, 122 Wing, the Americans had all the Mustangs and that bloody great Thunderbolt!

Reference to the tactical air force is opportune for our purposes. The Mustang relieved the Spitfire of long-range bomber escort missions, but the Spitfire's contribution was far from over.

The control of the Mediterranean was also bitterly contested during the first half of the war, this struggle beginning when Italy entered the war on the Axis side in June 1940. Geographically the key to that theatre was the tiny island of Malta, which was on the supply route to North Africa where British and German forces were engaged, and the Italians lost no time in trying to neutralise British resistance. For three weeks the island's defence was undertaken by three antiquated Gladiator biplanes, known as 'Faith', 'Hope' and 'Charity'; at the end of June 1940 four Hurricanes arrived and throughout the following month these seven fighters resisted the best efforts of some 200 enemy aircraft based in Sicily. So furiously did the defenders fight that eventually the Italians, like the Germans over England, were forced to operate only at night. More Hurricanes arrived but by March 1942 the Italians had been joined by superior Luftwaffe units and the contest was at its height. That month fifteen Spitfires flew off the aircraft carrier HMS Eagle, landing at Takali. Within three days the Spitfires had destroyed their first enemy aircraft, but the very fact that Spitfires were on the island incensed the enemy. Time after time Takali was bombed, and by 2 April not one complete section of Spitfires was operational. Indeed, the defenders thought themselves lucky if they could field six fighters at any one time, two for airfield defence and four to intercept. Incredibly, sometimes the RAF pilots had no ammunition, it being in such short supply, but the Germans could never be sure, so always treated the Spitfires with respect.

On 15 April 1942, Malta was awarded the George Cross, and five days later forty-seven more Spitfires reach the besieged island. Following intense attacks, a day later only eighteen Spitfires were serviceable; two days later none were airworthy. For some unknown reason, however, the Luftwaffe then made another classic tactical blunder, as it had at a crucial moment in the Battle of Britain, and eased off the pressure. This enabled sixty-four Spitfires, flying off USS Wasp and HMS Eagle, to get through to Malta, and a clever system was devised to rapidly turn the aircraft around to prevent them being caught on the ground: six Spitfires were up again within just six minutes of landing! It is perhaps worthy of note that the Air Officer in command of Malta was none other than Air Vice-Marshal Sir Keith Park, commander of 11 Group during the Battle of Britain, and the 'Boss' Controller was Group Captain A. B. 'Woody' Woodhall of Duxford and Tangmere fame. A Spitfire pilot famously described the action over Malta as making the 'Battle of Britain seem like child's play', but still the island held out. By 23 October 1942, Rommel had been defeated in the desert, and soon, after the Americans landed, the Allies were rolling up North Africa from both directions. The defence of Malta has rightly become legendary, but Spitfire operations from the island are important for another reason: it was from Malta that Spitfire fighter-bombers first flew, two 500 lb bombs carried beneath their wings, attacking enemy airfields in Sicily. As we have seen R. J. Mitchell designed the Spitfire as a defensive fighter, but early in the war it had to perform as an offensive escort fighter; now came another unexpected task which reflected the airframe's great strength and flexibility. Spitfires too had flown in the Desert Air Force during the North African campaign, and many of these units now gathered on Malta ready for the push into Europe via Sicily. From Malta the Spitfire wings swept over Sicily in an attempt to bring German fighters to battle, in much the same way as was happening over northern France. Flight Lieutenant Ron Rayner was on Malta with 43 Squadron:

> On 10 July 1943, the Allied invasion of Sicily, Operation HUSKY, commenced, and on that day we actually landed our Spitfires at Comiso. I remember it well as I parked my Spitfire in a dispersal area adjacent to a runway - my aircraft was next to a Stuka with Italian markings which had tipped over on its back with the two dead crew members still hanging upside down from their straps!
>
> In Sicily we started the slog up the western coast, and flew patrols of Augusta and Catania, eventually landing at the latter. From there we began escorting American daylight bombers attacking targets in Italy itself. We were escorting Mitchells and Bostons, and in addition to this escort work we were attacking the retreating Germans ourselves. As they tried to escape up the coast to Messina, we strafed them in what looked like the equivalent vessel to our tank landing craft. We were then transferred to an airstrip which had been made for us on the northern side of Sicily and continued patrolling Messina and Augusta. Eventually we arrived at Falcone, another strip prepared for us by army engineers.
>
> It was in Sicily that we received our Spitfire Mk IXs, rushed through to combat the FW 190 threat that had caused serious problems for

Fighter Command in England. The IXs were marvellous, absolutely incredible. I remember that on my first flight in a Mk IX, an air test, I went up to 35,000 feet, just for the joy of experiencing what it was like to operate at high altitude. It was definitely a different aircraft altogether at high altitude compared to the Mk V, it really was quite something. We only received, certain quantity of Mk IXs at first, so we flew a mixture of Vs and IXs. In fact the IXs were not even painted with an individual aircraft letter, they were just given a number. My personal aircraft at this time remained a Mk V, and I always flew FT-J.

The arrival of the Spitfire Mk IX was a major milestone in Spitfire history. Air Marshal Johnnie Johnson:

> The Mk IX was more powerful that the V, the Merlin 61 perfectly matched the airframe, there being no undue torque or bad flying characteristics like there was later with Griffon engined Spitfires. In my opinion the IX was the best Spitfire, we had the upper hand back then, which did for the 190s.

Squadron Leader Dan Browne:

> Although I was an American, I joined Johnnie's Canadian Wing at Kenley in 1943. I was delighted to find that we had Spitfire Mk IXs, which had a two-stage, two-speed engine. When you got up to about 19,000 feet the second stage kicked in, at which point it was your air and no longer the Germans' air.

Flight Lieutenant Ron Rayner:

> On 8 September 1943, we were assembled and told that the invasion of Italy was to commence the next day. Our role was to support the army, which was landing on a beach in the bay of Salerno. On 9 September, therefore, our patrol area was Salerno, about 170 miles across the sea from our base at Falcone. We patrolled the beaches, milling about with German aircraft attacking the ground forces, and whilst the navy shelled German positions inland. This went on until 15 September, by which time the army had secured the beach-head, and a landing strip, called 'Roger', had been pushed up parallel to the beach at Salerno. We were then able to land at Salerno itself, but not without danger as not only were the Germans still shelling us but the trajectory of our own artillery also went across our new airfield!

Also operating over Salerno were Seafires, the carrier version of Mitchell's Spitfire. Indeed, as early as 1936, the designer had considered a naval version of his fighter but, as we know, he died in 1937. No further interest was shown in a sea-going Spitfire until 1941 when the Admiralty decided there was an urgent need for such an aircraft to operate from carriers in the Fleet Air Defence role. Subsequently a number of elderly Spitfires were transferred from the RAF to the Fleet Air Arm, for trials and training, and from the data arising these aircraft were converted to Seafires. The modifications necessary for the Spitfire to operate from a carrier at sea included the fitting of an arrester hook, four spools for catapult launches and a strengthened airframe to cope with the extra strains imposed by such rapid acceleration and deceleration. Later, folding wings were also introduced to facilitate the storage of more aircraft below deck. Sub-Lieutenant Basil King flew Seafires and remembers the difficulties of deck landings:

> For some reason I was not given the opportunity to try a simulated deck landing on dry land at RNAS Yeovilton, but instead went straight to 808 Squadron on HMS Battler. The CO was not at all pleased. How I came to envy RAF pilots who could put down on dry land! We had to approach the narrow deck of the carrier, which left no room for error. Because of the Seafire's approach angle our view of the deck was virtually nil - we could only see about two feet of it and the Batsman, who used coloured bats, one in each hand, and gave the pilot signals to tell you whether you were coming in OK. Fortunately I landed safely on most occasions.

Ron Rayner continues:

> We continuously patrolled the battlefront, making sure that the army was not troubled too much by the Luftwaffe. Eventually the Germans got the message that we were not going to be pushed out of our beach-head and so the pressure started to ease off, as the army pushed inland and north towards the town of Salerno and then on to Naples. On 19 September we swept over the enemy airfield at Foggia, just to show the Germans that we were in control.
>
> The fighting in Italy for what were just small hills was intense. I once walked over one with the Squadron Padre and found it littered with bodies. Truckloads of bodies were also driven past our landing strips as the battlefields were cleared. For us it was a time of living in tents, often in deep mud, very uncomfortable to say the least. We were largely engaged in ground attack against the German army, strafing columns of their motor transport and armour. This entailed flying very low, so low that once I returned to base trailing a length of telegraph wire from my wingtip; the airfield cleared rapidly!

The experience of all three services during the invasions of Sicily and Italy provided crucial experience for the later Allied liberation of enemy occupied France. Having recognised that there was an impending change of role for RAF fighter pilots, in that come the invasion they would be required to provide tactical support to the advancing British and Canadian armies, it was necessary to re-organise the existing service structure. Consequently the 2nd Tactical Air Force was created in June 1943, the concept being to provide a composite force of fighters, bombers, fighter-bombers and army co-operation aircraft which was independent of existing commands. This new air force would exist exclusively for deployment in support of the Allied Expeditionary Force which would undertake the proposed invasion.

The Italian campaign also provided experience, as Ron Rayner has related, of whole airfields living under canvas and keeping on the move to support the ground forces. So it was that in August 1943, many Spitfire squadrons of 2nd TAF left their comfortable Sector Stations to begin operating under canvas. Canadian Wing Commander Bob Middlemiss was flying with Johnnie Johnson's Kenley Wing at the time:

> We had to leave the luxuries of batmen, soft beds, hot showers, good food, nice bar and lounge, and a short ride by electric train to the bright lights and excitement of London night life. We traded all this for tents, canvas beds, canvas wash basins, cold water for shaving, damp, cool nights and the general lack of amenities that we had become accustomed to. The 'Mess Hall' was a large tent, for example, where we ate off tin plates and sat at great wooden tables. The idea was to prepare and train us for the eventual landing in France and the mobile aerial and ground warfare that an eastward Allied advance would dictate. These primitive living conditions were not exactly what we had bargained for, however!

The Kenley Wing became known as '127 Wing', that numerical designation being the airfield at Lashenden where the Canadians now lived under canvas. The Spitfire's wings, however, were not strong enough to carry a couple of 500 lb bombs and auxiliary fuel tanks, so a compromise was reached with just one external fuel tank fitted between the inboard wheel wells and beneath the pilot's cockpit. Rather than bombs, however, most pilots would have preferred to see extra fuel, thus enabling penetrations deep into enemy territory and the welcome prospect of some decent air fighting. It was not to be, though, as times were changing. The Luftwaffe in the West was fighting the American heavy bombers by day, the RAF by night, so gone were the days of opposing fighters clashing on sweeps. Gone too would be the days of 'Big Wings'; Johnnie Johnson:

> Big wings of 36 Spitfires were OK for pre-planned offensive operations, but we knew that this would have to change once the invasion started. The time factor would not allow for such a large number of aircraft to take off and form up and if the Germans struck at low level there would be no warning whatsoever. Also, we knew that after the invasion our main task would be flying in support of our advancing armies, which meant a fundamental change

as our role would be that of a fighter-bomber rather than a bomber escort or offensive fighter. It meant that we would have to respond quickly to calls for help from the army, and the only way to do this would be to operate smaller formations tactical level, such as a flight or squadron, as opposed to an entire wing.

When bombing you had to put the Spitfire into a steep dive, aim it at the target and release the bomb as you pulled out. Allowances had to be made for wind strengths etc because the bomb had not same flying characteristics as a Spitfire. As there was no dedicated sight for this kind of work it was a case of developing our own technique of how to time the bomb release so that the target was hit. In Sicily and Italy it had been discovered that bridges were easier to hit with dive-bombers rather than light or medium bombers.

2nd TAF's fighter-bombers prowled over northern France, seeking out targets of opportunity. Naturally enemy airfields were always a popular choice, but on 21 April 1944, Wing Commander Johnnie Johnson and his Canadians nearly bit off more than they could chew:

The tactical bombers were operating in the Paris area so I led a section of Spitfires back down to the deck to sweep the numerous airfields scattered around the French capital. After twenty minutes at level I was lost, although I knew we were a few miles south of Paris. I put away the map and concentrated on flying the various courses I had worked out before leaving base. About another five minutes on this leg and then a turn to the west to avoid getting too close to Paris. Our horizon was limited to three miles over level country but was considerably reduced as we dipped into a valley.

We crossed a complicated mass of railway lines which indicated that we were close to Paris. We across a wide river and ahead of us was a heavily wooded slope, only a few feel above the top branches, and found ourselves looking straight across a large grass airfield with several large hangars on the far side.

The German gunners were ready and waiting. Shot and shell came at us from all angles, for son the gun positions were on the hangar roofs and they fired down at us! I had never before seen tin of this barrage. It would have been folly to turn back and make for the shelter of the wooded slop the turn would have exposed the vulnerable bellies of our Spitfires. Enemy aircraft were parked and there, but our only thought was to get clear of this inferno. There was no lime for radio orders, it was every man for himself, and each pilot knew that he would only get clear by staying at the lowest height.

It seemed that our exits were sealed with a concentrated criss-cross pattern of fire from every gun; only hope of a getaway lay in the small gap between two hangars. I pointed the Spitfire at this hurtled through it and caught a glimpse of the multiple barrels of a light flak gun swinging round from one of the parapets. Beyond lay a long, straight road with tall poplars either side, and I belted the Spitfire down the road with the trees forming some kind of screen. Tracer was still bursting over the cockpit, but with luck I would soon be out of range. I held down the Spitfire so she was only a few feet above the cobbled roadway. Half a dozen cyclists were making their way up the road, low arc airfield. They flung themselves from their bicycles in all directions. If you're a Frenchman, then I am sorry, but I've had a bigger fright than you!

I pulled up above the light flak and called up the other pilots. Miraculously they had all come through the barrage, and when the last one answered I pulled up the Spitfire into a climbing roll with the sheer joy of being alive.

Johnnie and his pilots landed at Tangmere, and were enjoying a cigarette and cup of NAAFI tea when General Eisenhower himself appeared, on an official visit with Air Chief Marshal Leigh-Mallory, commander of the new 2nd TAF, and Air Vice-Marshal Harry Broadhurst, commanding 83 Group. Seeing that Johnnie had just landed from an operational flight, Broadhurst introduced the Supreme Allied Commander to the Spitfire pilots; Johnnie:

Elsenhower said to me 'Did you have any luck over there?'

I thought quickly, for we had not actually fired a shot and what words could accurately describe our desperate encounter with the flak?

'No Sir', I answered, 'Our trip was uneventful'.

At last the invasion came on 6 June 1944, a vast Allied armada crossing the Channel in secret and landing American, British and Canadian troops on the Normandy beaches near Cherbourg. Flight Lieutenant Bob Beardsley DFC described to the press what he had seen from the cockpit of his Spitfire:

The sky over the target was absolutely packed with aircraft. Fighters and bombers seemed to fill the air, wingtip to wingtip. From above we fighter pilots could see the bombs go down. The whole target area was a mass of flames. It was both an impressive and terrifying sight and I for one was glad not to be a German soldier.

A Norwegian Spitfire wing leader added that:

Looking down on the target area was like looking down into hell.

Flying Officer Kazek Budzik, a Pole, had flown Spitfires operationally since

1941. On D-Day he flew with 317 Squadron:

> We must have been amongst the first fighter aircraft over the beach-head as dawn was just breaking on our arrival. The invasion armada was enormous. Most of the landing craft were still in the sea, heading towards the beaches, it really was quite a spectacle. There was flak everywhere, though, mostly from the Allied fleet, and that was quite frightening. Watching the start of Europe's liberation was a fantastic experience, particularly the naval bombardment. You could see the guns fire and the shells hitting the coastline, getting further inland the more our troops advanced. It was amazing.

In spite of this massive bombardment from both air and sea, D-Day was far from one sided and American casualties were exceptionally heavy on 'Omaha' beach. By nightfall the Allies remained on the continent and were moving inland; Johnnie:

> In August 1943 the Luftwaffe had reacted swiftly and ferociously to the Canadian and British landing at Dieppe. That was an isolated landing hut this time the stakes were infinitely higher. We expected the German fighters to respond in numbers on D-Day but they did not. So, awesome though the sight of our invasion fleet was, from our perspective as fighter pilots the landings were an anti-climax.

The German chain of command was in confusion, so reaction to the landings was slow. The Allies flew a staggering 14,000 sorties on D-Day, with a loss ratio of 1.1%; the Luftwaffe flew but 319 sorties and suffered 6.9% casualties.

Once the Allied armies began moving inland, the 2nd TAF fighter-bombers were constantly above the battlefield, dive-bombing and strafing the enemy wherever he could be found. Sturmann Karl Heinz Decker was an eighteen-year-old grenadier in the 12th SS Hitlerjugend Panzer Division:

> The Mustangs and Spitfires fired at everything that moved, and Typhoons poured rockets down on us. It became only safe for us to move by night.

On D-Day plus 3, Johnnie Johnson's 144 Wing actually landed and re-fuelled in Normandy:

> We received news that an airstrip, B-3, had been created at St Croix-sur-Mer by our engineers, just inland of the beach-head, and 144 Wing was given the honour of being the first Spitfires to land in France. I sent Squadron Leader Dal Russell and three other 442 Squadron Spitfires to go across from our base at Ford and ensure that all was well at St Croix. It was and so I took the whole Wing across to B-3 to re-fuel and re-arm before sweeping further

south. The chance of operating from Normandy itself was welcome indeed, because we knew mat there were concentrations of enemy aircraft based south of the River Loire, which was hitherto beyond our limited range.

> We first made a low pass over St Croix familiarising ourselves with the location, and then made a light circuit to a void barrage balloons protecting the beach-head. It was a strange experience, landing in what had been enemy territory and from which we had experienced all manner of hostile shot and shell. We touched down and RAF Servicing Commandos attended to our Spitfires. As we pilots gathered together the Airfield Commander came over and told us not to stray too far because of minefields and snipers. The Airfield Control system had been established in an adjacent orchard where we were soon approached by a delegation from St Croix. The villagers brought with them gifts of fruit, flowers and wine. Whilst we and the French rejoiced, dead German soldiers lay all around.

How fitting it was that Spitfires should be the first Allied aircraft to land in Normandy. By 19 August, Field Marshal Montgomery considered the Battle for Normandy to be over. By that time the Americans had advanced along the Contentin peninsula and broken through the *bocage* country, the British and Canadians had broken out into the open countryside beyond Caen and the Germans were trapped as if by a giant pincer. After the enemy counter-attack failed at Mortain, the Germans had no option but to retreat across the Dives, 80,000 men struggling to reach the River Seine via the 'Falaise Gap'. The battlefield was completely dominated by rocket-firing Typhoons and other fighter-bombers. Time and time again the Spitfires took off to pound the enemy in the 'Corridor of Death'. The aircraft flew in pairs to facilitate a rapid turnaround. As all pilots involved knew the area well, there was no need for lengthy briefings, this also increasing the number of sorties possible. Pilots were flying up to six or seven trips a day to the killing ground. 127 Wing's diary indicates just how busy things were:

> It was the busiest day in the history of the Wing. Approximately 290 operational hours were flown by our aircraft. About 30,001 rounds of 20 mm ammunition were expended on the Hun. Nearly 500 enemy vehicles were destroyed or damaged by our squadrons.

This was a terrible crescendo to the bloody Battle for Normandy, complete proof of the total tactical aerial superiority enjoyed over the battlefield by the Allies. On that last day, Flying Officer Peter Taylor of 65 Squadron wrote in his log book: 'Forcing on with big strafe. Sifta Section dive-bombed. Not so dusty but too many Spitfires.' Of another sortie later that same day, the young Scot complained bitterly that the area was 'getting clapped. Too many Tiffies and too few trucks'. Aircraft from both 2nd TAF and the American 9th Air Force continued attacking until it was too dark to aim their bombs and guns. The withdrawal became a rout, and Allied pilots maintain that the stench of death even permeated their cockpits a thousand feet above the 'Shambles'. The gap was sealed by the Polish Armoured Division linking up with the US 90th Division at Chambois, by which time total German losses numbered some 300,000 men. Although the victory was both definite and decisive, it was not actually complete because before the gap was closed 20,000 German troops escaped.

After Normandy life continued in much the same vein for the Spitfire pilots of 2nd TAF, flying in support of the armies advancing through Belgium and Holland into Germany itself. There were fighter-to-fighter engagements but these were increasingly rare given that the Luftwaffe was by now an overstretched and all but spent force. There was still danger, however, mainly from light flak which harried the Allied fighter-bombers wherever they appeared. Kazek Budzik was a flight commander in 308 Squadron when he was shot down by flak near the Breda-Dortrecht bridge in Holland on 29 October 1944:

> It was a low-level strafing attack and I was leading a section of four Spitfires. I think that the target was a flak position. I went in first, got hit, turned back and crash landed safely. There were another four Polish Spitfires doing a similar job nearby and their leader was also shot down; Flight Lieutenant Krzemanski was killed whereas for some unknown reason I survived.

Two days later Budzik was back in action but was again shot down by flak during a dive-bombing attack against a train on the Zwolle-Mardewijk line. Again luck was on Kazek's side and he survived a wheels up forced landing near Gorinchem. Just a few days later he was, needless to say, back in action over the Arnhem area.

Another menace combated by Spitfires during 1944 were the pilot-less V-1 robot bombs, known as 'Doodlebugs', at first launched on England from 'No Ball' sites in the Pas-de-Calais. By now there were yet more new Spitfires on the scene, the Mk XII and XIV, powered not by a Merlin but a Griffon engine, and these machines out performed even the popular Mk IX. In their Griffon Spitfires, pilots chased and destroyed many V-1s, some even drawing level with the flying bombs and using their wingtips to tip the Doodlebug over, upsetting its sensitive gyroscope, and causing the bomb to crash harmlessly. As the Allies advanced, the V-1 launch sites were moved east, first to Belgium and then to Holland. Hitler's next secret weapon was the V-2 rocket, which also caused havoc but was a threat beyond the capability of any fighter aircraft.

German technology was ever impressive, and over Germany Allied fighter pilots were astonished by a new and incredibly fast shape in the sky: the Me 262 jet fighter. On 5 October 1944, the first Me 262 to be destroyed was shot down by Spitfires of 401 Squadron, an incredible achievement. Flying Officer Tony Minchin flew Mustangs with 122 Squadron, and remembers seeing an Me 262 take off from Paderborn: 'He must have seen us for he opened the tap and just left us standing, even though we were doing over 500 mph in the dive!' Although Hitler completely mismanaged this potent resource, the appearance of such a fighter heralded the Spitfire's swansong. The days of piston engine fighters were drawing to a close, the jet engine providing far greater performance in every respect.

Still the war in Europe went on, and on New Year's Day 1945 the Luftwaffe mounted its last offensive: Operation BODENPLATTE, a surprise attack on Allied airfields in Holland. Although successful to a degree, the Luftwaffe was unable to deliver any kind of decisive hammer blow so the operation really was a last gasp show of strength. The Allied war machine ground ever eastwards, whilst the Russians advanced west. On 8 May 1945, Germany signed an unconditional surrender. Hitler was dead, his empire destroyed; the war in Europe was finally over.

In the Far East, however, the Japanese menace had yet to be beaten. The RAF air component serving in that theatre is often referred to as the 'Forgotten Air Force', with just cause. It was Hurricanes, though, that arrived in theatre first, and held the fort admirably until the arrival of Spitfires and American P-47 Thunderbolts in 1944. Spitfires had, however, reached Australia in 1943, and the Port Darwin Wing Leader, Clive 'Killer' Caldwell, frequently led his pilots into action against the enemy Mitsubishi Zero, with success. The Zero was a light and high maneuverable fighter but unable to withstand a beating from Caldwell's Mk Vs which had 20 mm cannon. Seafires too operated in the Far East, and by July 1945 the carriers of Task Force 37 were in the Pacific just 130 miles from Tokyo. One offensive sweep was flown before the order came to cease all aerial activity due to a special operation: the B-29 Superfortresses 'Boxcar' and 'Enola Gay' were poised to drop atom bombs on Hiroshima and Nagasaki. The result stunned the world, and on 15 August 1945, the Allies celebrated victory against the Japanese. The Second World War was over at last.

Nevertheless, the Spitfire's fighting days were not yet over. In 1948 came the Malayan Emergency, two Spitfires destroying a terrorist base that July. The Spitfire force in Malaya flew a total of 1,800 operational sorties during the campaign. Although no Spitfires fought in the Korean War, Seafire F.47s did. Most incredibly, Spitfire fought Spitfire over the Middle East: the Egyptian Air Force operated LF Mk IXs, which attacked Tel Aviv on 15 May 1948, the day on which Israel was born. RAF Spitfires were based in Israel, to provide support to the new state, and 32 and 208 Squadron were strafed by the Egyptians at Ramat David. The next time the Egyptian Mk IXs appeared, three were shot down by RAF Spitfires. Perhaps even more amazing is the fact that Spitfires operated alongside FW 190s in the Turkish Air Force, and with Me 109s in Israel! Spitfires flew operationally over the Middle East until 1953, in fact, when Syria replaced its F.22s with jets.

The following year was the Seafire's last in operational service, although the RAF continued to use PR.19s for non-operational work. Those aircraft gathered data for the Temperature & Humidity Testing Flight, based at Woodvale near Manchester, making the very last Spitfire service flight in June 1957, by which time military aviation was completely dominated by the jet.

It is interesting that the Spitfire was eventually developed through twenty-four different marques, which included a complete engine change. Although designed purely as a short range defensive fighter, the Spitfire had performed its intended roll admirably but had also been pressed into service as an offensive escort fighter, fighter-bomber and photographic reconnaissance aircraft, all evidence of the incredible potential and flexibility of R. J. Mitchell's inspired design. Would this have happened had Mitchell lived? It has often been said that he was more an innovator than developer, so it is suspected that instead of continually upgrading the Spitfire R. J. Mitchell would have created new designs, purpose built for the job in hand. Certainly this is what the Hurricane's designer, Sydney Camm, did; although the Hurricane was developed, and also carried bombs, rockets and cannons, it was nothing like the process applied to the Spitfire. Instead Camm applied himself to the creation of new aircraft, such as the Typhoon and Tempest. The Spitfire, however, like no other icon, became the absolute symbol of defiance and freedom during the Second World War, and has earned its place in both history and legend.

Dilip Sarkar MBE FRHistS

1

FLYING THE SPITFIRE: *PILOT'S NOTES*

All aircrew were volunteers, their route to the cockpit various. In the peacetime RAF, before the Air Expansion Scheme of 1934, pilots were almost exclusively officers, all of whom were graduates of the RAF College Cranwell. The Expansion Scheme, however, looked to recruit officers on a Short Service Commission basis of three years, whilst the RAF Volunteer Reserve, effectively the airborne equivalent of the Territorial Army, recruited young men who remained in their civilian occupations full-time but were trained to fly at the weekend. In the 'VR' pilots were both commissioned and non-commissioned from the outset, the minimum rank being that of sergeant. When war was declared, however, those engaged on Short Service Commissions had their engagements extended 'for the duration of hostilities' and reservists were called to full-time service. Their training, however, differed.

Those who had learned to fly either before or early on in the war did so at Flying Training Schools in Britain before being posted to their squadrons where fledgling pilots would receive instruction and experience on the type of aircraft they would be flying operationally. Losses sustained during the Fall of France, however, meant that fighter squadrons were too busy to provide such training to new pilots and so operational training units – OTUs – were created. In 1940, for example, there were two Spitfire training schools, 5 OTU at Aston Down in Gloucestershire and 7 OTU at Hawarden near Chester. There pilots would report upon completion of Service Flying Training, and aspire to Spitfire flight. First, though, instruction would be given on the two-seater North American Harvard, after which the pupil would fly solo before taking the controls of a Spitfire. This operational training included dogfight practice, altitude climbs, aerobatics, navigation exercises and formation flying but, during the very early war years, little air-to-ground firing and no air-to-air firing practice – so short was ammunition in supply. Neither were pilots provided practical parachute training; Warrant Officer Peter Fox: 'The first time I pulled a ripcord was when I was shot down over the Dorset coast during the Battle of Britain. No-one had really explained in detail what the procedure was, so when I was clear of my Hurricane I counted to ten and pulled for all I was worth! There was then one hell of a jolt and there I was floating gently earthwards under a parachute'. Instructors at the OTUs were combat veterans, who strived to pass on their experience in the hope that this would increase the replacement pilots' chances of survival. During the Battle of Britain, most OTU pupils received ten hours on Spitfires before being posted to a fighter squadron; if they were lucky they went to a squadron recuperating in the north, where there was little action and where more experience could be gained in relative safety – otherwise it was a posting to southern England and the front line: some were lucky and learned sufficiently quickly to survive, but many died bewildered and disorientated in that dangerous spider's web of vapour trails.

Flying training was conducted in the western half of the British Isles, safe from marauding enemy fighters, but many pilots were killed through inexperience or technical malfunction – their machines often being exhausted old hacks that had already seen much combat and many flying hours. Later the Empire Air Training Scheme came into being, under the auspices of which pilots received all of their flying training overseas, at bases in Canada and America,

Every RAF aircraft was subject to a set of *Pilot's Notes*, an Air Ministry publication identifying and explaining the flying controls, surfaces and exactly how to safely take-off, fly and land said service aircraft. The Spitfire was no exception, each marque of which was subjected, with amendments, to *Pilot's Notes*. Reproduced here is 'Air Publication I 565 B', otherwise known as *Pilot's Notes for the Spitfire IIA and IIB Aeroplanes and Merlin XII Engine*. Before soaring aloft on that first, thrilling, Spitfire flight every pilot would have to study – and understand in detail – the content of this vital document.

AIR PUBLICATION 1565 B
Pilots Notes

PILOT'S NOTES

SPITFIRE IIA and IIB AEROPLANES
MERLIN XII ENGINE

Prepared by direction of the
Minister of Aircraft Production

A. Rowlands

Promulgated by order of the Air Council.

[signature]

AIR MINISTRY

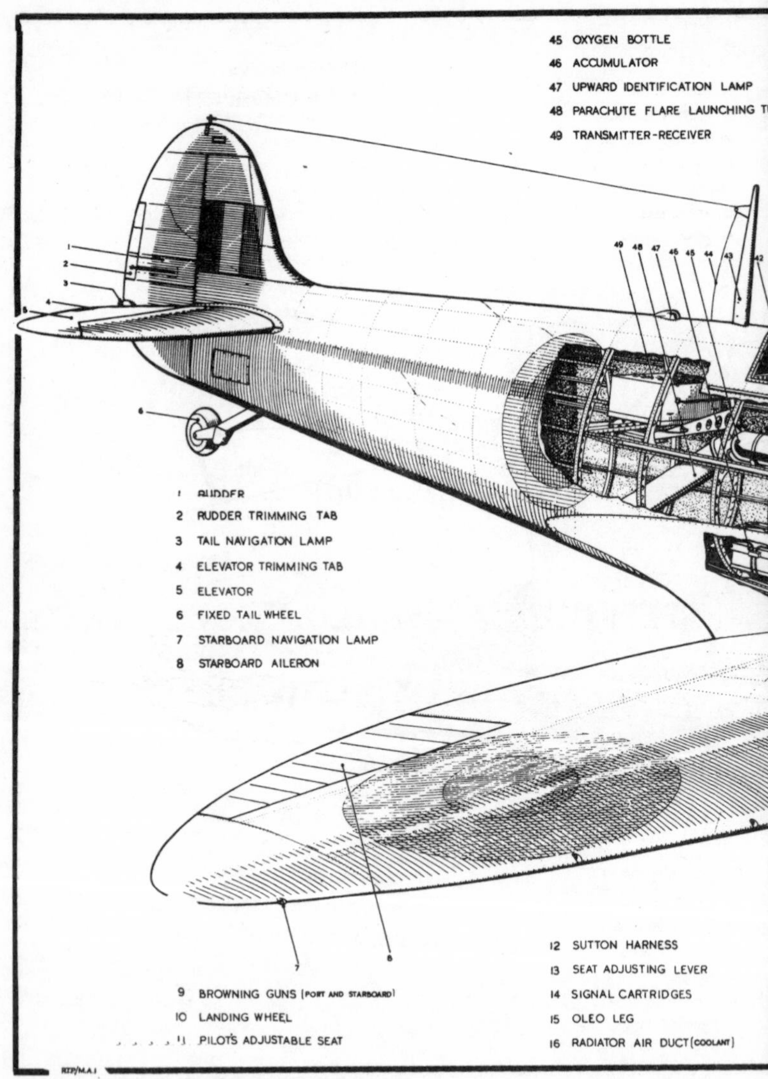
45 OXYGEN BOTTLE
46 ACCUMULATOR
47 UPWARD IDENTIFICATION LAMP
48 PARACHUTE FLARE LAUNCHING TU
49 TRANSMITTER-RECEIVER
1 RUDDER
2 RUDDER TRIMMING TAB
3 TAIL NAVIGATION LAMP
4 ELEVATOR TRIMMING TAB
5 ELEVATOR
6 FIXED TAIL WHEEL
7 STARBOARD NAVIGATION LAMP
8 STARBOARD AILERON
9 BROWNING GUNS (PORT AND STARBOARD)
10 LANDING WHEEL
11 PILOT'S ADJUSTABLE SEAT
12 SUTTON HARNESS
13 SEAT ADJUSTING LEVER
14 SIGNAL CARTRIDGES
15 OLEO LEG
16 RADIATOR AIR DUCT (COOLANT)
RTP/M.A.I

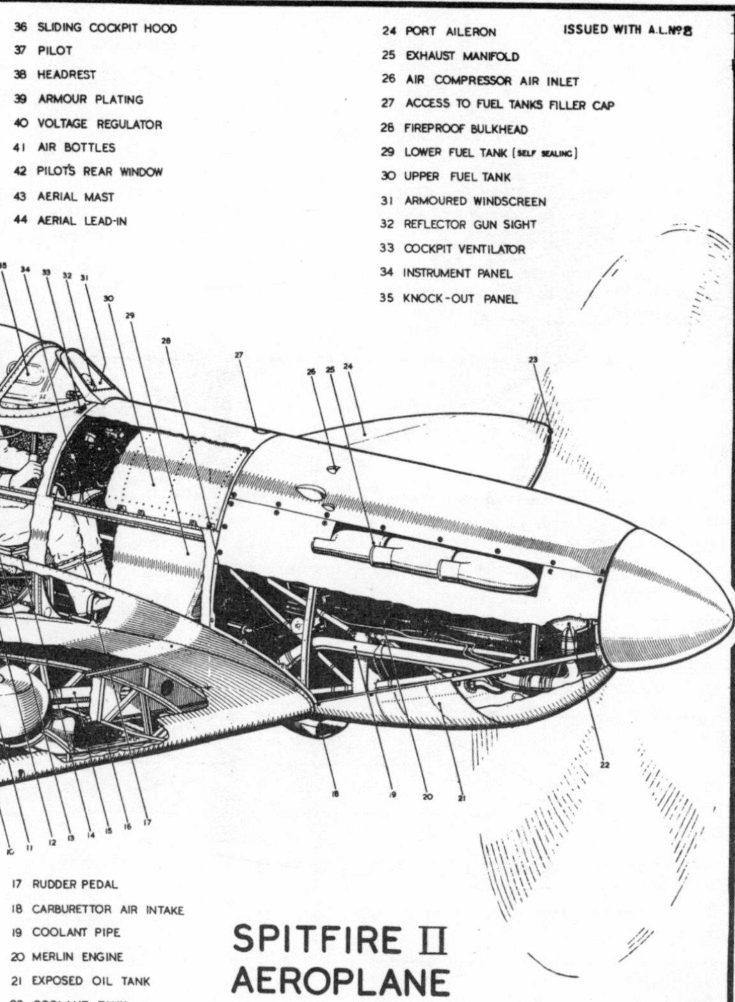
ISSUED WITH A.L.Nº8
36 SLIDING COCKPIT HOOD
37 PILOT
38 HEADREST
39 ARMOUR PLATING
40 VOLTAGE REGULATOR
41 AIR BOTTLES
42 PILOT'S REAR WINDOW
43 AERIAL MAST
44 AERIAL LEAD-IN
24 PORT AILERON
25 EXHAUST MANIFOLD
26 AIR COMPRESSOR AIR INLET
27 ACCESS TO FUEL TANKS FILLER CAP
28 FIREPROOF BULKHEAD
29 LOWER FUEL TANK (SELF SEALING)
30 UPPER FUEL TANK
31 ARMOURED WINDSCREEN
32 REFLECTOR GUN SIGHT
33 COCKPIT VENTILATOR
34 INSTRUMENT PANEL
35 KNOCK-OUT PANEL
17 RUDDER PEDAL
18 CARBURETTOR AIR INTAKE
19 COOLANT PIPE
20 MERLIN ENGINE
21 EXPOSED OIL TANK
22 COOLANT TANK
23 PORT NAVIGATION LAMP
SPITFIRE II
AEROPLANE
A.P. 1565 B. VOL.I.
FRONTISPIECE

AIR PUBLICATION ....

Volume I

Pilot's Notes

AMENDMENT CERTIFICATE

Incorporation of an amendment list in this publication should be certified by inserting the amendment list number, initialling in the appropriate column and inserting the date of incorporation.

Holders of the Pilot's Notes will receive only those amendment lists applicable to the Preliminary Matter, and Sections 1 and 2.

Amendt. List No.	6	8	9	10	11	11A	14		19 F	19 L
Prelimy. matter		✓				✓				
Leading Partics.										
Introducn.					✓					
Section 1	✓				✓				✓	
Section 2	✓		✓	✓			✓			✓
Section 3										
Section 4										
Section 5										
Section 6										
Section 7										
Section 8										
Section 9										
Section 10										
Section 11										
Date of incorpn.				JUNE			1	9	4	3

Amendt. List No.	22 H	23 J	25 K							
Prelimy. matter										
Leading Partics.										
Introducn.										
Section 1										
Section 2	✓	✓	✓							
Section 3										
Section 4										
Section 5										
Section 6										
Section 7										
Section 8										
Section 9										
Section 10										
Section 11										
Date of incorpn.	1/42	5/42	8/42							

NOTES TO OFFICIAL USERS

Air Ministry Orders and Vol. II leaflets as issued from time to time may affect the subject matter of this publication. It should be understood that amendment lists are not always issued to bring the publication into line with the orders or leaflets and it is for holders of this book to arrange the necessary link-up.

Where an order or leaflet contradicts any portion of this publication, an amendment list will generally be issued, but when this is not done, the order or leaflet must be taken as the overriding authority.

Where amendment action has taken place, the number of the amendment list concerned will be found at the top of each page affected, and amendments of technical importance will be indicated by a vertical line on the left-hand side of the text against the matter amended or added. Vertical lines relating to previous amendments to a page are not repeated. If complete revision of any division of the book (e.g. a Chapter) is made this will be indicated in the title page for that division and the vertical lines will not be employed.

LIST OF SECTIONS

(A detailed Contents List is given at the beginning of each Section)

R.T.P./592.3550.6/40

SECTION 1.

CONTROLS AND EQUIPMENT FOR PILOT

LIST OF CONTENTS

SECTION I

PILOT'S CONTROLS AND EQUIPMENT

INTRODUCTION

1. The Spitfire IIA and IIB are single seat, low wing monoplane fighters each fitted with a Merlin XII engine and a de Havilland 20° (P.C.P.) or Rotol 35° constant speed airscrew.

MAIN SERVICES

2. Fuel System -

Fuel is carried in two tanks mounted one above the other (the lower one is self-sealing)forward of the cockpit and is delivered by an engine driven pump. The tank capacities are as follows:

Top tank:	48 gallons
Bottom tank:	37 gallons

The top tank feeds into the lower tank, and the fuel cock controls (38 and 39), one for each tank, are fitted below the instrument panel.

3. Oil System -

Oil is supplied by a tank of 5.8 gallons capacity fitted below the engine mounting, and two oil coolers in tandem are fitted in the underside of the port plane.

4. Hydraulic System -

An engine-driven hydraulic pump supplies the power for operating the under-carriage.

5. Pneumatic system -

An engine-driven air compressor feeds two storage cylinders for operation of the flaps, brakes, guns and landing lamps. The cylinders are connected in series, each holding air at 200 lb/sq.in pressure.

6. Electrical System -

A 12 Volt generator, controlled by a switch (56) above the instrument panel, supplies an accumulator which in turn supplies the whole of the electrical installation. There is a voltmeter (55) on the left of the switch.

AEROPLANE CONTROLS

7. **Primary flying controls and locking devices**

(a) The control column (37) is of the spade-grip pattern and incorporates the brake lever and gun and cannon firing control. The rudder pedals (41) have two positions for the feet and are adjustable for leg reach by rotation of star wheels (42) on the sliding tubes.

(b) Control locking struts are stowed on the right hand side of the cockpit, behind the seat. To lock the control column, the longer strut should be clamped to the control column handle at one end and the other end inserted in a key-hole slot in the right hand side of the seat. The fixed pin on the free end of the arm attached to this strut at the control column end should then be inserted in a lug (72) on the starboard datum longeron, thus forming a rigid triangle between the column, the seat and the longeron.

(c) To lock the rudder pedals, a short bar with a pin at each end is attached to the other struts by a cable. The longer of the two pins should be inserted in a hole in the starboard star wheel bearing and the shorter in an eyebolt (77) on the fuselage frame directly below the front edge of the seat. The controls should be locked with the seat in its highest position.

8. **Flying instruments**

A standard blind flying instrument panel is incorporated in the main panel. The instruments comprise airspeed indicator (28), altimeter (30), directional gyro (31), artificial horizon (29), rate of climb and descent indicator (49), and turn and bank indicator (48).

9. **Trimming tabs**

The elevator trimming tabs are controlled by a hand wheel (7) on the left hand side of the cockpit, the indicator (21) being on the instrument panel. The rudder trimming tab is controlled by a small hand wheel (3) and is not provided with an indicator. The aeroplane tends to turn to starboard when the hand wheel is rotated clockwise.

10. **Undercarriage control and Indicators (visual and audible)**

(a) The undercarriage selector lever (75) moves in a gated quadrant, on the right hand side of the cockpit. An automatic cut-out in the control moves the selector lever into the gate when it has been pushed or pulled to the full extent of the quadrant.

(b) To raise the undercarriage

The lever is pushed forward, but it must first be pulled back and then across to disengage it from the gate. When the undercarriage is raised and locked, the lever will spring into the forward gate.

(c) To lower the undercarriage

The lever is pulled back, but it must be pushed forward and then across to disengage it from the gate. When the undercarriage is lowered and locked, the lever will spring into the rear gate.

(d) Electrical visual indicator

The electrically operated visual indicator (22) has two semi-transparent windows on which the words UP on a red background and DOWN on a green background are lettered; the words are illuminated according to the position of the undercarriage. The switch for the DOWN circuit of the indicator is mounted on the inboard side of the throttle quadrant and is moved to the ON position by means of a striker on the throttle lever; this switch should be returned to the OFF position by hand when the aeroplane is left standing for any length of time. The UP circuit is not controlled by this switch.

(e) Mechanical position indicator

A rod that extends through the top surface of the main plane is fitted to each undercarriage unit. When the wheels are down the rods protrude through the top of the main planes and when they are up the top of the rods, which are painted red, are flush with the main plane surfaces.

(f) Warning horn

The push switch controlling the horn is mounted on the throttle quadrant and is operated by a striker on the throttle lever. The horn may be silenced, even though the wheels are retracted and the engine throttled back, by depressing the push button (9) on the side of the throttle quadrant. As soon as the throttle is again advanced beyond about one quarter of its travel the push-button is automatically released and the horn will sound again on its return.

11. Flap control

The split flaps have two positions only, up and fully down. They cannot therefore, be used to assist take-off. They are operated pneumatically and are controlled by a finger lever (25). A flap indicator was fitted only on early Spitfire I aeroplanes.

12. Undercarriage emergency operation

(a) A sealed high-pressure cylinder containing carbon-dioxide and connected to the undercarriage operating jacks is provided for use in the event of failure of the hydraulic system. The cylinder is mounted on the right hand side of the cockpit and the seal can be punctured by means of a red painted lever (76) beside it. The handle is marked EMERGENCY ONLY and provision is made for fitting a thin copper wire seal as a check against inadvertent use.

(b) If the hydraulic system fails, the pilot should ensure that the undercarriage selector lever is in the DOWN position (this is essential) and push the emergency lowering lever forward and downward. The angular travel of the emergency lever is about 100° for puncturing the seal of the cylinder and then releasing the piercing plunger; it must be pushed through this movement and allowed to swing downwards. NO attempt should be made to return it to its original position until the cylinder is being replaced.

13. Wheel brakes

The control lever (35) for the pneumatic brakes is fitted on the control column spade grip; differential control of the brakes is provided by a relay valve (43) connected to the rudder bar. A catch for retaining the brake lever in the on position for parking is fitted below the lever pivot. A triple pressure gauge (18), showing the air pressures in the pneumatic system cylinders and at each brake, is mounted on the left hand side of the instrument panel.

ENGINE CONTROLS

14. Throttle and mixture controls

The throttle and mixture levers (10 and 11) are fitted in a quadrant on the port side of the cockpit. A gate is provided for the throttle lever in the take-off position and an interlocking device between the levers prevents the engine from being run on an unsuitable mixture. Friction adjusters (8) for the controls are provided on the side of the quadrant.

15. **Automatic boost cut-out**

The automatic boost control may be cut out by pushing forward the small red painted lever (14) at the forward end of the throttle quadrant.

16. **Airscrew controls**

The control lever (12) for the de Havilland 20° or Rotol 35° constant speed airscrew is on the throttle quadrant. The de Havilland 20° airscrew has a Positive Coarse Pitch position which is obtained in the extreme aft position of the control lever, when the airscrew blades are held at their maximum coarse pitch angles and the airscrew functions as a fixed airscrew.

17. **Radiator flap control**

The flap at the outlet end of the radiator duct is operated by a lever (40) and ratchet on the left hand side of the cockpit. To open the flap, the lever should be pushed forward after releasing the ratchet by depressing the knob at the top of the lever. The normal minimum drag position of the flap lever for level flight is shown by a red triangle on the top of the map case fitted beside the lever. A notch beyond the normal position in the aft direction provides a position of the lever when the warm air is diverted through ducts into the main planes for heating the guns at high altitude.

18. **Slow-running cut-out**

The control on the carburettor is operated by pulling the ring (74) on the right hand side of the instrument panel.

19. **Fuel cock controls and contents gauges**

The fuel cock controls (38 and 39), one for each tank, are fitted at the bottom of the instrument panel. With the levers in the up position the cocks are open. Either tank can be isolated, if necessary. The fuel contents gauge (46) on the instrument panel indicates the contents of the lower tank, but only when the adjacent push button is pressed.

20. **Fuel priming pump**

A hand-operated pump (44) for priming the engine is mounted below the right hand side of the instrument panel.

21. **Ignition switches**

The ignition switches (17) are on the left hand bottom corner of the instrument panel.

F.S/4

22. Cartridge starter

The starter push-button (47) at the bottom of the instrument panel operates the L.4 Coffman starter and the booster coil. The control (70) for reloading the breech is below the right-hand side of the instrument panel and is operated by slowly pulling on the finger ring and then releasing it.

23. Hand starting

A starting handle is stowed behind the seat. A hole in the engine cowling panel on the starboard side gives access for connecting the handle to the hand starting gear.

24. Engine instruments

The engine instruments are grouped on the right hand side of the instrument panel and comprise the following: engine-speed indicator (58), fuel pressure gauge (59), boost gauge (61), oil pressure gauge (69), oil inlet temperature gauge (67), radiator outlet temperature gauge (63) and fuel contents gauge (46).

COCKPIT ACCOMMODATION AND EQUIPMENT

25. Pilot's seat control

The seat is adjustable for height by means of a lever on the right hand side of the seat.

26. Safety harness release

In order that the pilot may lean forward without unfastening his harness, a release catch (73) is fitted to the right of the seat.

27. Cockpit door

To facilitate entry to the cockpit a portion of the coaming on the port side is hinged. The door catches are released by means of a handle at the forward end. Two position catches are incorporated to allow the door to be partly opened before taking off or landing in order to prevent the hood from sliding shut in the event of a mishap.

28. Hood locking control

The sliding hood is provided with spring catches for holding it either open or shut; the catches are released by two finger levers at the forward end of the hood. From outside, with the hood closed, the catches can be released by depressing a small knob at the top of the windscreen. Provision is made on the door to prevent the hood from sliding shut if the aeroplane over-turns on landing.

29. **Direct vision panel** -

A small knock-out panel is provided on the right hand side of the hood for use in the event of the windscreen becoming obscured.

30. **Cockpit lighting** -

A floodlight (62) is fitted on each side of the cockpit and is dimmed by a switch (34) immediately below the instrument panel.

31. **Cockpit heating and ventilation** -

A small adjustable flap on the starboard coaming above the instrument panel is provided for ventilation of the cockpit. The flap is opened by turning a knurled nut (57) underneath the flap.

32. **Oxygen** -

A standard regulator unit (23) is fitted on the left hand side of the instrument panel and a bayonet socket (65) is on the right hand side of the cockpit. A separate cock is provided in addition to the regulato

33. **Mirror** -

A mirror providing a rearward view is fitted at the top of the windscreen.

34. **Map cases** -

A metal case (6) for a writing pad and another (2) for maps, books etc. are fitted on the left hand side of the cockpit. Stowage (71) for a height-and-airspeed computor is provided below the wireless remote contacto

OPERATIONAL EQUIPMENT AND CONTROLS

35.(a) **Guns and cannon** -

The eight machine guns on the Spitfire IIA are fired pneumatically by a push-button on the control column spade grip. The compressed air supply is taken from the same source as the brake supply, the available pressure being shown by the gauge (18). The push-butto is surrounded by a milled sleeve which can be rotated by a quarter of a turn to a safe position in which it prevents operation of the button. The SAFE and FIRE positions are engraved on the sleeve and can also be identified by touch as the sleeve has an indentation which is at the bottom when the sleeve is in the SAFE position and is at the side when the sleeve is turned to the FIRE position.

(b) The guns and cannon on the Spitfire IIB are fired pneumatically by a triple push-button on the control column spade grip. A milled finger lever extending from the bottom of the push button casing provides the means of locking the button in the SAFE position, SAFE and FIRE being engraved on the adjacent casing. When the lever is in the FIRE position a pip extends also from the top of the casing enabling the pilot to ascertain by feel the setting of the push button.

(c) To prevent accidental firing of the cannon on the ground, a safety valve is fitted in the firing system. This is mounted below the undercarriage control unit and is coupled to the undercarriage locking pin cable in such a way that the cannon firing system is inoperative when the wheels are locked down. For practice firing at the butts however, a finger lever on the safety valve can be operated to allow the use of the firing system.

(d) The cannons are cocked pneumatically by a cocking valve mounted on the right-hand side of the cockpit.

36. Reflector gun sight

a) For sighting the guns and cannon a reflector gun sight is mounted on a bracket (53) above the instrument panel. A main switch (50) and dimmer switch (51) are fitted below the mounting bracket. The dimmer switch has three positions marked OFF, NIGHT and DAY. Three spare lamps for the sight are stowed in holders (60) on the right hand side of the cockpit.

b) When the sight is used during the day the dimmer switch should be in the DAY position in order to give full illumination, and if the background of the target is very bright, a sun-screen (54) can be slid behind the windscreen by pulling on the ring (52) at the top of the instrument panel. For night use the dimmer switch should be in the NIGHT position; in this position a low-wattage lamp is brought into circuit and the light can be varied by rotating the switch knob.

37. Camera

(a) A G.42B cine-camera is fitted in the leading edge of the port plane, near the root end and is operated by the cannon-firing button on the control column spade grip, a succession of exposures being made during the whole time the button is depressed, provided the selector switch (5) on the left-hand side of the cockpit is ON.

(b) A footage indicator and an aperture switch are mounted on the wedge plate above the throttle lever. The switch enables either of two camera apertures to be selected, the smaller aperture being used for sunny weather. A stowage clip is provided to receive the electrical cable (13) when the indicator and switch are not fitted.

NAVIGATIONAL, SIGNALLING AND LIGHTING EQUIPMENT

38. Wireless

(a) The aeroplane is equipped with a combined transmitter-receiver, either type T.R.9D or T.R.1133, and an R.3002 set.

(b) With the T.R.9D installation a type C mechanical controller (19) is fitted on the port side of the cockpit above the throttle lever and a remote contactor (66) and contactor master switch are fitted on the right hand side of the cockpit. The master contactor is mounted behind the pilot's headrest and a switch controlling the heating element is fitted on the forward bracket of the mounting. The heating element should always be switched OFF when the pilot leaves the aeroplane. The microphone/telephone socket is fitted on the right hand side of the pilot's seat.

(c) With the T.R.1133 installation the contactor gear and microphone/telephone socket are as for the T.R.9D installation, but the type C mechanical controller is replaced by a push-button electrical control unit.

39. Navigation and identification lamps

(a) The switch (24) controlling the navigation lamps is on the instrument panel.

(b) The upward and downward identification lamps are controlled from the signalling switchbox (64) on the right hand side of the cockpit. This switchbox has a switch for each lamp and a morsing key, and provides for steady illumination or morse signalling from each lamp or both. The switch lever has three positions: MORSE, OFF and STEADY.

(c) The spring pressure on the morsing key can be adjusted by turning the small ring at the top left hand corner of the switchbox, adjustment being maintained by a latch engaging one of a number of notches in the ring. The range of movement of the key can be adjusted by opening the cover and adjusting the screw and locknut at the centre of the cover.

40. Landing lamps

The landing lamps, one on each side of the aeroplane, are housed in the undersurface of the main plane. They are lowered and raised by a finger lever (36) below the instrument panel. Each lamp has an independent electrical circuit and is controlled by a switch (16) above the pneumatic control lever (36) with the switch in the central position both lamps are off; when the switch is moved to the left or to the right, the port or the starboard lamp respectively, is illuminated. A lever (15) is provided to control the dipping of both landing lamps. On pulling up the lever the beam is dipped.

41. Signal discharger

A straight pull of the toggle control on the left hand side of the cockpit fires one of the cartridges out of the top of the fuselage, aft of the cockpit.

DE-ICING EQUIPMENT

42. Windscreen de-icing

(a) A tank containing the de-icing solution is mounted on the left-hand side of the cockpit directly above the bottom longeron. A cock is mounted above the tank, and a pump and a needle valve to control the flow of the liquid are mounted below the undercarriage emergency lowering control. Liquid is pumped from the tank to a spray at the base of the windscreen, from which it is sprayed upwards over the front panel of the screen.

(b) The flow of liquid is governed by the needle valve, after turning ON the cock and pushing down the pump plunger to its full extent. The plunger will return to the extended position on its own, and if required it can be pushed down again. When de-icing is no longer required the cock should be turned to the OFF position.

43. Pressure head heater switch

The heating element in the pressure head is controlled by a switch (4) below the trimming tab handwheels. It should be switched off on landing in order to conserve the battery.

F.S/7

EMERGENCY EQUIPMENT

44. **Hood jettisoning**

The hood may be jettisoned in an emergency by pulling the lever mounted inside the top of the hood in a forward and downward movement, and pushing the lower edge of the hood outboard with the elbows. On aeroplanes not fitted with a jettison type hood, a crowbar is provided to assist in jettisoning the hood.

45. **Forced landing flare**

A forced landing flare is carried in a tube fixed inside the fuselage. The flare is released by means of a ring grip (1) on the left of the pilot's seat.

46. **First aid**

The first aid outfit is stowed aft of the wireless equipment and is accessible through a hinged panel on the port side of the fuselage.

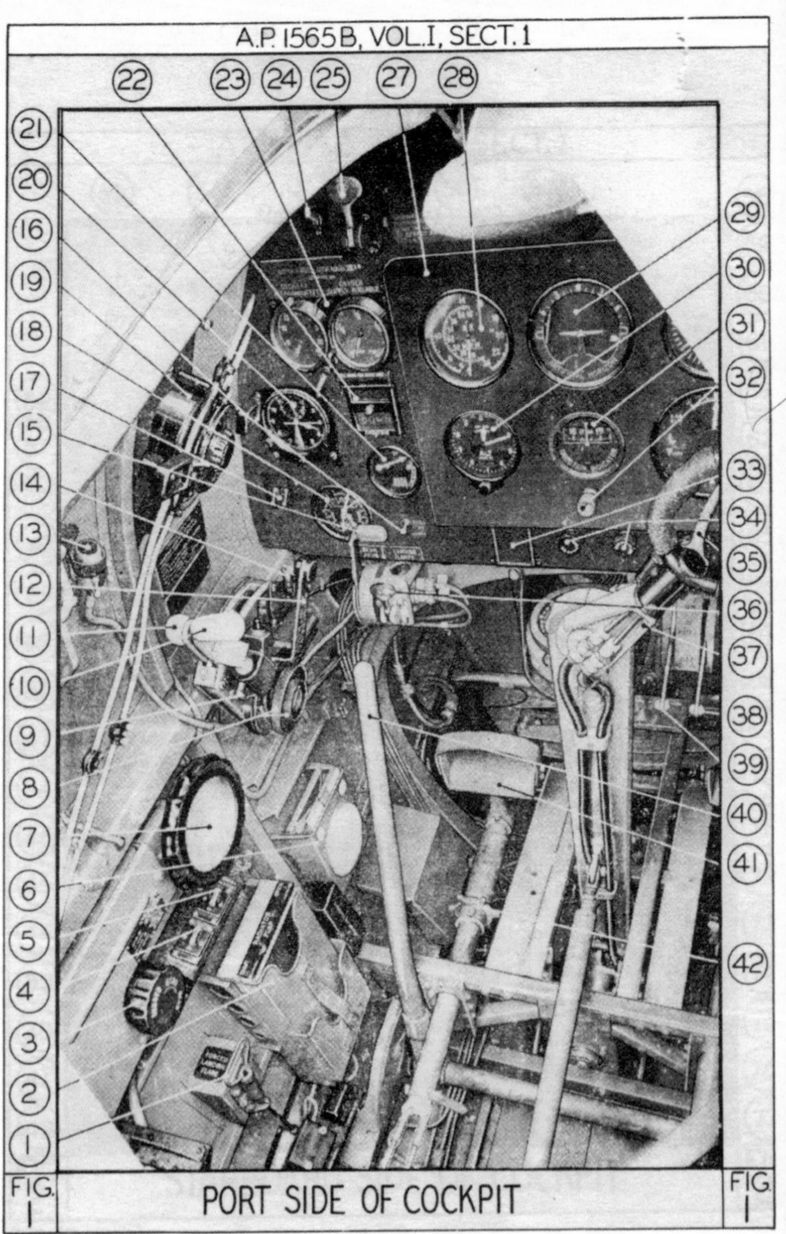

FIG. 1 PORT SIDE OF COCKPIT FIG. 1

F.S./8

Key to fig. 1

Port side of cockpit

1. Flare release control
2. Map stowage box
3. Rudder trimming tab control
4. Pressure head heating switch
5. Camera-gun master switch
6. Writing pad container
7. Elevator trimming tab control
8. Throttle and mixture friction adjusters
9. Push switch for silencing warning horn
10. Throttle lever
11. Mixture lever
12. Airscrew control lever
13. Connection for cine-camera footage indicator
14. Boost cut-out control
15. Landing lamp dipping lever
16. Landing lamps switch
17. Main magneto switches
18. Brake triple pressure gauge
19. Wireless remote controller
20. Clock
21. Elevator trimming tabs position indicator
22. Undercarriage position indicator
23. Oxygen regulator
24. Navigation lamps switch
25. Flaps control

27. Instrument-flying panel
28. Airspeed indicator
29. Artificial horizon
30. Altimeter
31. Direction indicator
32. Setting knob for (31)
33. Compass deviation card holder
34. Cockpit lamp dimmer switches
35. Brake lever
36. Landing lamp lowering control
37. Control column
38. Fuel cock lever (top tank)
39. Fuel cock lever (bottom tank)
40. Radiator flap control lever
41. Rudder pedals
42. Rudder pedal leg reach adjusters

FIG. 2 STARBOARD SIDE OF COCKPIT FIG. 2

F.S./9

Key to fig. 2

Starboard side of cockpit

29. Artificial horizon
31. Direction indicator
34. Cockpit lamp dimmer switch
38. Fuel cock lever (top tank)
39. Fuel cock lever (bottom tank)
43. Brake relay valve
44. Priming pump
45. Compass
46. Fuel contents gauge
47. Engine starting pushbutton
48. Turning indicator
49. Rate of climb indicator
50. Reflector sight main switch
51. Reflector sight lamp dimmer switch
52. Lifting ring for dimming screen
53. Reflector gun sight mounting
54. Dimming screen
55. Ammeter
56. Generator switch
57. Ventilator control
58. Engine speed indicator
59. Fuel pressure gauge
60. Spare filaments for reflector sight
61. Boost gauge
62. Cockpit lamp
63. Radiator temperature gauge
64. Signalling switch box
65. Oxygen socket
66. Wireless remote contactor mounting and switch
67. Oil temperature gauge
68. Engine data plate
69. Oil pressure gauge
70. Cartridge starter reloading control
71. Height and airspeed computor stowage
72. Control locking lug
73. Harness release
74. Slow-running cut-out control
75. Undercarriage control lever
76. Undercarriage emergency lowering lever
77. Control locking lug

SECTION 2

HANDLING AND FLYING NOTES FOR PILOT

AMENDED BY AL.10

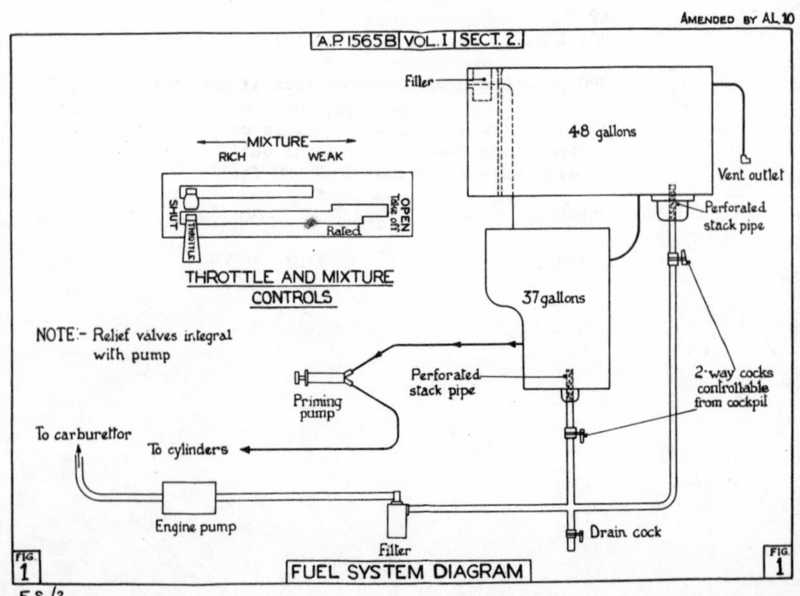

FUEL SYSTEM DIAGRAM

F.S./2

SECTION 2

HANDLING AND FLYING NOTES FOR PILOT

1. ENGINE DATA: MERLIN XII

(i) Fuel: 100 octane (the reduced limitations for use with 87 octane fuel are shown in brackets)

(ii) Oil: See A.P.1464/C.37.

(iii) Engine limitations:

	R.p.m.	Boost lb/sq.in.	Temp. °C Clnt.	Temp. °C Oil
MAX. TAKE-OFF TO 1,000 FEET	3,000	+12½(+7)	-	-
MAX. CLIMBING 1 HR. LIMIT	2,850	+ 9 (+7)	125	90
MAX. RICH CONTINUOUS	2,650	+ 7 (+5)	105*	90
MAX. WEAK CONTINUOUS	2,650	+ 4 (+2½)	105*	90
COMBAT 5 MINS. LIMIT	3,000	+12 (+7)	135	105

* 115°C permitted for short periods if necessary

Note: +12 lb/sq.in. combat boost is obtained by operating the boost control out-out and is effective up to about 10,500 feet.

OIL PRESSURE: MINM. IN FLIGHT: 30 lb/sq.in.

MINM. TEMP. FOR TAKE-OFF: OIL: 15°C
COOLANT: 60°C

FUEL PRESSURE: NORMAL: 2½-3 lb/sq.in.

F.S/3

(iv) Other limitations:

Diving: Maximum r.p.m. : 3,600
3,000 r.p.m. may be exceeded only for 20 seconds, with the throttle not less than one-third open.

(v) Combat concession:

3,000 r.p.m. may be used above 20,000 feet for periods not exceeding 30 minutes.

2. FLYING LIMITATIONS

(i) Maximum speeds (m.p.h. I.A.S.):

Diving:	450
Undercarriage down:	160
Flaps down:	140
Landing lamps lowered:	140

(ii) A.S.R. dinghy:

Aircraft carrying air/sea rescue dinghy equipment must be fitted with an inertia weight in the elevator control circuit. Aerobatics and violent manoeuvres are not permitted until the equipment is dropped.

3. PRELIMINARIES

On entering the cockpit check:

Undercarriage selector lever - DOWN
(Check that indicator shows DOWN; switch on light indicator and check that green lights appear).

Flaps - UP

Landing lamps - UP

Contents of lower fuel tank.

4. STARTING THE ENGINE AND WARMING UP

(i) Set:

Both fuel cock levers - ON
Throttle - ½ inch open
Mixture control - RICH
Airscrew speed control - Fully back DH 20°
Rotol 35° Propellor. Lever fully forward.
Radiator shutter - OPEN

(ii) Operate the priming pump to prime the suction and delivery pipes. This may be judged by a sudden increase in resistance of the plunger.

(iii) Prime the engine, the number of strokes required being as follows:

Air temperature °C:	+30	+20	+10	0	-10	-20
Normal fuel:	3	4	7	13		
High volatility fuel:				4	8	15

(iv) Switch ON ignition and pull out the priming pump handle.

(v) Press the starter push button and at the same time give one stroke of the priming pump. The push button also switches on the booster coil and should be kept depressed until the engine is firing evenly.

Note: If the engine fails to start on the first cartridge, no more priming should be carried out before firing the second, but another stroke should be given as the second cartridge is fired.

(vi) As soon as the engine is running evenly, screw down the priming pump.

5. TESTING ENGINE AND INSTALLATIONS

(i) While warming up, exercise the airscrew speed control a few times. Also make the usual checks of temperatures, pressures and controls. Brake pressure should be at least 120 lb/sq.in.

(ii) See that the cockpit hood is locked open and that the emergency exit door is set at the "half-clock" position.

(iii) After a few minutes move the airscrew speed control fully forward.

(iv) After warming up, open the throttle to give maximum boost for cruising with WEAK mixture and test the operation of the constant speed airscrew.

(v) Open the throttle to give maximum boost for cruising with RICH mixture and check each magneto in turn. The drop in r.p.m. should not exceed 150.

(vi) Open the throttle fully momentarily and check static r.p.m., boost and oil pressure.

(vii) Warming up must not be unduly prolonged because the radiator temperature before taxying out must not exceed 100°C.

When engines are being kept warm in readiness for immediate take-off, de Havilland 20° C.S. propeller should be left in fine pitch - control lever fully forward.

6. TAXYING OUT

It may be found that one wing tends to remain down while taxying. This is due to stiffness in the undercarriage leg, especially in a new aeroplane.

FINAL PREPARATION FOR TAKE-OFF - DRILL OF VITAL ACTIONS

7. Drill is "T.M.P., Fuel, Flaps and Radiator".

T - Trimming Tabs	-	Elevator about one division nose down from neutral. Rudder fully to starboard.
M - Mixture control	-	RICH
P - Pitch	-	Airscrew speed control fully forward.
Fuel	-	Both cock levers ON and check contents of lower tank.
Flaps	-	UP
Radiator shutter	-	Fully open.

TAKE-OFF

8. (i) Open the throttle slowly to the gate (RATED BOOST position). Any tendency to swing can be counteracted by coarse use of the rudder. If taking off from a small aerodrome with a full load, max. boost may be obtained by opening the throttle through the gate to the TAKE-OFF BOOST position.

(ii) After raising the undercarriage, see that the red indicator light - UP - comes on (it may be necessary to hold the lever hard forward against the quadrant until the indicator light comes on).

(iii) Do not start to climb before a speed of 140 m.p.h. A.S.I.R. is attained.

CLIMBING

9. Up to 15,000 feet the maximum rate of climb is obtained at 160 m.p.h. A.S.I.R. but for normal climbing the following speeds are recommended:-

Ground level to 13,000 feet	185 m.p.h. A.S.I.R.
13,000 feet to 15,000 feet	180 " "
15,000 feet to 20,000 feet	160 " "
20,000 feet to 25,000 feet	140 " "
25,000 feet to 30,000 feet	125 " "
30,000 feet to 35,000 feet	110 " "

F.S/5

GENERAL FLYING

10. **Stability and control**

(i) This aeroplane is stable. With metal covered ailerons the lateral control is much lighter than with the earlier fabric covered ailerons and pilots accustomed to the latter must be careful not to overstress the wings. Similar care is necessary in the use of the elevators which are light and sensitive.

(ii) For normal cruising flight the radiator shutter should be in the minimum drag position.

(iii) Change of trim

Undercarriage down	-	nose down
Flaps down	-	nose down

(iv) Maximum range is obtained with WEAK mixture, 1,700 r.p.m. and at 160 m.p.h. A.S.I.R.

(v) Maximum endurance is obtained with WEAK mixture, 1,700 r.p.m. and at the lowest speed at which the machine can be comfortably flown.

(vi) For combat manoeuvres, climbing r.p.m. should be used.

(vii) For stretching a glide in the event of a forced landing, the airscrew speed control should be pulled right back and the radiator flap put at the minimum drag position.

STALLING

11. (i) At the stall one wing will usually drop with flaps either up or down and the machine may spin if the control column is held back.

(ii) This aeroplane has sensitive elevators and, if the control column is brought back too rapidly in a manoeuvre such as a loop or steep turn, stalling incidence may be reached and a high-speed stall induced. When this occurs there is a violent shudder and clattering noise throughout the aeroplane, which tends to flick over laterally and, unless the control column is put forward instantly, a rapid roll and spin will result.

(iii) Approximate stalling speeds when loaded to about 6,250 lb. are:-

Flaps and undercarriage	UP	73 m.p.h. A.S.I.R.
" " "	DOWN	64 " "

SPINNING

12. (i) Spinning is permitted by pilots who have written permission from the C.O. of their squadron (C.F.I. of an O.T.U.). The loss of height involved in recovery may be very great, and the following height limits are to be observed:-

(a) Spins are not to be started below 10,000 feet.

(b) Recovery must be started not lower than 5,000 feet.

(ii) A speed of over 150 m.p.h. I.A.S. should be attained before starting to ease out of the resultant dive.

AEROBATICS

13. (i) This aeroplane is exceptionally good for aerobatics. Owing to its high performance and sensitive elevator control, care must be taken not to impose excessive loads either on the aeroplane or on the pilot and not to induce a high-speed stall. Many aerobatics may be done at much less than full throttle. Cruising r.p.m. should be used, because if reduced below this, detonation might occur if the throttle is opened up to climbing boost for any reason.

(ii) The following speeds are recommended for aerobatics:-

Looping

Speed should be about 300 m.p.h. I.A.S. but may be reduced to 220-250 m.p.h. when the pilot is fully proficient.

Rolling

Speed should be anywhere between 180 and 300 m.p.h. I.A.S. The nose should be brought up about 30° above the horizon at the start, the roll being barrelled just enough to keep the engine running throughout.

Half roll off loop

Speed should be 320-350 m.p.h. I.A.S.

Upward roll

Speed should be about 350-400 m.p.h. I.A.S.

Flick manoeuvres

Flick manoeuvres are not permitted.

DIVING

13a. (i) The aeroplane becomes very tail heavy at high speed and must be trimmed into the dive in order to avoid the dangers of excessive acceleration in recovery. The forward trim should be wound back as speed is lost after pulling out.

(ii) A tendency to yaw to the right should be corrected by use of the rudder trimming tab.

APPROACH AND LANDING

14. (i) During the preliminary approach see that the cockpit hood is locked open, and the emergency exit door is set at half-cock position. Take care not to get the arm out into the airflow.

(ii) Reduce speed to 140 m.p.h. I.A.S. and carry out the Drill of Vital Actions "U.M.P. and flaps".

U - Undercarriage - DOWN (Watch indicators and check green lights)

M - Mixture control - RICH

P - Pitch - Propeller speed control fully forward.

Flaps - DOWN

(iii) When lowering the undercarriage hold the lever fully forward for about two seconds. This will take the weight off the locking pins and allow them to turn freely when the lever is pulled back. The lever should then be pulled back smartly to the down position; if it cannot be pulled fully back, hold it forward again for at least two seconds. If it becomes jammed it may generally be released by a smart blow of the hand. If this fails it is necessary to take the weight of the wheels off the locking pins, either by pushing the nose down sharply or by inverting the aeroplane. The lever can then be pulled straight back.

(iv) If the green indicator light does not come on, hold the lever fully back for a few seconds. If this fails, raise the undercarriage and repeat the lowering. If this fails also, use the emergency system (see Section 1, Para. 12).

Note: Before the emergency system can be used, the control lever must be in the down position. It may be necessary to push the nose down or invert the aeroplane in order to get the lever down.

(v) Correct speeds for the approach:-

Engine assisted	-	about 85 m.p.h. I.A.S.
Glide	-	" 90 " "

(vi) Sideslips may be performed quite satisfactorily with the flaps either up or down.

MISLANDING

15. Climb at about 120 m.p.h. I.A.S.

LANDING ACROSS WIND

16. The aeroplane can be landed across wind but it is undesirable that such landings should be made if the wind exceeds about 20 m.p.h.

AFTER LANDING

17. (i) After taxying in, set the propeller control fully back and open up the engine sufficiently to change pitch to coarse. DH 20°

(ii) Allow the engine to idle for a few seconds, then pull the slow-running cut-out and hold it out until the engine stops.

(iii) Turn OFF the fuel cocks and switch OFF the ignition.

FLYING AT REDUCED AIRSPEEDS

18. Reduce the speed to about 120 m.p.h. I.A.S. and lower the flaps. The radiator shutter must be opened to keep the temperature at about 100°C and the propeller speed control should be set to give cruising r.p.m.

F.S/7

POSITION ERROR TABLE

19. The corrections for position error are as follows:-

	m.p.h. I.A.S.									
From To	100 110	110 120	120 130	130 140	140 150	150 165	165 180	180 195	195 220	220 and over
Add Subtract	10	8	6	4	2	- -	 2	 4	 6	 8

FUEL AND OIL CAPACITY AND CONSUMPTION

20. (i) <u>Fuel and oil capacities</u>

Fuel capacity:-

2 Main tanks - top tank		48 gallons
	bottom tank	37 gallons
Total effective capacity		85 gallons

Oil capacity:-
Effective capacity 5.8 gallons

(ii) <u>Fuel consumption</u>

Max r.p.m. and boost for:	Height feet	Approximate Consumption galls/hr.
Climbing	13,000	94
Cruising RICH	13,000	78
" WEAK	18,000	56
All-out level	14,500	98

OIL DILUTION IN COLD WEATHER

21. See A.P.2095/4. The dilution period should be:

Atmospheric temperatures above -10°C : 1½ minutes
Atmospheric temperatures below -10°C : 2½ minutes

2

FORM 414: PILOT'S FLYING LOG BOOK

Every service pilot was obliged by the Air Ministry to keep 'an accurate and detailed record… of all flights'. These were to be recorded in the Pilot's Flying Log Book, the blue, hard cover 'Form 414'. In addition to flights, a record was also maintained of types flown, airfields at which the pilot had landed, and a 'Record of Service', that being the pilot's promotions and units. Every month the log was endorsed by the pilot's senior officer, and commendations and punishments were also recorded, an endorsement in green ink being for commendable flying, such as saving an aircraft under difficult circumstances, but 'blacks' – RAF slang for a faux pas – such as landing with wheels up, were recorded in red. Flying assessments were also pasted into the log book, the style of which differed from squadron to squadron. Some pilots were encouraged to maintain their log as a very personal document and record, pasting in newspaper cuttings and snapshots, whilst others were recorded in minimal detail.

The log book opens out into a double-page entry, going left to right across both pages, for each day, columns being year and date, aircraft type, individual serial number, identity of pilot, details of the sortie, times up and down, total time of sortie and total number of flying hours. Additionally, pilots would record victories, losses and any other remarkable detail. After the war, most survivors were able to retain their log books as a souvenir, but unless relatives requested them and apart from a small number preserved for posterity (now available for public scrutiny at The National Archive), the logs of casualties were destroyed.

The pages reproduced here are from the log book number three belonging to Johnnie Johnson, the RAF's top scoring ace of World War Two, and covering the period March 1944 – May 1945. A unique document from Britain's greatest fighter pilot, this really is inspirational material.

T7351 Wt. 11351 28,000 Bks. 2/40—Sir J. C. & S. Ltd.—18

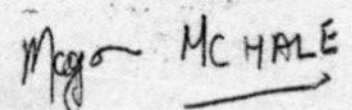

INSTRUCTIONS

[see K.R. & A.C.I., para. 786]

1. This book is an official document and is the property of His Majesty's Government.

2. An accurate and detailed record is to be kept in the log of all flights undertaken by the individual to whom it relates.

3. Monthly flying will be analysed by aircraft types and inserted in red ink. The stamp will be inserted on the left-hand page appropriately aligned to the ruling.

4. The annual summary and assessment will be completed on Form 414 A and inserted in the appropriate page of the log. This form will also be used when a pilot is posted or attached to another unit for flying duties.

CERTIFICATES OF QUALIFICATION AS FIRST PILOT

[K.R. & A.C.I., para. 805, clause 5.]

Name J.E. Johnson. *Rank* W/Cdr.

(i) Certified that the above named has qualified as a first pilot (day only)

On (Type)	Date	Unit	Signature and Rank

(ii) Certified that the above named has qualified as a First Pilot

On (Type)	Date	Unit	Signature and Rank

YEAR		AIRCRAFT		PILOT, OR 1ST PILOT	2ND PILOT, PUPIL OR PASSENGER	DUTY (INCLUDING RESULTS AND
MONTH	DATE	Type	No.			
–	–	—	–	—	—	TOTALS BROUGHT
						Enemy
		1941 – 616 Sqn. A.A.F				
June	26	1	Me	109	Destroyed.	1
July	6	1	Me	109	Destroyed.	2
July	14	1	Me	109	Destroyed.	3
Aug	9	$\frac{1}{2}$	Me	109	Destroyed.	$3\frac{1}{2}$
Aug	9	1	Me	109	Destroyed.	$4\frac{1}{2}$
Sep	21	2	Me	109s	Destroyed.	$6\frac{1}{2}$
		1942 – 610 Sqn AAF				
Aug	19	1	FW	190	Destroyed	$7\frac{1}{2}$
Aug	19	$\frac{1}{3}$	Me	109	Destroyed	$7\frac{5}{6}$
		1943 Kenley & 127 Wings.				RCAF
April	3	1	FW	190	Destroyed.	$8\frac{5}{6}$
May	11	1	FW	190	Destroyed.	$9\frac{5}{6}$
May	13	1	FW	190	Destroyed.	$10\frac{5}{6}$
May	13	$\frac{1}{3}$	FW	190	Destroyed	$11\frac{1}{6}$
May	14	1	FW	190	Destroyed.	$12\frac{1}{6}$
June	1	$\frac{1}{2}$	Me	109	Destroyed.	$12\frac{4}{6}$
June	15	2	FW	190s	Destroyed.	$14\frac{4}{6}$
June	17	1	FW	190	Destroyed	$15\frac{4}{6}$
June	24	1	FW	190	Destroyed.	$16\frac{4}{6}$
June	27	1	FW	190	Destroyed.	$17\frac{4}{6}$

GRAND TOTAL [Cols. (1) to (10)] ....Hrs..........Mins.

TOTALS CARRIED

3

Single-Engine Aircraft				Multi-Engine Aircraft						Pass-enger	Instr/Cloud Flying [Incl. in cols. (1) to (10)]	
Day		Night		Day			Night					
Dual	Pilot	Dual	Pilot	Dual	1st Pilot	2nd Pilot	Dual	1st Pilot	2nd Pilot		Dual	Pilot
(1)	(2)	(3)	(4)	(5)	(6)	(7)	(8)	(9)	(10)	(11)	(12)	(13)

Destroyed.

July 15 1 Me 109 Destroyed 18 $\frac{4}{6}$

July 25 1 Me 109 Destroyed 19 $\frac{4}{6}$

July 30 $\frac{1}{2}$ Me 109 Destroyed 20 $\frac{1}{6}$

Aug 12 1 Me 109 Destroyed 21 $\frac{1}{6}$ (1 stepped up from $\frac{1}{2}$ Me 109 on evidence of cine film)

Aug 17 $\frac{1}{4}$ Me 110 Destroyed 21 $\frac{5}{12}$

Aug 23 1 Me 109 Destroyed 22 $\frac{5}{12}$

Aug 26 1 FW 190 Destroyed 23 $\frac{5}{12}$

Sept 4 1 FW 190 Destroyed 24 $\frac{5}{12}$.

1944 144 x 127 Wings RCAF

Mar 28 $\frac{1}{2}$ unidentified twin engined aircraft destroyed. 24 $\frac{11}{12}$

April 25 2 FW 190s Destroyed. 26 $\frac{11}{12}$

May 5 1 FW 190 Destroyed 27 $\frac{11}{12}$

June 16 1 FW 190 Destroyed 28 $\frac{11}{12}$

June 22 1 Me 109 Destroyed 29 $\frac{11}{12}$

June 28 2 Me 109s Destroyed 31 $\frac{11}{12}$

June 30 1 Me 109 Destroyed. 32 $\frac{11}{12}$

July 5 2 FW 190s Destroyed 34 $\frac{11}{12}$

Aug 23 2 FW 190 Destroyed 36 $\frac{11}{12}$

Sept 27 1 Me 109 Destroyed. 37 $\frac{11}{12}$ 38

(1)	(2)	(3)	(4)	(5)	(6)	(7)	(8)	(9)	(10)	(11)	(12)	(13)

YEAR 1944		AIRCRAFT		PILOT, OR 1ST PILOT	2ND PILOT, PUPIL OR PASSENGER	DUTY (INCLUDING RESULTS AND REMARKS)
MONTH	DATE	Type	No.			
FORD.	–	–	–	–	–	— TOTALS BROUGHT FORWARD
June.	3	Spitfire IX	MK.392.	Self.		Cannon Test.
June	3.	Spitfire IX.	MK. 392.	Self.	29	LEADING 443 SQD. GROUND STRAFFING IN COURTRAI AREA.
June	3.	Spitfire IX	MK.392.	Self.		To Reamsby.
June	4.	Spitfire IX	MK.392.	Self.		From Reamsby.
June	6.	Spitfire IX	MK.392	Self.	30	PATROL ASSAULT BEACHES.
June	6	Spitfire IX	MK.392.	Self	31	do
June	6	Spitfire IX	MK.392	Self	32	do
June	6.	Spitfire IX	MK 392.	Self.	33	do.
June	7	Spitfire IX	MK.392	Self	34	do
June	7.	Spitfire IX	MK.392.	Self.	35	do
June	8	Spitfire IX	MK.392	Self	36	do
June	8	Spitfire IX	MK.392	Self.	37	do.
June	10	Spitfire IX	MK.392.	Self.	38	SWEEP. LANDED AT ST. CROIX sur MER.
June	10	Spitfire IX	MK.392.	Self.	39	PATROL BEACHES.

GRAND TOTAL [Cols. (1) to (10)]
1567 Hrs. 45 Mins.

TOTALS CARRIED FORWARD

Single-Engine Aircraft				Multi-Engine Aircraft						Pass-enger	Instr/Cloud Flying [Incl. in cols. (1) to (10)]	
Day		Night		Day			Night					
Dual	Pilot	Dual	Pilot	Dual	1st Pilot	2nd Pilot	Dual	1st Pilot	2nd Pilot		Dual	Pilot
(1)	(2)	(3)	(4)	(5)	(6)	(7)	(8)	(9)	(10)	(11)	(12)	(13)
·35	1454·05											
	·30									56		
			11 Transports Destroyed.									
	1·50											
	1·00											
	1·00											
	2·00			"D" DAY. British & American Forces								
	2·00						invade Normandy.					
	2·00											
	·2·00											
	2·15		1 Me 109 Destroyed. F/Lt Russell & F/O Ockenden.									
	2·15											
	2·15											
	2·15											
	2·15		First Wing to touch down in France.									
	2·15											
3·35	1479·55											
(1)	(2)	(3)	(4)	(5)	(6)	(7)	(8)	(9)	(10)	(11)	(12)	(13)
	25·50											

Year 1944 Month	Date	Aircraft Type	Aircraft No.	Pilot, or 1st Pilot	2nd Pilot, Pupil or Passenger	Duty (Including Results and Remar
—	—	—	—	—	—	— Totals Brought Forw
FORD						
June	11	Spitfire IX	MK.392	Self	40	PATROL BEACHES.
June	12	Spitfire IX.	MK.392.	Self.	41	do.
June	12.	Spitfire IX.	MK.392.	Self.	42	do
June	14	Spitfire IX	MK.392.	Self.	43	SWEEP West of PARI
June	15	Spitfire IX	MK 392	Self.		TO CROIX SUR MER.
CROIX SUR MER — FRANCE.						
June	16.					
June	16	Spitfire IX	MK.392.	Self.	44	PATROL CAEN AREA.
June	17	Spitfire IX.	MK.392	Self.	45	PATROL. DREUX - ARGENT.
June	22	Spitfire IX	MK 392	Self.	46	SCRAMBLE. LEADING 442 SQD.

GRAND TOTAL [Cols. (1) to (10)]
1581 Hrs. 40 Mins.

Totals Carried Forw

Single-Engine Aircraft				Multi-Engine Aircraft						Pass-enger	Instr/Cloud Flying [Incl. in cols. (1) to (10)]	
Day		Night		Day			Night					
Dual	Pilot	Dual	Pilot	Dual	1st Pilot	2nd Pilot	Dual	1st Pilot	2nd Pilot		Dual	Pilot
(1)	(2)	(3)	(4)	(5)	(6)	(7)	(8)	(9)	(10)	(11)	(12)	(13)
3.35	1479.55											
	2.15	Trains & Ground Targets attacked. (27)										
	2.20											
		Pilot who ... his aircraft.										
	2.00											
	2.30	1 Do 217 Destroyed. S/Ldr McLeod. 443										
		1 Do 217 Destroyed. P/O Hodgins. 443										
	.40											
		1 Me Hancock – 2 months late.										
		1 Me 109 Destroyed. F/Lt Walz. 443 Sqd. 29										
	1.10	Manoeuvring his FW 190s about. Self – 1 FW 190 Destroyed										
		S/Ldr McLeod – 1 Me 109 Destroyed										
		443 S/Ldr Hall, F/Lt Russell, F/Lt Walz, P/O Perez-Gomez – missing										
	2.00	Awarded Second Bar to D.S.O.										
	1.00	1. Me 109 Destroyed. Self. (30)										
		1. Me 109 Destroyed P/O Weeks. 442										
		1 Me 109 Destroyed. P/O Young. 442										
		1. FW 190 Destroyed. F/Lt Marriott. 442.										
		1. FW 190 Destroyed. F/O Fleming. 441.										
		1. FW 190 Destroyed shared. F/O Brown, F/O Clausen, F/Sgt McMillan. 441.										
3.35	1493.50											
	13.55											

YEAR 1944		AIRCRAFT		PILOT, OR 1ST PILOT	2ND PILOT, PUPIL OR PASSENGER	DUTY (INCLUDING RESULTS AND REMAR
MONTH	DATE	Type	No.			
ST CROIX SUR MER.				—	—	— TOTALS BROUGHT FORWA
June	23	Spitfire IX.	MK. 392.	Self.	47	SWEEP ALENCON AREA
June	24	Spitfire IX.	MK. 392.	Self.	48	ARMED RECCO ARGENTAN AREA.
June	24	Spitfire IX	MK. 392	Self.	49	ARMED RECCO. EVREUX AREA.
June	26	Spitfire IX	MK. 392.	Self.	50	Weather Recco.
June	26	Spitfire IX	MK. 392.	Self.	51	ARMED RECCO. AGENTAN AREA.
June	26	Spitfire IX	MK. 392.	Self.	52	PATROL with S/Ldr McLeod.
June	27	Spitfire IX.	MK. 392.	Self.	53	PATROL with 441 SQD.
June	28	Spitfire IX.	MK. 392.	Self	54	ARMED RECCO with 442 SQD.

GRAND TOTAL [Cols. (1) to (10)] 1589 Hrs. 20 Mins. TOTALS CARRIED FORW

Single-Engine Aircraft				Multi-Engine Aircraft						Pass-enger	Instr/Cloud Flying [Incl. in cols. (1) to (10)]	
Day		Night		Day			Night					
Dual	Pilot	Dual	Pilot	Dual	1st Pilot	2nd Pilot	Dual	1st Pilot	2nd Pilot		Dual	Pilot
(1)	(2)	(3)	(4)	(5)	(6)	(7)	(8)	(9)	(10)	(11)	(12)	(13)
53·35	1493·50											
	1·20.		443	S/Ldr McLeod.			2 FW 190's Destroyed.					
			443	F/Lt Shenk.			1. FW. 190. Damaged.					
	1·20.			Transport shot-up.						58		
	1·00											
	·20											
	1·10.			6 Transports Destroyed 441 Sqd.								
				5 " " Damaged.						442 Sqd.		
							F/Lt Dowding.			2 Me 109's Dest.		
	·30						F/O McLarty.			2 Me 109's Dest.		
	1·00			7 E/A. Sighted but contact not close.								
	1·00			7 E/A. (109's) engaged.							443 Sqd	
				Self. 2 Me 109's Destroyed. 31 32						1 FW 190 Dest. F/O Stephen.		
	-			F/O Robillard 1 Me 109 "						1 FW 190 " F/O Gilbert.		
				F/O Goodwin. 1. Me 109 "						1 FW 190 Dam. F/L Shenk.		
				F/O O'Sullivan. 1 Me 109 Probably Dest.								
				F/O Burn. 1. Me 109 Damaged.								
53·35	1501·30											
(1)	(2) 7·40	(3)	(4)	(5)	(6)	(7)	(8)	(9)	(10)	(11)	(12)	(13)

Year 1944.		Aircraft		Pilot, or 1st Pilot	2nd Pilot, Pupil or Passenger	DUTY (Including Results and Remark[s])
Month	Date	Type	No.			
ST. CROIX- SUR- MER.				—	—	—— Totals Brought Forwa[rd]
June	28	Spitfire IX	MK. 392.	Self.	55	ANTI - RECCO with 441.
June	29	Spitfire IX.	9G. W.	Self.	56	ARMED RECCO with 44[1]
June	30	Spitfire IX.	9G. W.	Self.	57	FRONT LINE PATROL.
				Summary for JUNE 1944. 144 Wing. 17 Sector. R.C.A.F. J.E. Johnson. W/Cdr. 1 July 1944.		Spitfire IX.

GRAND TOTAL [Cols. (1) to (10)]
1592 Hrs. 40 Mins.

Totals Carried Forwa[rd]

Single-Engine Aircraft				Multi-Engine Aircraft						Pass-enger	Instr/Cloud Flying [Incl. in cols. (1) to (10)]	
Day		Night		Day			Night					
Dual	Pilot	Dual	Pilot	Dual	1st Pilot	2nd Pilot	Dual	1st Pilot	2nd Pilot		Dual	Pilot
(1)	(2)	(3)	(4)	(5)	(6)	(7)	(8)	(9)	(10)	(11)	(12)	(13)
3.35	1501.30											
	1.20									59		
	1.00		Several M.E.T. attacked.									
	1.00		441 S/Ldr Browne. 1 F.W. 190 Destroyed.									
			Self. 1 Me 109 "									
			441 F/Lt Johnstone 1. Me 109 " + 1 Me 109 Damaged.									
			441 F/O Mott. 1. Me 109 "									
			442 F/O Young. 1. Me 109 Destroyed									
			442 F/Lt Roseland 1½. Me 109's Destroyed.									
			442. F/O [illegible] ½ Me 109 Destroyed.									
	50.45		Operational Hours for JUNE. 1944. 47.45.									
			Total Operational Hrs this tour. 95.05.									
			E/A Destroyed this tour. 8½.									
			E/A Destroyed Previously. 24 5/12.									
			Total E/A Destroyed. 32 11/12 (includes ½ Destroyed)									
	J. E. Johnson. W/Cdr.											
3.35	1504.50											
(1)	(2)	(3)	(4)	(5)	(6)	(7)	(8)	(9)	(10)	(11)	(12)	(13)
	3.20											

YEAR 1944. MONTH	DATE	AIRCRAFT "FINALE". Type	No.	PILOT, OR 1ST PILOT	2ND PILOT, PUPIL OR PASSENGER	DUTY (INCLUDING RESULTS AND REMAR
ST CROIX SUR MER				—	—	— TOTALS BROUGHT FORWA
July	2	Spitfire IX	MK.392.	Self.	58	Front Line Patrol. (442
July	3	Spitfire IX	MK.392.	Self.	59	Front Line Patrol (443)
July	5	Spitfire IX.	MK.392.	Self.	60	Front Line Patrol (441
July	5	Spitfire IX.	MK.392	Self.	61	Patrol. Argentan-Alençon Area.
	7	[illegible]	[illegible] – 890		[illegible]	
July	8	Spitfire IX.	MK.392	Self.	62	Patrol Beaches.
July	9	Spitfire IX	MK.392.	Self.	63	Armed Recce. 441 Sqd.
July	10	Spitfire IX	MK.392.	Self.	64	Armed Recce. 442 Sqd
July	12	Spitfire IX	MK.392	Self		To Tangmere
July	15	Spitfire IX	MK.392.	Self.		from Tangmere.
July	16	"				

GRAND TOTAL [Cols. (1) to (10)] 1600 Hrs. 50 Mins.

TOTALS CARRIED FORW

Single-Engine Aircraft				Multi-Engine Aircraft						Pass-enger	Instr/Cloud Flying [Incl. in cols. (1) to (10)]	
Day		Night		Day			Night					
Dual	Pilot	Dual	Pilot	Dual	1st Pilot	2nd Pilot	Dual	1st Pilot	2nd Pilot		Dual	Pilot
(1)	(2)	(3)	(4)	(5)	(6)	(7)	(8)	(9)	(10)	(11)	(12)	(13)
3.35	1504.50											
	1.15	443. F/Lt Roseland. 1. Me 109 Destroyed; 441. F/Lt Moore. 2½ Me 109. Destroyed.; 441. F/O Lake. 2½. Me 109. Destroyed.										
	1.10											
	1.15											(60)
	1.00		Engaged 10 FW 190's. Self 2 FW 190s Destroyed. (34 3½); S/Ldr Brannagan 1. FW 190 Destroyed & 1 FW 190 Damaged									
	.40		F/Lt Mott 1. FW 190 Destroyed & 1 FW 190 Damaged.; F/O Neil. 1 FW 190 Destroyed.; F/O Kimball 1 FW 190 Destroyed; F/O Clowes 1 FW 190 Destroyed (missing); F/O McKenzie. 1 FW 190 Damaged.; F/O Hill. 1 FW 190. Damaged.									
	1.10.		M.E.T attacked.									
	.20		Hit by heavy flak in fuselage!!									
	.40											
	.40		July 14. 144 Wing disbanded.									
3.35	1513.00											
(1)	(2)	(3)	(4)	(5)	(6)	(7)	(8)	(9)	(10)	(11)	(12)	(13)
	8.10											

3

FORM 'F': PILOT'S PERSONAL COMBAT REPORT

Naturally all engagements with enemy aircraft were recorded in detail: kills had to be claimed and verified, and details of enemy tactics, aircraft types and markings were important to collating an overall picture of enemy operating procedures and deployment. Every squadron had an Intelligence Officer, known as the 'Spy', usually an older man, too old to fly and sometimes veterans of the Great War. After each air battle, upon landing the pilot would immediately complete his Form 'F', sometimes in longhand or dictated to the 'Spy' or his clerk seated at his manual typewriter.

The examples reproduced here include two from the Battle of Britain, one typed the other handwritten, and several personal combat reports by Wing Commander Johnnie Johnson, leader of 144 (Canadian) Wing during the D-Day period. Finally an overall report for an engagement by 144 Wing on 28 March 1944, is faithfully reproduced, this being based upon pertinent extracts from the individual pilots' combat reports. All such reports are now preserved at The National Archive in AIR 50, and are essential primary sources to historians when re-creating the action of yesteryear.

P/O WHITBREAD

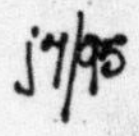

SECRET. FORM "F" 148

COMBAT REPORT.

Sector Serial No.	(a)	
Serial No. of order detailing Patrol.	(b)	
Date.	(c)	7. 9. 40
Flight, Squadron.	(d)	'B' 222 Squadron
No. & type of enemy aircraft.	(f)	Various formations of 30 & 50 ME 109's, 110's, DO 215's, etc
Time attack was delivered.	(g)	
Place attack was delivered.	(h)	London area
Height of enemy.	(j)	25,000 feet - actual formation attacked
Enemy casualties.	(k)	Destroyed --
		Probable --
		Damaged 1 DO 215
Our casualties. Aircraft	(l)	--
Personnel	(m)	--
Searchlights.	(n) (i)	--
A.A. Guns. Assistance.	(ii)	--
Fire from fighters.	(p)	Range opened
		Length of burst
		Range closed
		No. of rounds fired.

SECRET

P/O WHITBREAD.

During combat on 31 August 1940 at 1330 hours I encountered a M.E. 109 at 16,000 feet over Sittingbourne. I manoeuvred till it appeared in my sights - the M.E. climbing slowly away not having seen me it appeared. I fired at about 400 yards range which rapidly closed to within 50 yards when I could see the bullets entering the fuselage from tail to cockpit. The M.E. half rolled onto its back and remained in that attitude flying quite slowly with a little white smoke issuing from it. It eventually nosed slowly downwards when I was obliged to lose sight of it having noticed an aircraft approaching my tail which turned out to be a Spitfire.

H.R. Whitbread P/O.

SECRET.

FORM "F" R.A.F. Form 1151.

j20/5

COMBAT REPORT.

Sector Serial No.	(A)	
Serial No. of Order detailing Flight or Squadron to Patrol	(B)	
Date	(C)	20-9-40
Flight, Squadron	(D)	Flight: "B" Sqdn. 72.
Number of Enemy Aircraft	(E)	50+ ME109's
Type of Enemy Aircraft	(F)	ME 109's
Time Attack was delivered	(G)	12-10
Place Attack was delivered	(H)	Ashford-Canterbury
Height of Enemy	(J)	26,000 to 30,000 feet.
Enemy Casualties	(K)	1 ME109 destroyed
Our Casualties — Aircraft	(L)	Nil
Personnel	(M)	Nil
SEARCH LIGHTS ~~GENERAL REPORT~~ Was enemy illuminated if not, were they in front or behind Target	(N)	
General Report	(R)	

I was Red 2 in a section that was told to intercept the enemy fighters. We took off at 10·40 and after having done a patrol by ourselves we were told to rejoin the rest of the squadron as the leading section. We did this and met the enemy near Canterbury. We were climbing up towards one batch of ME109's when we were told by our rearguard that another lot were diving down on us. We kept on climbing into the sun and the rest of the squadron had used evasive action to get rid of the ME109's. I soon found myself by Ashford and couldn't not

Signature

O.C. { Section / Flight / Squadron } Squadron No.

(1611) Wt. 33246—2323 400 Pads 12/38 T.S. 700

see any of our squadron near me. I was flying along at 22,000 feet when I saw what appeared to be a Spitfire or Hurricane diving down to about 16,000 to 18,000 and then climbing up again. I decided to have a look at it so I got into the position so that I had the sun behind me and could see the machine clearly. As it came up in the climb I saw plainly that it was a ME109. with yellow nose and yellow fin. I let it climb up again and waited thinking perhaps it would dive again. It did so and then I dived out of the sun on to its tail and waited till it started to climb before I pressed the tit to fire. I let it have about 3 secs. fire and the ME109 did a stall turn to starboard and I followed it. I saw a large black peice break away from the side of the cockpit on the port side. I got it in my sight again as it turned and let it have another 4 sec burst. This time I saw the smoke and what appeared to be oil & water come from underneath it. It turned to dive and as it did I let them have a final burst when the whole lot of the cockpit dropped away and the rest dropped down towards the cloud. This was at 12,000 feet. I flew through the cloud and made for the aerodrome as I had only 10 gallon of petrol left. I marked the spot where the machine went in and it was near WYE between a wood and lake as far as I could make out from my own position. I landed back with 3 gallon of petrol and a leaky glycol rad.

Sgt. W Rolls.

"72" Squadron.

"B" Flight

Red. 2.

W/C J.E. Johnson, D.F.C.

Ramrod 831

MAIN H.Q. 83 GROUP
51
INTELLIGENCE.

PERSONAL COMBAT REPORT

From:- 144 Airfield Intelligence.

To:- Main H.Q., No. 83 Group.

Date	A -	5th May, 1944.
Squadron	B -	144 Airfield Wing.
Type and Mark of Aircraft	C -	Spitfire IX B.
Time up and Time Down	D -	0700 - 0910.
Time of Attack	E -	0745.
Place of Attack	F -	Douai Area.
Height of Enemy on First Sighting	G -	2000 ft.
Own Height on First Sighting	H -	8000 ft.
Our Casualties	I -	Nil.
Enemy Casualties (State Claim)	J -	1 F.W. 190 destroyed.

PERSONAL NARRATIVE (All Details of Tactical Value):-

I was leading 144 Airfield on Ramrod 831 sweeping in the Lille Area. When over Douai I saw 6 F.W. 190s flying over the town at ground level. I detached 443 Squadron (S/L McLeod) to go down and search for these e/a. About 5 minutes afterwards I saw a F.W. 190 flying west at 2000 ft. I closed from his port side and opened fire from 300 yards, closing from 20° angle off to 5° angle off. After 1-second burst e/a jettisoned hood and tank and pieces were seen to fly off. I continued to fire and the pilot baled out at 400 ft. and unfortunately landed safely by parachute. E/A crashed in a field 3 miles East of Douai. Claimed as destroyed.

Rounds Fired: Cannon 100 M.G. 480 Cine Used

4488

Senior Intelligence Officer,
No. 144 (RCAF) Airfield [illegible]

Pilot
144 Airfield

W/Cmdr. J.E. Johnson D.S.O. D.F.C.

144 Wing R.C.A.F.

PERSONAL COMBAT REPORT

MAIN H.Q. ... 52 AIR INTELLIGENCE

From:-

To:-

Date	A -	16 June 1944
Squadron	B -	144 Wing
Type and Mark of Aircraft	C -	Spit. IX B
Time up and Time Down	D -	2035 - 2213
Time of Attack	E -	2110
Place of Attack	F -	N.E. Villers - Bocage
Height of Enemy on First Sighting	G -	ground level
Own Height on First Sighting	H -	4000 feet
Our Casualties	I -	Nil.
Enemy Casualties (Combat Claim)	J -	1 FW190 destroyed.

PERSONAL NARRATIVE (All Details of Tactical Value):-

I was on patrol 2 miles south of Caen when I saw 4 FW190's flying South West at ground level. I dived down and opened fire on the starboard e/a who was slightly behind the other 3 e/a. Opened fire at 150 yards with a 3 second burst of cannon and MG fire from dead astern and slightly above. Strikes were seen on the engine cowling and cockpit of the e/a who dived into the ground and disintregrated. I then broke away and climbed into cloud as I was being engaged by intense and accurate light flak.

Cine film used.

I claim one FW190 Destroyed.

Senior Intelligence Officer,
No. 144 (RCAF) Airfield H.Q.

Pilot
144 Airfield

MAIN H.Q. 83 GROUP
Ref:
29 JUL 1944 36
AIR
INTELLIGENCE.

PERSONAL COMBAT REPORT

From:- 144 Wing Intelligence.

To:- 83 Group

Date	A -	July 5/- 1944
Squadron	B -	144 Wing RCAF
Type and Mark of Aircraft	C -	Spit IX B
Time Up and Time Down	D -	1815 - 1915
Time of Attack	E -	1840
Place of Attack	F -	Alencon Area,
Height of Enemy on First Sighting	G -	5000 ft.
Own height on First Sighting	H -	8000 ft.
Our Casualties	I -	Nil
Enemy Casualties (State Claim)	J -	2 FW 190s Destroyed.

7313

PERSONAL NARRATIVE (All Details of Tactical Value):-

I was leading 441 Sqdn on a patrol in the Alencon Area. We sighted 12(plus) FW 190s flying beneath cloud. I led the Sqdn in th attack, and a general dog fight ensued. I got on the tail of a 190 who was hitting F/Lt Copeland's aircraft; opened fire from 250 yds, closing to 100 yds, climbing steeply, angle of 25 deg. Strikes were seen on cockpit and engine cowling and e/a burst into flames and crashed. At this time I saw another FW 190 spiral down and crash in the area S.E. of Alencon. I then chased another FW 190 at ground level and after a 20 mile chase at 16 lbs boost, I came within range (350 yds) and touched him on the fusleage with a few cannon shells. E/a broke starboard and climbed steeply and I had no difficulty in getting on his tail. Then followed a series of aileron turns, half-rolls, dives and zooms, but my a/c was superior in every respect and I continued to get in the occasional burst. I saw several strikes in the cockpit and e/a went straight in from 4000 ft.

Claim: 2 FW 190s destroyed.

Cine Film used.

PERSONAL COMBAT REPORT: Fighter Sweep. SECRET

35

DATE:	23rd, August 1944
SQUADRON:	Denver Leader.
TYPE OF A/C:	Spit IX.B
TIME UP: DOWN:	1241 - 1438
TIME OF ATTACK:	1335
PLACE OF ATTACK:	SENLIS area.
HEIGHT OF ENEMY:	9-10,000 feet.
OWN HEIGHT:	8-10,000 feet.
OUR CASUALTIES:	3 Spit IX.B(N.Y.R.)
ENEMY CASUALTIES:	2 FW. 190's Destroyed

NARRATIVE:

I was leading 443 and 421 Squadrons on a Fighter Sweep in the PARIS area. When in the Senlis area I saw between 60 to 80 enemy aircraft approaching head on. I instructed 421 Squadron to engage the highest e/a (approximately 1,000' above me and 1,000' below 421 Squadron) and to remain at that height to provide top cover (9,000'). I then led 443 Squadron in to engage between 30 to 40 e/a flying 1,000' below 443 Squadron. I attacked a FW. 190 firing short bursts from line astern closing to 150 yards; e/a caught fire and went down completely enveloped in flames. I then chased another FW. 190 flying at ground level and opened fire from 300 yards. I saw five or six strikes on the cockpit of this e/a and he pulled up steeply and baled out at 1,000 feet. A series of individual combats then ensued as by this time the wing had been split up. I was attacked by six short nosed 190's who possessed an exceptional rate of climb; by turning in to each attack, I managed to evade most of their fire power only receiving one hit in the starboard wing root. They stayed with me until my supercharger came in at 13,000' when I was able to out-climb them and return to base. FW. 190's and ME. 109's were usual black and grey camouflage and carried black and white markings on their spinners. After the initial combat they seemed keen to engage but probably only because they out-numbered the wing by 4 to 1. I claim 2 FW. 190's Destroyed. Cine gun used. No Gyro Sight fitted.

W/C. J.E. Johnson (83267)

(C. Johnson) Flight Lieutenant,
Senior Intelligence Officer,
No. 127 Wing Headquarters.

SECRET

PERSONAL COMBAT REPORT:

34

DATE	: 27th September, 1944.
SQUADRON	: 443
TYPE OF A/C	: Spitfire IX B.
TIME UP: DOWN	: 1218 - 1350 hrs.
TIME OF ATTACK	: 1250 hrs.
PLACE OF ATTACK	: REES ON RHINE
HEIGHT OF ENEMY	: 3 - 4000 feet.
OWN HEIGHT	: 3 - 4000 feet.
OUR CASUALTIES	: Nil
ENEMY CASUALTIES	: 1 Me. 109 Destroyed.

NARRATIVE:

I was leading 443 Squadron on patrol at 7000 feet when I saw nine Me. 109's flying at ground level immediately below me. I led the squadron down to attack but e/a saw us and broke upwards into the attack and a general melee ensued. I closed on a Me. 109 turning to port and closed to 250 yards firing short bursts of cannon and machine-gun. Strikes were seen on port wing of e/a and he peeled away and crashed into the ground. Cine-gun used. G.M.2 sight fitted. I claim 1 Me. 109 destroyed.

J. E. Johnson.

83267 W/C JOHNSON, J.E.

(C. Johnson), Flight Lieutenant,
Senior Intelligence Officer,
No. 127 Wing Headquarters.

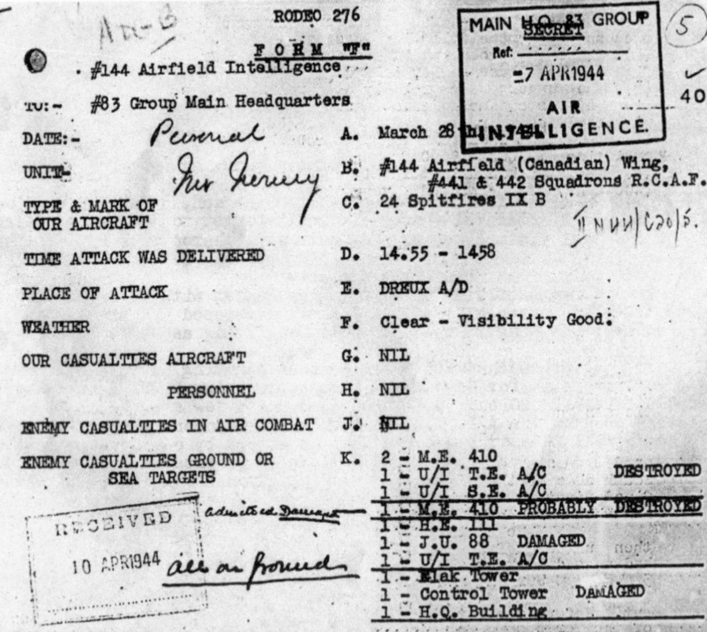

RODEO 276

MAIN H.Q. 83 GROUP
SECRET
Ref:
7 APR 1944
AIR
INTELLIGENCE.

FORM "F"

#144 Airfield Intelligence

TO:- #83 Group Main Headquarters

DATE:-	A.	March 28th, 1944
UNIT-	B.	#144 Airfield (Canadian) Wing, #441 & 442 Squadrons R.C.A.F.
TYPE & MARK OF OUR AIRCRAFT	C.	24 Spitfires IX B
TIME ATTACK WAS DELIVERED	D.	14.55 - 1458
PLACE OF ATTACK	E.	DREUX A/D
WEATHER	F.	Clear - Visibility Good.
OUR CASUALTIES AIRCRAFT	G.	NIL
PERSONNEL	H.	NIL
ENEMY CASUALTIES IN AIR COMBAT	J.	NIL
ENEMY CASUALTIES GROUND OR SEA TARGETS	K.	2 - M.E. 410 / 1 - U/I T.E. A/C DESTROYED / 1 - U/I S.E. A/C / ~~1 - M.E. 410 PROBABLY DESTROYED~~ / ~~1 - H.E. III~~ / 1 - J.U. 88 DAMAGED / 1 - U/I T.E. A/C / ~~1 - Flak Tower~~ / 1 - Control Tower DAMAGED / 1 - H.Q. Building

RECEIVED 10 APR 1944

Wing led by W/C Johnson, D.S.O. & BAR, D.F.C. & Bar, airborne Holmsley South at 13.06 hours, landed at Tangmere to refuel. Airborne Tangmere at 14.04 hours, flying on the deck until 35 miles off of the French Coast where they climbed to 10,000 ft. W/C Johnson developed radio trouble and Wing was taken over by W/C Wells, D.S.O., D.F.C. & Bar. Crossed the French Coast near St. Valery and flew on course to St. Clair, arriving there at approximately 14.45 hours. Changed course to Chartres and when in the vicinity of DREUX A/D at approximately 10,000 ft. 20 to 30 mixed enemy aircraft were sighted on the A/D, parked around the perimiter.

W/C Johnson states:-

I was leading #144 A/F on Rodeo #276. Off St. Valery I developed R.T. trouble so I handed over the leadership to W/C Wells, and continued flying on his port side. W/C Wells led uneventfully to St. Clair where he turned slightly starboard on 205 Magnetic. Shortly afterwards the A/D at DREUX was sighted and as we flew by on the west side many twin-engined A/C could be seen in the dispersals. W/C Wells instructed #442 Squadron (top squadron) to remain at altitude as a decoy and top cover and himself led #441 Squadron from up-sun to attack. We crossed the southern boundary of the A/D at 400 mph. each pilot selecting his target on the western side. I attacked a twin-engined A/C (probably a Ju. 88) with cannon and machine gun with a five-second burst. Many hits were registered on the e/a and after crossing the northern boundary of the A/D I climbed steeply to 7000 ft. in orderto see the results of "B" flight's attack and to see the second flight, "A" Flight, make their attack. During this climb I was fired at continually by intense light flak, but the gunners were under-deflecting, probably due to very high speed and rate of climb. I saw three twin-engined a/C burning and a fourth, single-engined E/A had its back broken and was smoking badly. "A" Flight carried out their attack but unfortunately they tooattacked the western dispersal instead of the eastern dispersal where there were several more e/a including two ME 109 taxying on the perimeter track. "A" flight continued at ground level and the Wing reformed several miles to the North and returned to Tangmere uneventfully.

As I was not leading the Wing at the time of the attack, I had a good opportunity of observing W/C Well's tactics and method of ~~attack on this well-defended target. In my opinion the attack was~~

attack on this well-defended target. In my opinion the atta... was successful for the following reasons:-
(1). The enemy probably did not anticipate a front-gun attack b[illegible]s/e fighters on a base so far inland.
(2). The gunners were probably at a relaxed state, as three combat Wings of Fortresses had just passed to the west of the A/D on their withdrawl.
(3). The light flak gunners were probably watching the decoy squadron orbitting at 8000 - 9000 ft.
(4). The attacking fighters attacked from the sun, at a very high speed (400 mph.) and presented a very difficult target to the ground defences.

I claim one T.E. A/C Destroyed, shared with F/O McLachlan.

41

W/C Wells states:-

I was flying as Deputy Wing Leader with #144 A/F on Rodeo #276. Near the French Coast W/C Johnson developed R/T trouble and handed over the Wing to me. He continued flying as White 3 on my port side.

We reached St. Clair without sighting any e/a and turned out 205° magnetic for Chartres. When approaching DREUX A/F at about 9000 ft. between 20 and 30 twin-engined and a few s/e a/c could be plainly seen on the A/F. It was such a very concentrated target and being so well inland, I decided that an attack by one squadron out of the sun and at a very high speed would give profitable results.

Accordingly, having #442 Squadron above (8000 ft.) as both a decoy and top cover, I turned #441 Squadron into the sun and eschel-oned them starboard. Then we dived very fast to ground level on the South side of the A/F and made an extremely fast run across it. I fired first at a Flying Control building which was in my line of flight and then fired at a Me! 410, on which I saw strikes.

We continued low down and fast for a couple of miles and then pulled up fast and reformed without trouble. W/C Johnson who had had a good look at the A/F after the first six A/C had attacked, saw 3 T.E. A/C burning and a S/E A/C collapsed and smoking.

The Wing then returned to Tangmere without further incid-ent. Before the attack on this enemy A/F, I considered the withdrawl of the Forts some few minutes before and the fact that the enemy probably didn't think that a front gun attack was imminent.

I claim one Me. 410 destroyed (in flames) after checking positions of burning A/C with W/C Johnson.

F/O T.A. BRANNAGAN states:-

I was flying White 5. The W/C Flying positioned the Wing into sun and gave the OK to attack DREUX A/D. I attacked the west side of the field, going from south to north. I fired at an army vehicle outside the field but was behind and short. I approached the A/D at 400 mph. right on the tree tops. A gun was firing from my right and I had a squirt. Next I fired at a flak tower on the left and straight-ened out and saw a S/E A/C on the left. I had a short burst and then had to pull up the nose to avoid trees. I had noticed a twin-engined A/C sitting in front of the hanger at the north-west end of the field. I came into the clear, pushed the nose down and fired, then had to pullup to avoid hangers. I did not observe the results of my fire on either A/C.

I claim one Me.410 Destroyed-
and
one S/E A/C Destroyed-
On the results seen by W/C Johnson.

F/O MacLachlan states:-

I was flying White 2 to W/C Johnson. On the attack I eschel- starboard, opening fire slightly after the W/C. The front part of the A/C which I believe was a Ju.88, was obscured with dust and smoke from the cannon strikes from the W/C's attack. I continued firing at this A/C until forced to break off, seeing strikes all over the front part of the A/C. I claim one twin-enggined A/C destroyed (shared with W/C Johnson) on the results seen by W/C JOhnson.

F/L L.A.Moore states:-

As leader of Black section, I took my chaps into attack shortly after W/C Wells took his section in. Isaw strikes on an He.111 and also all over an Me410 that I attacked. The Me410 was seen smoking by F/O Lake who was my No. 2. I claim one Me.410 Probably destroyed, shared with F/L Mott and F/O Lake, and one He.111 damaged.

F/O R.Lake states:-

I was flying black 2 and followed Black 1, F/L Moore down on the A/D. F/L Moore fired on a twin engined A/C and I fired at the A/C beside the one he attacked. I gave a short burst at this A/C and saw strikes on the wing and fuselage. While pulling out of my dive and turning to follow Black 1, I fired a short burst at a hut at the side of the field and then fired at an Me.410 which Black 1 was just breaking away from. I saw quite a few strikes when Black 1 fired and strikes when I gave a burst. There was a bit of smoke rising from this A/C and as I broke away another Spitfire, Black 5 was firing at the same A/C. I claim an Me.410 probably destroyed, shared with F/L Moore and FL Mott and one twin-enginened A/C damaged.

F/L Mott states:-

I was flying Black 5 and led my section in behind Black 1 & 2 firing a short burst of cannon and machine gun at a Headquarters building and then fired a longer burst at an Me.410 which was behind some low trees and in front of a hanger. I saw flashes on and around the Me.410 and on the hanger. This A/C was seen smoking by F/O Lake ~~and F/L Moore.~~ I claim one Me.410 probably destroyed, shared with F/O Lake and F/L Moore.

P/O D.H.Kimball states:-

I was flying Black 4 and followed my section Leader down (F/O Graham). I fired cannons and machine guns at a twin engined A/C presumably a Ju.88, & saw strikes on wings and fuselage.

I claim a Ju.88 damaged.

A flak tower was also attacked and damaged by F/O Graham and F/O Fleming, a control tower attacked and damaged by F/O McKenzie and a H.Q. Building attacked and damaged by F/O Cashman. Wing reformed and returned to Tangmere via Evreux and Cabourg. Moderate heavy flak was encountered at Dieppe, at Evreux and Le Havre. Intense light flak encountered at Dreux A/D. Transport was seen travelling North West on the Paris-Roen road and also in and around the town of Lisieux. Two fairly large boats were seen in Le Havre harbour. W/C Johnson saw a special target site South East of St. Clair which was reported to Tangmere ~~at 1552~~. Refuelled and returned to base pancaking at 1750 hrs.

	Claims on Ground Targets	Rds. Fired Cannon	M.G.	Cine Gun
W/C J.E.Johnson, D.S.O. & Bar, D.F.C. & Bar	1 U/I T.E. A/C DEST. shared with F/O McLachlan	100	300	used
W/C E.P.Wells, D.S.O., D.F.C. & Bar	1 Me.410 DEST.	126	300	used
#441 Squadron (R.C.A.F.)				
F/O T.A.Brannagan J 10762	1-Me.410 Dest. 1-U/I T.E. A/C DESTROYED	280	1360	used

4

FORM 78: AIRCRAFT MOVEMENT CARD

Each RAF aircraft had a 'Form 78' or 'Movement Card', this providing a record of which units the machine was issued to, any damage and repairs, and its fate. This document is the starting point for any historian reconstructing the story of any Spitfire, in this case a Mk IIB, P8208. Built at CBAF, this Spitfire was first issued to 12 Maintenance Unit on 26 March 1941, before allocation to 303 Squadron of Northolt's Polish Wing on 12 May. Flown on operations over France, after being damaged in combat, P8208 was repaired but never flew with a front line squadron again. Flying with a number of rear echelon units, the Spitfire suffered minor damage during several flying accidents before being issued to 52 OTU at Aston Down on 10 October 1942. Although written off with 'Category E damage' on 3 February 1943, this, as Les Howard of the Air Historical Branch added in 1985, was an error: P8208 collided with P8207 during an air-to-air firing exercise over the Severn Estuary on 26 January 1943. The Canadian pilot, Sergeant Caldwell, was posted missing. Following initial crash site investigations by a local group in 1983, ten years later the Malvern Spitfire Team recovered the substantial wreckage off this Spitfire, including the maker's plate confirming the aircraft's identity. A new Spitfire is now being built around this important artifact, meaning that, in due course, Spitfire P8208 will once more soar and roll 'high in the sunlit silence' – it will be a tribute not only to today's dedicated aero-engineers who refurbish and recreate Spitfires but more so Sergeant Caldwell and the thousands like him who made the ultimate sacrifice before ever firing a shot in anger.

A.M. Form 78.

AIRCRAFT

Contract No.

Type Spitfire IIB R.A.F. No. P8208 Contractor

Type of Engine Merlin XII Engine Nos.

	(1)	(2)	(3)	(4)	(5)	(6)	(7)	(8)	(9)
Taken on Charge of	12 MU.	303 Sqn	43 Sqn 3A	8 MU	1 CaCF.	R.O.S. at ac. FA	1 CaCF.	CAT. A.C. FA	1.C. R.W R.1.W
Date taken on Charge	26/3/41	12.5.41	14.6.41	11.10.41	24.12.41	2.1.42	20.1.42	25.3.42	1.4.42
Authority	1632 D/A	1623A	1623 D/	1623A	1623A	CRO	CRO	A138	CRO

	(10)	(11)	(12)	(13)	(14)	(15)	(16)	(17)	(18)
Taken on Charge of	A.W./CN. (CRO 27/6)	9 M.U.	52 O.T.U.	CAT. E.					
Date taken on Charge	10.5.42	30.6.42	9.10.42	3.2.43					
Authority	F.653.	1632 D/A	1623A/186.	1623.213					

Date	Unit to whom allotted	Authority	Date	Unit to whom allotted	Authority
				The ORB for 52 OTU records that the accident occurred on 26 Jan 43. 28 Oct 85	(AIR 27/681) L. Howard AHB 3 (RAF)
				SEE ALSO P8207	

(2301) Wt.44020 25m (3) 1/40 Gp.697 C&SLtd

5

FORGET-ME-NOTS FOR FIGHTERS

Numerous instructional booklets were issued to trainee RAF fighter pilots throughout World War Two, this one, *Forget-Me-Nots for Fighters* being a combination of short but essential points emphasised by simple but amusing cartoons. Issued by 13 Group, responsible for protecting the north of England, the foreword by Air Vice-Marshal 'Birdie' Saul is succinct, concluding that 'Air fighting is a combination of skill and courage, which, allied with confidence and experience, makes the Fighter Pilot the master of his trade'.

FORGET-ME-NOTS
for
FIGHTERS
by
NO 13 GROUP
RAF

FOREWORD

"All for one and one for all"

THIS BOOK is the outcome of discussion amongst the Training Staff, on the best and simplest way to bring to the notice of new Fighter Pilots certain salient points in air fighting, which it is essential that they should master before taking their places as operational pilots in Fighter Squadrons.

The various points illustrated are by no means fully comprehensive, and it must be clearly understood that only the main points which a new Fighter Pilot should know before going into action are included. These have been compiled on the advice and guidance of many well-known and proved Fighter Pilots, who have willingly co-operated in placing their knowledge and experience at the disposal of their younger brother pilots.

In selecting the motto of " The Three Musketeers " to put at the head of this Foreword, I have done so because it expresses what should be the creed of every Fighter Pilot. Never forget you are an essential cog in the wheel, and if you break or fail it will let down your brother pilots, and the grimness of war allows for no such weakness.

Air fighting is a combination of skill and courage, which, allied with confidence and experience, makes the Fighter Pilot master of his trade.

Good luck to each and every one of you.

R. E. Saul

Air Vice-Marshal,
Air Officer Commanding, No. 13 Group.

The need for vigilance

Never stop looking round. Many pilots shot down never saw the enemy fighter that got them. Out of every five minutes on patrol four should be spent looking over your shoulders. Whether you are by yourself or with a hundred others, never stop looking round. Mirrors are useful, but not infallible.

Start looking round as you taxi out to take off, and do not stop until you have taxied in—people have been shot taking off and landing.

NEVER STOP LOOKING ROUND

SOME PILOTS NEVER SAW THE ENEMY THAT GOT THEM

Search Formation and Weaving

The object of Search Formation is to provide the maximum and most effective look-out for enemy aircraft. Remember that your Leader can't always be expected to sight the enemy first, as he is a busy man. This responsibility must be shared by ALL members of the formation, and all your lives depend on the vigilance of your look-out. The Leader, and in some cases other Pilots are detailed to watch the area in front of the leading edge of their main planes, but there are always some Pilots whose duty is "Weaving," and it is on them that the responsibility for keeping a watch to the rear depends.

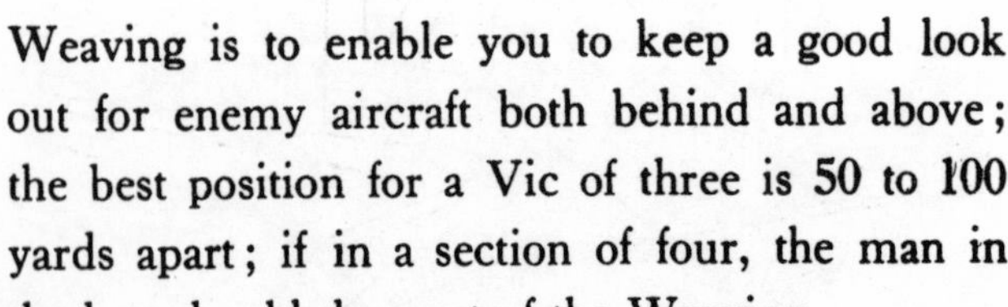

Weaving is to enable you to keep a good look out for enemy aircraft both behind and above; the best position for a Vic of three is 50 to 100 yards apart; if in a section of four, the man in the box should do most of the Weaving.

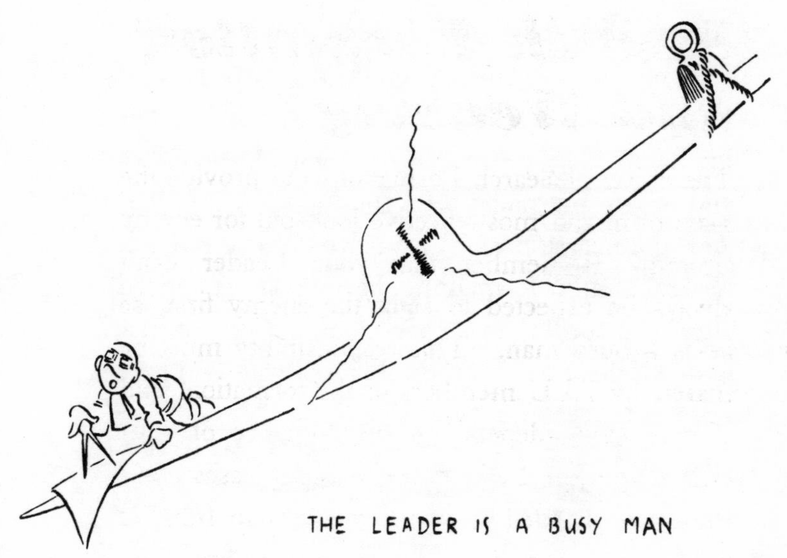

THE LEADER IS A BUSY MAN

THE MAN IN THE BOX

Always keep above your Leader: it will help you to come into formation quickly. This is vital for formation attacks. The man who is late lets the team down—sometimes right down. Try and weave alternately with your opposite number, and do not stop until you are over the base. Several times formations have been surprised after the order to "pancake." Take it for granted there is a HUN behind you. There often is!

Attacks

The advantage of height is half the battle. Always try to achieve it. Remember that the initial attack is the most successful. Keep together for it, and if possible after it; you may have another chance to go in together.

Attack forward of the Beam; it is the most effective, and you don't get hit often. Your breakaway must be a "HAM" manoeuvre downwards.

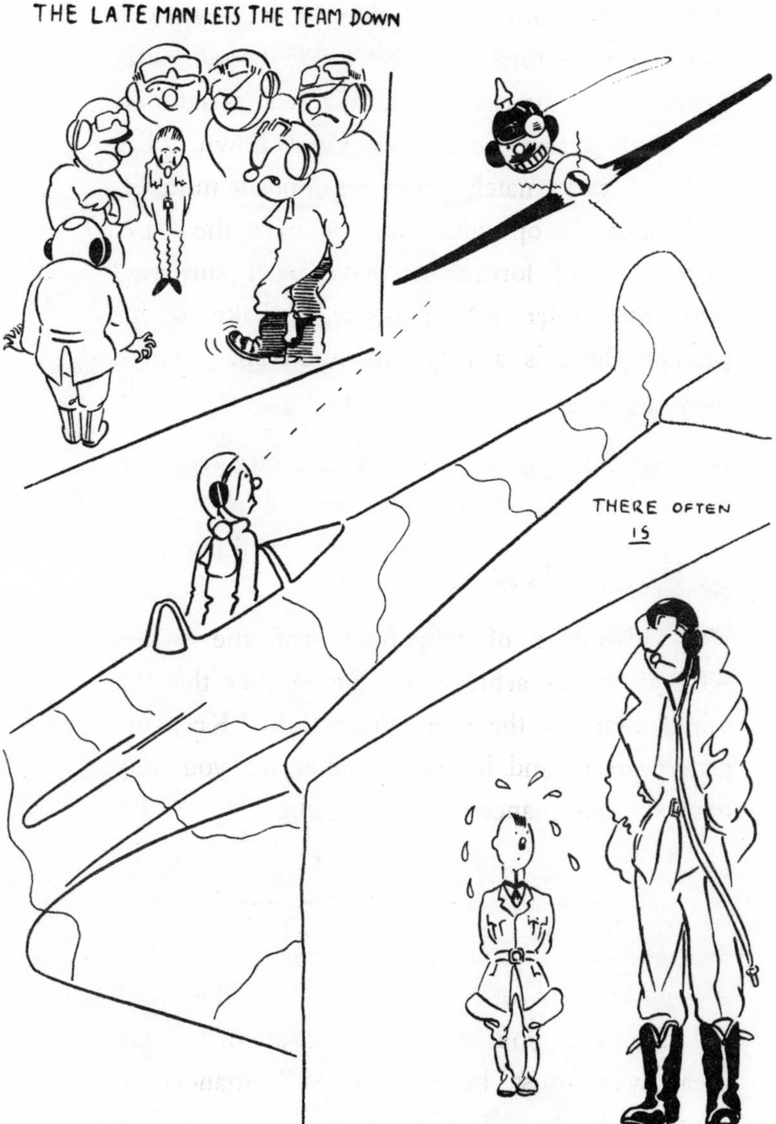

THE LATE MAN LETS THE TEAM DOWN

THERE OFTEN IS

THE ADVANTAGE OF HEIGHT.

Always stick together for as long as possible—you can then help each other when dog fights ensue.

When you have got separated from your Leader, individual attacks must be largely left to your own judgment, but here are a few tips :—

DON'T rush in without thinking how you are going to attack, but on the other hand, DON'T hang about trying to work out something very clever, as there is probably a " Messerschmitt " very close, and it would be such a pity if you didn't see him.

ALWAYS STICK
TOGETHER AS
LONG AS POSSIBLE.
DON'T HANG ABOUT
THINKING UP SOMETHING CLEVER.

The Almighty provided the Sun and Clouds for several reasons, take advantage of both. Remember there is no such thing as a "sitter."

The range is invariably twice what you think it is, so save your ammunition, and DON'T open fire too soon. You will probably need all your ammunition in a few moments.

Aim at 12 o'clock on your target, and use a head-on attack if possible against a formation. When using deflection always allow twice as much as you think necessary.

A three seconds burst is normally sufficient to shoot a German down, so look behind you every three seconds.

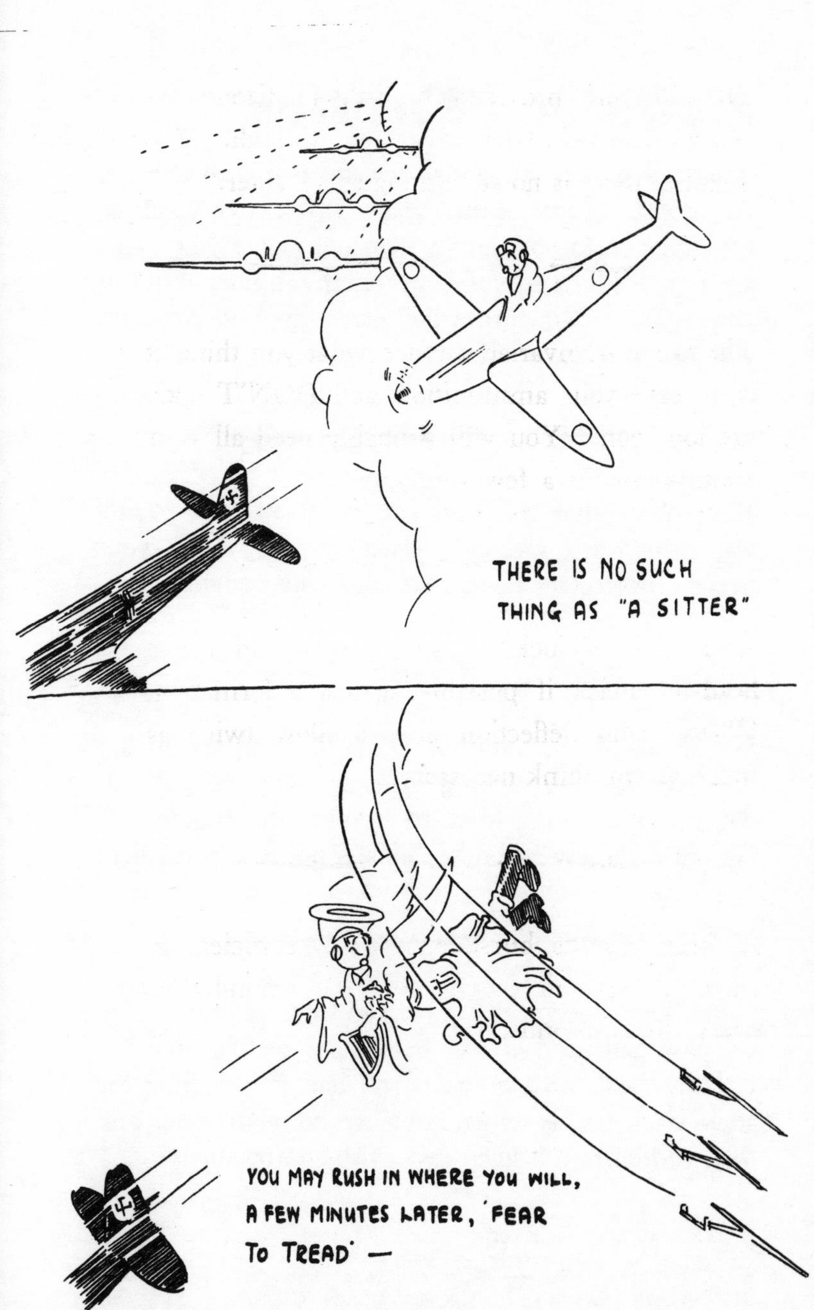
THERE IS NO SUCH
THING AS "A SITTER"
YOU MAY RUSH IN WHERE YOU WILL,
A FEW MINUTES LATER, 'FEAR
TO TREAD' —

Evasive Tactics

A barrelled aileron turn is very effective with fighters. An increasing rate of turn prevents the enemy getting his sights on to you, and will usually give you a shot at him. Try and face an enemy fighter who is above you. Climb into the Sun: this will also give you an attacking position.

Remember that the Sun can be your best friend, and your worst enemy. Used correctly he is your friend; neglected, he can be your worst enemy.

When out of ammunition DON'T hang about, but dive steeply with rocking turns to right and left. If you put your stick forward quickly the engine will cut out for a few seconds. This is not recommended.

If you have been really surprised by an enemy fighter on your tail, and if his bullets are getting uncomfortably close, do a quick barrel half roll, pulling the stick back firmly when you are on your side, and then rudder into a steep dive with aileron turns.

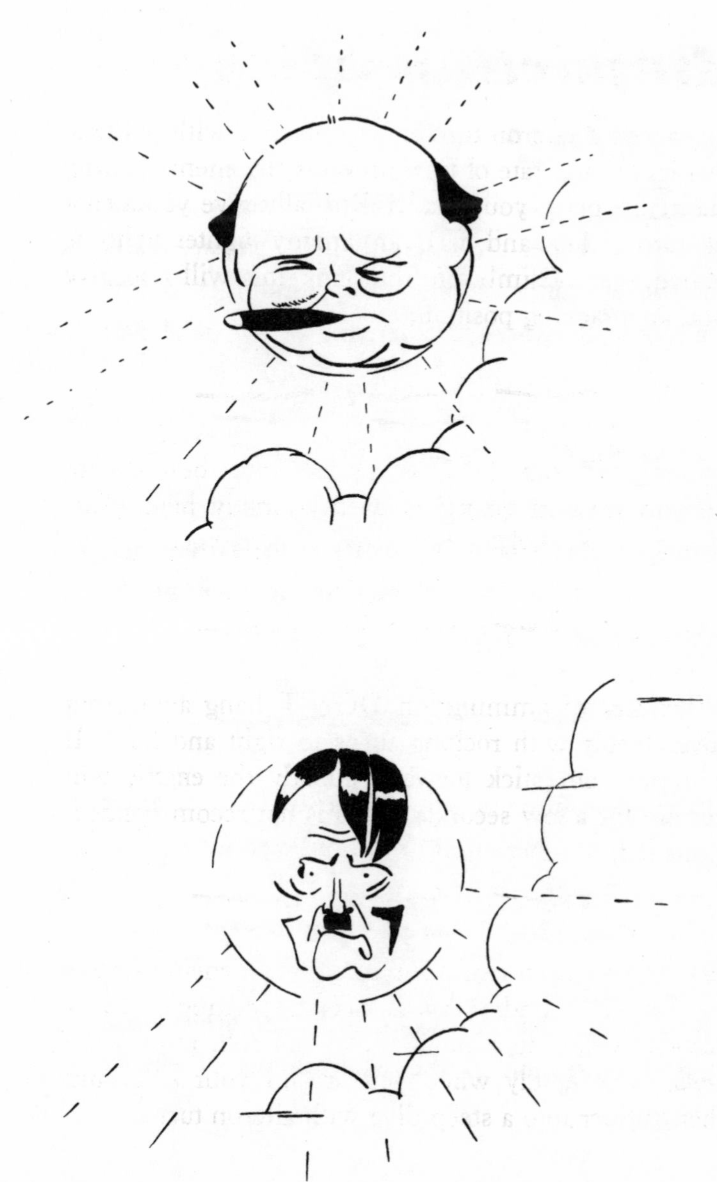

Reporting of enemy

DON'T get excited, and DON'T shout. Speak slowly and into the microphone. Report ALL hostile aircraft, not one group, and then a few minutes afterwards another one below or above.

If you see a formation of enemy aircraft look all round it, and report its escorts at the same time, using the clock system, and giving their height above or below you.

It is also quite a good idea when you have finished, to put your R/T set on to receive.

Remember that ACK-ACK bursts are often a useful indication of the whereabouts of enemy aircraft.

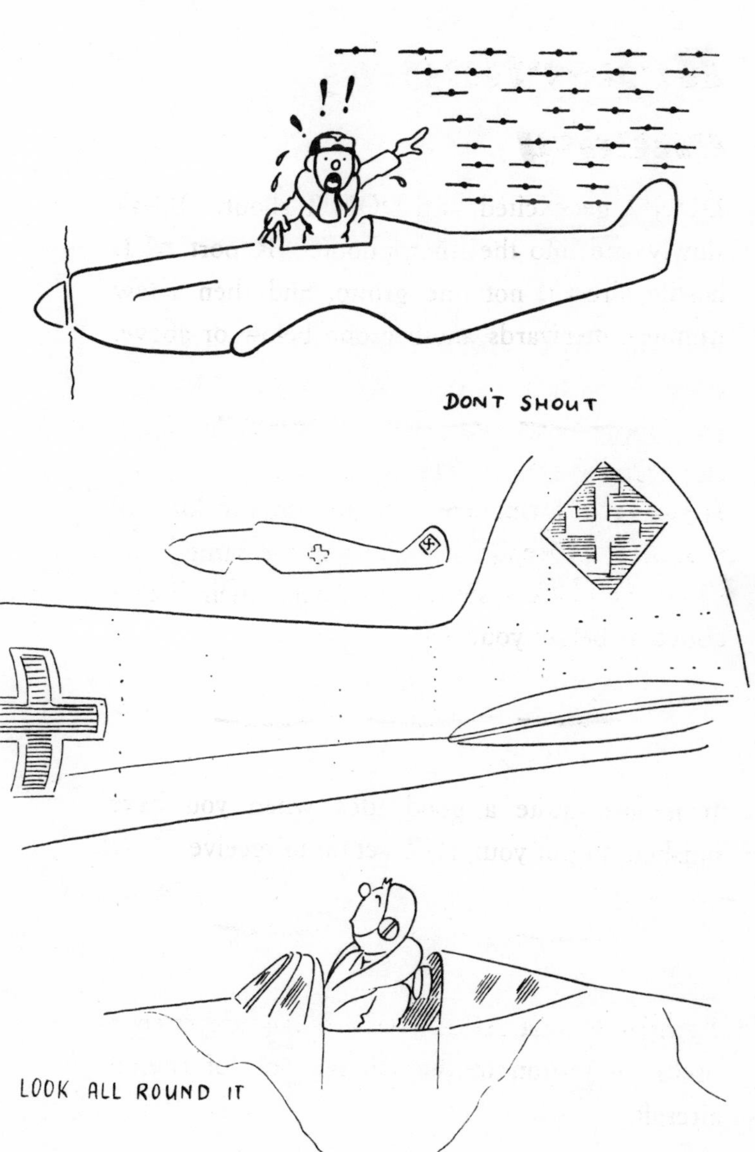
!!
DON'T SHOUT
LOOK ALL ROUND IT

R/T

Remember that "Silence is Golden."

Maintain R/T silence unless you have something important to say. Always say who you are; speak slowly—if it is really important speak slower than usual. This is quicker than having to repeat.

Use hand signals if you can. Remember that the Leader will tap his microphone if he thinks you have left your transmitter on. If you are guilty you had better avoid him when you get home.

DON'T LEAVE YOUR TRANSMITTER ON!

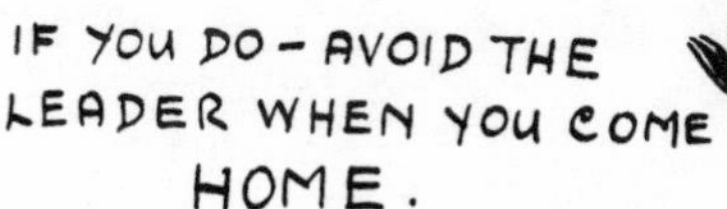

Baling out

The sequence of operations is most important, even if you are in a hurry. First, lift your seat to the full up position, slide back your hood and lock it fully open. Undo your harness, take hold of the parachute rip cord, and then either stand up on the seat and put the stick forward, or roll on to your back. Our old friends gravity and centrifugal force will have done the rest before you know they have started. If the aircraft is spinning get out on the inside of the spin.

If you are on fire DON'T open the hood until the last moment, as it will draw flames into the cock-pit.

If your clothes are soaked in petrol, switch off the engine switches, and leave the throttle open, otherwise as you get out the sparks from the exhaust may act like the flint in your cigarette lighter.

LOCK YOUR HOOD
FULLY OPEN.

DON'T OPEN YOUR HOOD TILL
THE LAST MINUTE.

Keep hold of the rip-cord as you leave the aircraft, but if you are very high there is no need to pull it for the time being. Pilots who have pulled the rip-cord immediately after getting out in a high speed dive have been badly injured. You will fall more slowly out of your aeroplane than in it, so do a delayed drop whenever you can. The "109" will also find you harder to hit with the umbrella shut than open. You only fall 1,000 feet in 5 seconds so there is really plenty of time.

If you have failed to keep hold of the rip-cord as you left the aircraft, it is quite easy to look down and find it. If for any reason you cannot see, pass your right hand down the centre of your chest till you come to the quick release knob, then move it left along the wide strap and you will find the rip-cord.

Flying boots, leather gloves and goggles will protect you if your clothing or the cock-pit should catch fire.

Your gloves are most important, as if your right hand were to get burnt you would not be able to feel the rip-cord.

THERE IS PLENTY OF TIME

General

If your aircraft has been hit, test the hydraulic system at a safe height. If it has broken you can nearly always get your wheels down by diving and pulling out quickly, or by rocking the aircraft with your rudder. If it still won't come down ask for orders over the R/T, since it might be possible to land with wheels up at your Maintenance Unit.

If your wing surface has been damaged by a cannon shell, or a panel has been lost, remember that the wing will stall first when holding off to land, so be ready for this, and try and do a wheel landing.

If you have been wounded and feel you may pass out before you get home, turn the oxygen full on—it will help you a lot.

TEST YOUR HYDRAULIC SYSTEM AT A SAFE HEIGHT
ROCK YOUR A/C WITH YOUR RUDDER.
IT MAY BE POSSIBLE TO LAND WITH WHEELS UP AT YOUR MAINTENANCE UNIT.

Don'ts

NEVER follow down a machine you have shot; there may be a kick still left in the air gunner, or he may have a pal in a M.E. 109 just behind you.

DON'T approach a friendly aircraft from astern; come in from the side, so that he can see your markings.

DON'T get out of your Leader's sight. He hates playing hide and seek.

DON'T open fire unless you are certain it is an enemy aircraft. If you are within range you can always see his markings.

NEVER break formation to do an individual attack. He who hunts on his own won't live long to enjoy it.

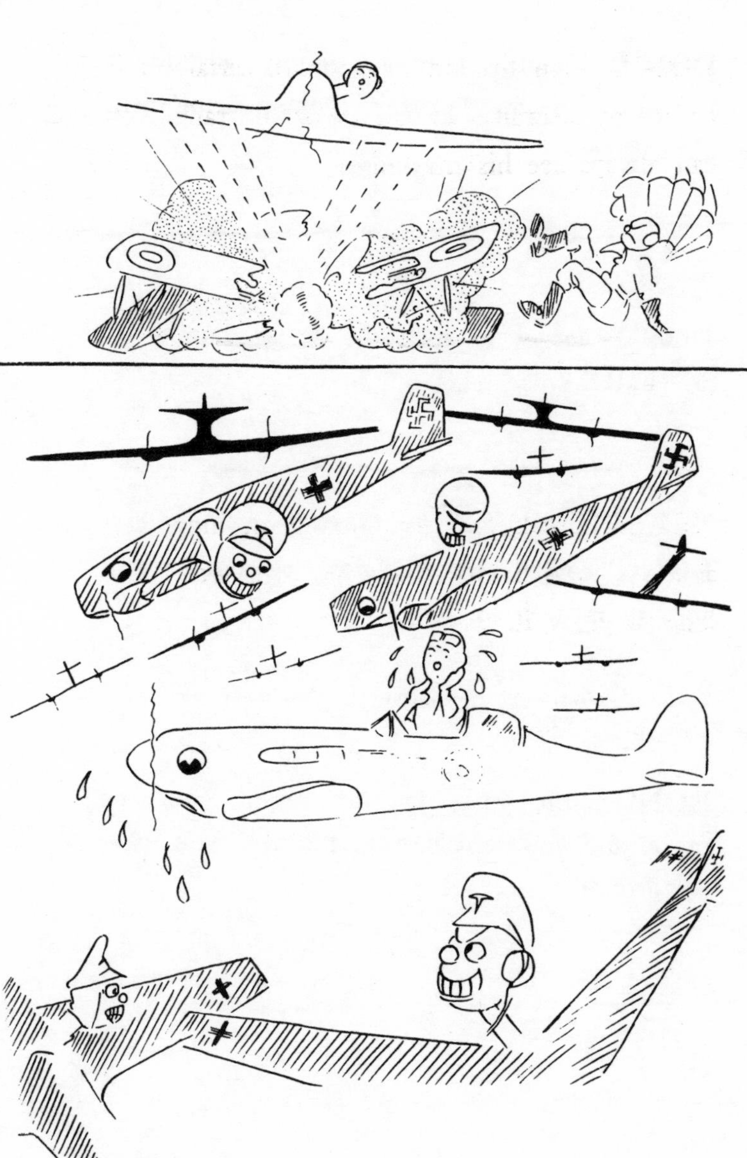

DON'T imagine that an enemy aircraft is "finished" if you see black smoke pouring from his engines.

DON'T forget to turn the firing button on to "FIRE."

DON'T forget your radiator; remember that your guns need keeping warm.

DON'T forget your oxygen at night; you need more, and you need it from the time you leave the ground.

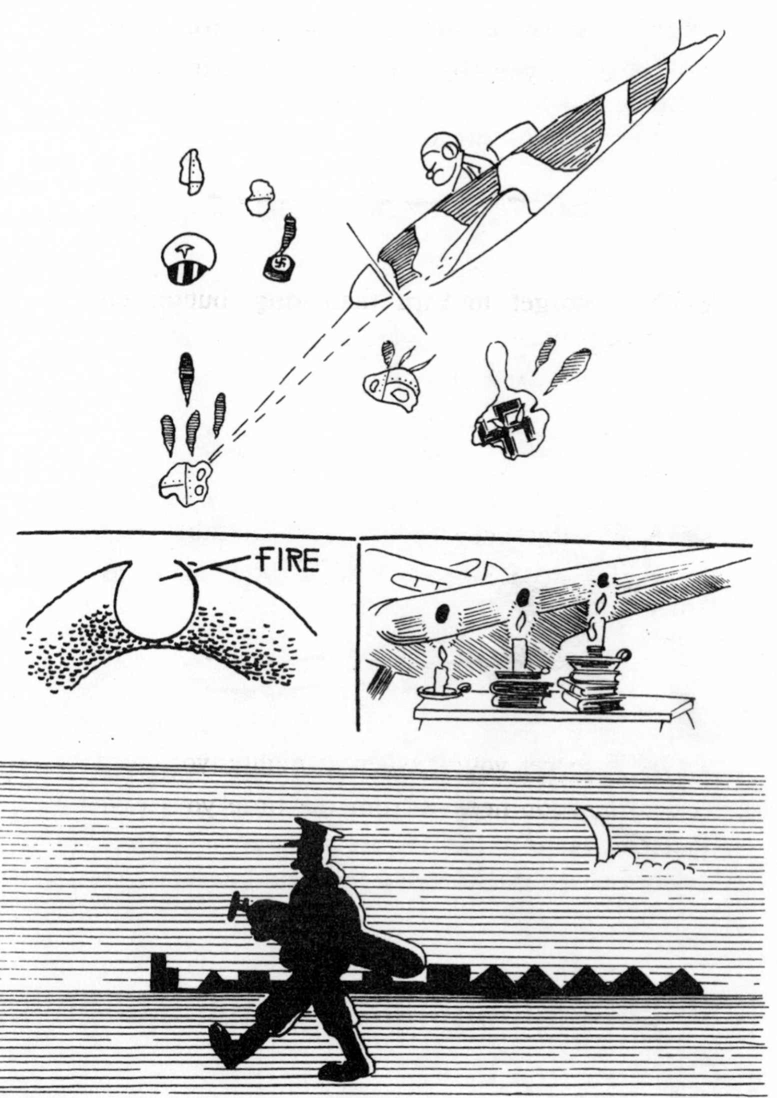
FIRE

DON'T go into a combat without goggles over your eyes. Splintered glass is not good for them, and some Pilots are now paying extra Insurance Premiums for their cars.

DON'T go off without your goggles, gloves and flying boots. They are a great help in case of fire in the cock-pit.

DON'T wind your oxygen tube around your neck. It may choke you if you have to "bale out."

DON'T "beat up" the aerodrome on your return, however pleased you are with yourself. It is bad manners, and some of those aerodrome defence chaps might take it the wrong way.

DON'T FORGET THESE

DON'T land with your wheels up after an exciting and successful combat. Some have.

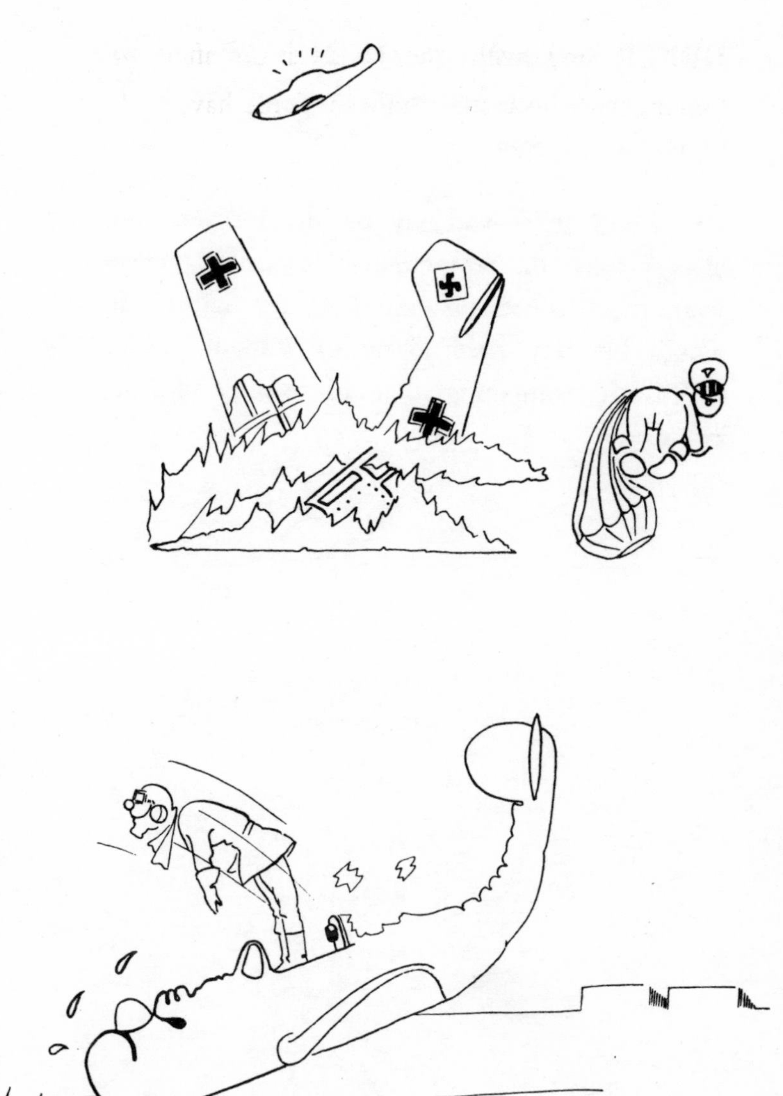

NEVER forget that the HUN is listening to nearly everything you say either on the R/T or in the "Local."

Be careful what you say on the former, and always resist the temptation of describing even your most successful patrol at the latter. It would be very hard to do so without telling HITLER something that he would like to know.

DON'T get shot down. YOU SHOULDN'T IF YOU TAKE THESE HINTS!

GOOD HUNTING!

6

GENERAL NOTES ON AIR GUNNERY AND AIR FIGHTING

In 1943, Wing Commander 'Teddy' Donaldson published this manual for fighter pilots. Donaldson was himself a successful fighter pilot during the Fall of France and initial stages of the Battle of Britain, destroying eight enemy aircraft and receiving the DSO for his leadership of 151 Squadron. In his manual, he also included *A Few Important Dont's* written by one of the RAF's greatest fighter pilots: the South African Wing Commander Adolf Gysbert 'Sailor' Malan DSO DFC, who also contributed his *Notes on Tactics and Air Fighting*. The thoughts of another exceptional Spitfire pilot were also included – the Polish 'Zura' Zurakowski – all of which represented absolutely essential advice and suggested tactical operating procedures which new pilots ignored at their peril.

GENERAL NOTES ON AERIAL GUNNERY

FIXED GUNS IN FIGHTERS.--The guns are fixed in the aircraft and harmonized so that they fire along the fore and aft axis of the ship. So that to aim the guns, it is necessary to point the whole ship, and aim the ship with the sight provided directly on your target at the correct range.

SIGHTING.--When shooting at a stationary target one merely has to aim directly at the target and pull the trigger in order to hit it. But should the target be apparently moving (that is, not flying directly to or from you, or is a stationary target on the ground) then several complicated points arise. You as a pilot have to judge:

(i) The distance from the target.

(ii) The speed of the target.

(iii) The distance to aim ahead because of the speed of the target to allow for the length of time the bullet takes to get from the gun to the target.

(iv) The angle that target is cutting with your own course.

Suppose the pilot has only an aiming point to direct his fire by, he has to then judge all the above points accurately. Supposing, however, he has a ring and bead type of sight (an explanation of which follows) he need not trouble about the point number (i) the distance from the target; or point number (iii) the distance to aim ahead of the target because the ring at once gives him an angle instead of the two distances. Your problems with a ring are therefore reduced to:

(i) Speed of the target, and

(ii) Angle of target's course to your own.

THE RING AND BEAD SIGHT.--The ring and bead sight consists of a bead sight mounted well forward toward the nose of the aircraft and a double ring sight mounted fairly close in front of the pilot's eye. The inner ring of the back sight is just larger than the bead of the foresight and thus if you, as pilot, align the inner ring of the back sight with the bead of the foresight, onto the target, you will then be aiming along the fore and aft axis of your aircraft, or, in other words, along your line of flight. With the same alignment, from your eye onto a target, the outer ring gives you an allowance basis for targets moving at any angle to your line of flight. The size you have the outer ring is immaterial but experienced pilots have preferred a ring designed for target speed of 100 miles per hour when flying at right angles to their line of flight. In other words if you are using a 100 m.p.h. ring sight and are approaching a target which is flying on a course 90° different from your own, you should, while holding your eye and the bead centralized in the inner ring, maneuver your aircraft so as to place the target on the outer ring of the sight but flying directly at the center bead. If you hold this aim, you should hit the target. The angle between the line of the pilot's eye and the outer ring to target and the line through the inner ring and the bead (which is the path of the bullets) is called the angle of deflection. So when a pilot fires at a target moving other than directly toward or away from him, he must allow an angle of deflection. Or as the Americans call it, he must LEAD the target.

The size of the outer ring can be calculated on certain standard data as follows:

(i) The distance you wish to have between your eye to the ring sight, in feet.

(ii) The average speed of the bullet, in feet per second.

(iii) The speed of the target in feet per second.

In this way:

$$\frac{\text{The distance from the eye in feet}}{\text{Bullet speed in feet per second}} \times \text{Speed of target in feet per second} = \text{The size in feet of the outer ring.}$$

An electrical sight designed on the basis of the ring and bead sight just described, shows a lighted image on the windshield of the ring and bead. This is called the Ring and Dot Reflector Sight. The Reflector sight has many good points over the ring and bead sight but the ring and bead sight has to be retained in case of failure of the electrical side of the reflector sight. To enumerate, these points are:

(i) In the ring and bead sight, because of the size of the outer ring has been calculated according to the distance the pilot's eye is from the ring sight, it is essential that he places his eye at this exact distance otherwise the basic allowance given by the outer ring will vary. For instance, if the distance of the sight from the pilot's eye be eight inches, a movement of two inches towards or away from the sight will give an error of 25 feet at 400 yards. This is not so with the reflector sight which automatically compensates for any distance the pilot may place his head from the sight.

(ii) In the ring and bead sight the pilot must align the bead of the fore sight in the inner ring of the back sight in his eye for every type of shot otherwise his "line of sight" will be incorrect. For instance, if the eye is 1/8" out of line it will give an error of 20 feet at 400 yards. Again this is not so with the reflector sight which, so long as it's image is visible on the windshield, it again automatically compensates for the position of the pilot's head.

(iii) The eye like a camera has to be in focus to see the object clearly, hence if the target is in focus the sights must be out of focus and are not seen distinctly. Not so with the reflector sight which gives the pilot the vision of the dot and ring's image being superimposed on the target.

DEFLECTION ALLOWANCES AND DIFFERENT ANGLES OF ATTACK.--When the target is flying at an angle of less than 90° to your aircraft the amount of deflection to be taken varies with the sine of the angle of attack. This is best shown diagramatically:

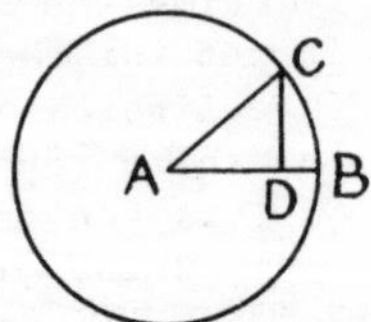

In the above diagram an aircraft flying across the ring sight from A to B at 90° to your course would therefore have to be positioned at the point B to allow for the target's movement during the time of the flight of the bullet over the target range. The distance AB is the full deflection allowed by the sight. An aircraft attacking along the line CA would be at 45°, would at first sight appear to be 1/2 that of 90°. This is not so, and it can be seen from the diagram that the allowance for 45° is DA, which is considerably more than 1/2 the line AB. That distance is of

410-2F-42

course allowed along the line of flight of the target.

But $\frac{AD}{AC}$ = sine 45°

and AC = AB which = full allowance

∴ AD (the allowance required) = full allowance X sine the angle of attack.

The following values for the sine of various angles may be studied at this point in order to derive what I consider the most important factor when shooting with deflection.

Sine 90°	= 1	Sine 45°	= .71
80°	= .98	30°	= .5
70°	= .94	20°	= .34
60°	= .87	10°	= .17
50°	= .76	5°	= .1

The factor that stands out from this is that from angles of 90° to 60° one still has to take the full allowance of deflection. I cannot emphasize sufficiently how important this point is. No pilot ever seems to take sufficient lead.

DENSITY.--When you fire at a target moving at an angle to your line of flight, you must turn your aircraft continually so that you hold the target at the correct deflection and sighting while you fire your guns. If you do not hold the aim, bullet hits the front of the airplane by the time the second bullet covers the distance to the target the target would have moved on its course 12 7/20 feet which equals 7 1/2 feet behind the first and the third round 7 1/2 feet behind the second, etc. From this you can see how important it is to hold your aim during your burst. IN OTHER WORDS YOU MUST TURN WITH THE TARGET AND KEEP YOUR SIGHTS ON. I realize, of course, that the fitting of multi-guns to fighters does produce a heavy concentration of fire at any moment, but modern aircraft are robust and heavily armored and it requires a great many hits to disable them. Likewise they would be going a great deal faster than 100 mph that I have shown in my example, so the faster the speed of the target the less is the concentration of your fire if you do not keep your sights on.

ACCURATE FLYING WHEN FIRING.--Even if you are able to take good aim and place your sights in the correct line ahead of your target, it is still very important indeed to fly accurately. ON NO ACCOUNT MUST YOU USE RUDDER ALONE TO CORRECT YOUR AIM. Your turns while keeping your sights on, must be accurate turns; that is the indicator bubble must be dead center. If you make either of these two faults; your airplane must have a slight sidewise velocity which obviously is imparted to the bullets as they are fired, this is sufficient to take them quite clear of the target. There is another natural tendency for your aircraft to turn out of line of its own. This is due to the fact that the airflow from the propeller rotates around the fuselage in a clockwise motion. To counteract this the makers of the ship place an offset fin. This allows your aircraft to fly hands off at its cruising speed. Should you dive or zoom in your ship, there is an immediate tendency due; in the first place, to the airflow straightening out, and the second place to the tightening of the corkscrew motion, around your fuselage as your propeller starts to thrash, for your ship to turn out of line. This must be corrected immediately by application of rudder. To fly your aircraft accurately without skidding requires infinite practice and skill. Practice doing this without altering the position of the trimming tabs, in combat with continual changes necessary, you will not have time. So practice without, and continually watch that slip bubble--always keep it dead center.

SKIDDING OF YOUR TARGET.--It has been pointed out that the line error in a deflection shot is caused by the pilot's failing to position the target aircraft so that it is flying towards the center of the sight or by failing to make accurate turns, or by using rudder alone to correct aim, when sighting or firing. The pilot must also be able to estimate the line of flight of the enemy, who may in extreme cases in individual combat, be skidding violently so that his aircraft is not in fact flying along the line in which the nose of the aircraft is pointing.

Unfortunately in a modern streamlined ship the application of rudder does not change the course of your ship, but only turns the nose of the ship away from the course. The ship in actual fact still proceeds along its original course slipping to one side. Therefore when firing at a ship try not to heed the direction the ship is pointing when deciding your line of sight, but try and access its general direction. When duck shooting in a high cross wind it is no use aiming ahead of the direction their beak and neck are pointing; because the duck, due to the high cross wind, is not actually proceeding in that direction at all. The same with an enemy aircraft flying with rudder applied. It is not easy to position the target in the sights so that it is flying towards the center of the target and a line error frequently occurs. This is a gunnery fault that firing with tracer ammunition will cure, as it is easy to see which side of the target your bullets are going. (See: Firing with Tracer.)

RANGE.--Range is one of the most important things of aerial gunnery. Obviously it is not quite so important when firing with only one gun mounted near the gun sight but with any form of guns carried in the wings which are considerable distance from the sight base, range is vitally important. The guns are harmonized so that all the bullets meet at a certain point in order to give you a concentration of fire which is the real reason you have this multiple armament. Therefore the range which the guns are harmonized to meet, is the best range to shoot. In practice you must do what you will have to do in combat; that is you must fire at your correct harmonized range. After ranges of more than 300 yards your bullets, even 50 caliber, start to lose their powers of penetration, and bullet drop enters into it. Another point to consider is the scattering of the bullets due to the vibration of the guns, this increases as the range increases. Against all this if you were close to any range of under 150 yards to an enemy bomber carrying rear gunners, I maintain that your chances of living to tell about it will be very slender. The danger point arises when you start your break-a-way after your attack. Firstly, because you are no longer firing at the bomber, this tends to buck-up the courage of the rear gunner, and secondly because you are turning your unarmored flank towards the gunner. I maintain that 150 yards is a minimum range for the attacking of bombers.

GRAVITY DROP.--An object is drawn towards the earth at an acceleration of 32 Ft. per second, per second, so that the bullets fly in a slight curve depending primarily upon the initial velocity. However, no allowance need be taken on any firing ranges up to 250 yards.

Owing to the fact that most of your guns are mounted below the line of sight, they must be canted up if they are to meet at the point of harmonization. This allows for considerable bullet drop when your ship is level about its horizontal axis, but when banked one must remember to aim up, and not ease the stick back to raise the nose, as this of course pulls the nose around the horizon and not up at all. It is recommended that no firing takes place at ranges of more than 300 yards.

BULLET GROUP.--Because of the slight inaccuracies in the gun itself, slight movement in the mounting and vibration of the aircraft, the bullets fired will roughly cover a circular area of approximately 20 feet in diameter at 400 yards. Without very careful thought, do not speed your guns when harmonizing them to get extra spreadage or you will loose too much concentration and your fire will be ineffective. A chapter of this manual gives guidance on this problem.

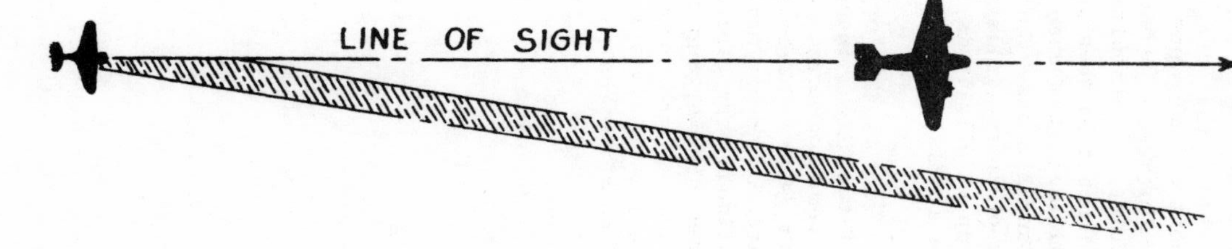

Although pilot took good aim this is path of bullets. Owing to fact that fighter pilot has failed to counteract correctly the tendency of his aircraft to swing to starboard whilst diving on target, this allowed the aircraft to attain a sideways velocity which is obviously imparted to bullets.

NOTES OF AIR FIRING PRACTICES (Fixed Gun)

Air Firing Practices against towed targets are not designed to teach potential fighter pilots any tactical methods of approaching hostile aircraft, but rather the final run onto the target, which includes (1) Judging of Range, (2) Aiming, (3) Firing, (4) Holding the sights on, (5) Correct deflection, (6) Correcting of flying faults. All the practices and exercises, however, have a very definite bearing on air combat and are essential in teaching the actual hitting of targets before the pilot has to go into action. These gunnery exercises must be made as realistic as possible.

There are two most important points which remain constant whatever the attack or exercise. In the case of deflection shooting (See Notes on the importance of deflection shooting) - it is obviously absolutely imperative that a pilot be able to assess automatically the angle between the course of the enemy aircraft and that of his own aircraft. Now in air firing against towed targets this is comparatively a simple task, as the towing aircraft, cable, and target give the attacker a definite indication of the direction in which the target is traveling. Unfortunately this is not as simple in combat, as the enemy aircraft need not necessarily be traveling in the direction in which he is pointing. For instance an enemy pilot might apply full rudder (and opposite stick to prevent banking and a turn) and point well to one side of the track he is making good. See diagram A I and A II.

In the case in diagram A II, it is most tempting for the fighter pilot to take a proper deflection shot at the enemy, assessing the amount of deflection on the APPARENT course of the enemy aircraft. So it is essential, through practice and experience, to be able to assess the amount of deflection to take by judging the amount of GENERAL MOVEMENT of the enemy compared with the fighter pilot, rather than by noting the direction in which the enemy aircraft is pointing.

Now there is the other important point and this point is absolutely vital whether in actual combat or on the practice range. This point is the "skidding" or "slip"

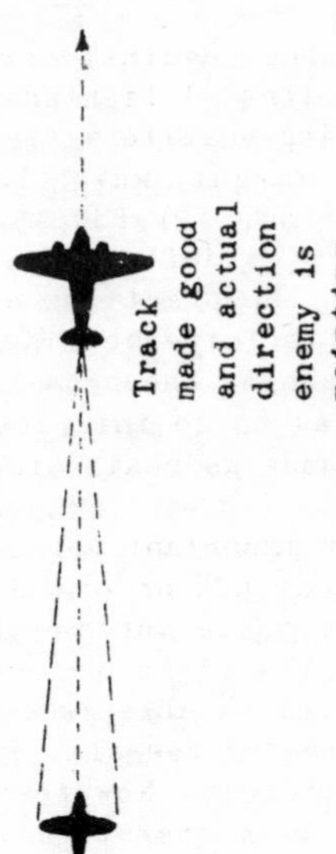
Track
made good
and actual
direction
enemy is
pointing

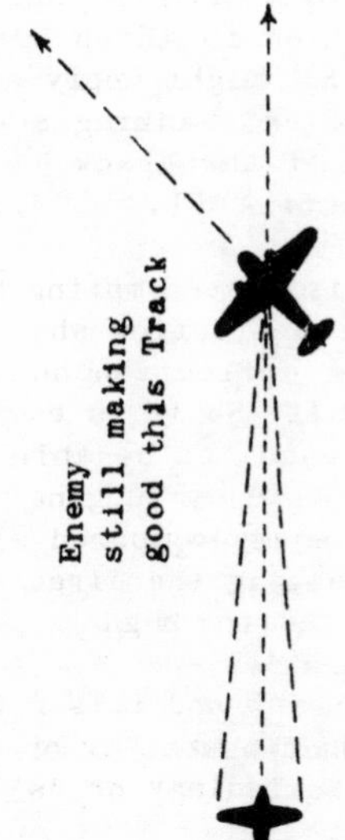
Enemy
still making
good this Track
Enemy pilot applied
rudder and is now
pointing at X but is
still making good ori-
ginal track as in A I.
Fighter pilot would be
very tempted to take a
full deflection shot.
but fighter pilot still takes
no deflection shot.

of the fighter aircraft. This can be caused in two ways, both are serious and must be overcome by instant action on the part of the pilot. Firstly a single engine fighter is drawn through the air by an airscrew, which to impart a forward movement to the aircraft, has to rotate. In rotating the airscrew sets up a corkscrew flow of air backwards and ROUND the fuselage. This corkscrew motion of air, strikes the side of the rudder and tends to turn the nose of the aircraft around its vertical axis. In other words the aircraft starts to "skid" or "slip". To keep the aircraft straight the pilot must apply rudder. However to avoid having to make the pilot fly around with continual pressure on the rudder bar, the makers of the aircraft fit a fin. This they "offset" enough to counteract the the corkscrew airflow motion; but of course this must be fixed. It is fixed so that the aircraft flies hands off at normal cruising speed, so that if any changes of air speed occur the pilot has to counteract either with rudder bias adjustment or by application of rudder. For instance, should the pilot dive his aircraft, the corkscrew airflow motion past the fuselage tends to straighten out; the fin, being offset (to counteract the normal corkscrew airflow) tends to swing the aircraft out of line. In other words the aircraft starts to "skid" and no longer proceeds in the direction in which it is pointing. This has to be counteracted at once by application of rudder. Another instance would be when the pilot starts to climb. At once the airscrew starts to thrash, blasting the air in a tighter corkscrew motion around the fuselage, so that the fin being set for a lesser "side blast", catches this extra blast from the side which tends to swing the nose of the aircraft, causing a skid to the opposite side. This again must be counteracted by application of rudder. See diagrams B I, B II and B III. This is the most IMPORTANT POINT IN AIR FIRING, FOR THIS REASON.

When an aircraft "skids" it has a speed to one side or other of the direction in which it is pointing. One can skid in a turn by having applied too much or too little rudder for bank applied. Therefore when the guns (which are fixed and fired dead down the line of the fuselage) are fired the bullets which come out of the guns have a velocity to the side of the same amount as that at which the aircraft is slipping to that side.

so that however careful your aim, the bullets you fire whilst slipping can never hit what you are aiming at, owing to the fact that they have this sideways velocity which, even though it be slight is enough to take them quite clear of the target. One can imagine that any combat at all, be it against bombers or fighters, must of necessity be one of continual dives, zooms or level flying. A fighter pilot must take great care that he is able automatically to counteract just sufficiently the slip caused by the offset fin. See diagram C I page 17. I must now take this argument a step further.

I HAVE MADE OUT IN THESE PRECEDING PARAGRAPHS THAT THIS SLIPPING AND SKIDDING WHICH OCCURS WHEN ONE DIVES AND ZOOMS IS VIOLENT, BUT THE DANGER IS THAT THEY ARE ACTUALLY INDISCERNABLE.

SECOND METHOD OF CAUSING "SKID".--Suppose you are taking the correct action to counteract this natural tendency of the aircraft to skid whilst zooming or diving to attack. As you approach your target and are all ready to open fire and are concentrating on aiming, you may find the sights are to one side or the other of your target. The natural tendency is to push on rudder in order to bring the sights to bear. This is a useless practice, as quite obviously, (although you actually bring your sights on to the target), you cause the aircraft to "skid". In other words the aircraft immediately has a movement to the side; this, of course, throws the bullets clear of the target. If one finds that one's sights are not dead on, one must use "bank" and rudder to bring them to bear.

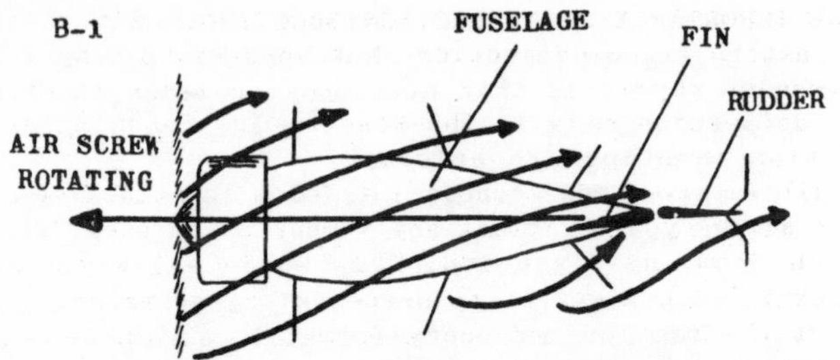

Corkscrew airflow Normal cruising with fin off set to counteract. Fin counteracting any tendency to swing.

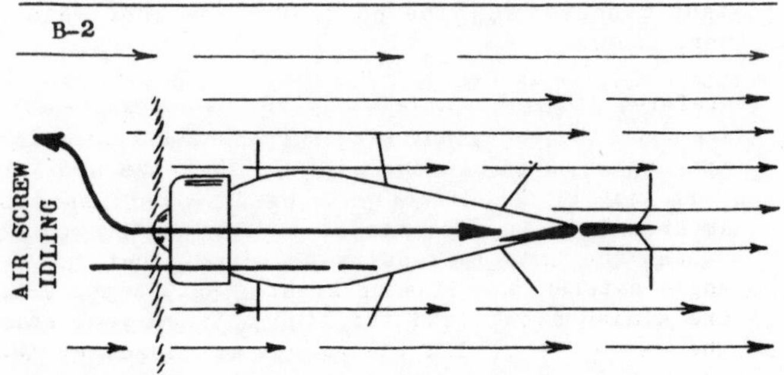

Aircraft diving airflow straightened out and striking off set fin swinging nose to starboard.

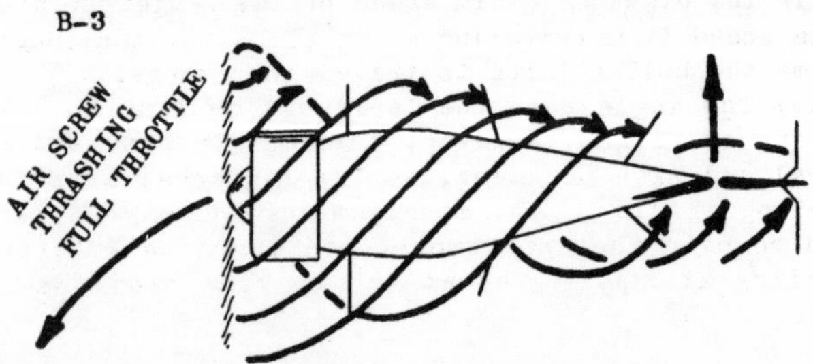

Aircraft climbing, airscrew starts to thrash more, corkscrew tightens, airflow airflow strikes side of fin which is not off set enough tending to swing to port.

THE IMPORTANCE OF DEFLECTION SHOOTING.--Since the dead astern or no deflection shot appears so easy you may wonder why it is ever necessary to learn to fire with deflection at all. The reasons for learning deflection shooting are briefly:

(i) It gives you technical freedom in attack, that is it allows you to attack any member of an enemy formation from any direction. This would allow you to attack in such a way as to screen with the target you select the rest of the enemy formation so that their supporting fire would be useless.

(ii) All the bullets fired from the side at enemy aircraft will enter into unarmored parts and therefore be very much more lethal.

(iii) In fighter vs. fighter combats, owing to the constant maneuvering, the no deflection shot seldom if ever, occurs.

Therefore, it is essential that you learn and be able to fire from the side. Any target you select which has an apparent movement to one side or the other of you (that is, not flying directly to or from you) one has to aim ahead of, in order to allow for the length of time which the bullets require to travel that range. The angle between the line of sight, that is the line you are aiming along, and the line between your ship and the target is called the amount of 'lead' or the 'angle of deflection'. There are four points which a pilot has to estimate. These are:

(i) The distance he is from the target.

(ii) The speed of the target.

(iii) The distance to aim ahead of the target because of the speed it is traveling at to allow for the length of time the bullet takes to travel that range.

(iv) The angle that the target is cutting to your own line of flight, however, this may be assessed as general sidewise movement, as for instance, a target traveling at 330 m.p.h. at right angles to your path would require the same amount of 'lead' as a target traveling at 200 m.p.h. at 45° to your own line of flight.

There is a fifth point which is always known to you which is your bullet speed and your own airplane speed;

that effects the length of time the bullet takes to travel the range that you have selected. The length of time is roughly 1/4 of a second for 250 yards, the airplane speed making no appreciable difference in this length of time.

With a ring and bead type of sight, be it electrical or standard iron ring and bead fixture, gives you the angle of deflection rather than the distances mentioned in point (i) and point (iii) above. The theory of this is well discussed in the opening chapter of this manual. There are one or two practical applications which the fighter pilot will find useful in combat. These points are as follows:

I. **THE FLY-THROUGH METHOD.**--Suppose that you are on beam at 250 yards range, flying in a straight line, at right angles to the enemy and that fire is opened whilst the allowance made is still too large and continued until the enemy has flown through the bullet stream. The fuselage of a bomber is about 50 feet long and, if its speed is 250 m.p.h., the bullet group sweeps the whole length of the fuselage in 0,14 seconds.

During this time four 20 m.m. guns fire 6 bullets so that the best that can be done by this method, even supposing that none of the bullets pass either above or below the enemy, is to put six bullets through the fuselage or 1 in 40 sq. ft.

Fire by this method cannot therefore be very effective though it may occasionally achieve a lucky success. Rather greater success may be expected from the method when fire is from a small angle from astern, since the bullets pass more lengthways through the fuselage and have more chance of doing damage. It is clear, however, that the adoption of the "fly-through" method amounts to a confession of weakness, since it throws away the much greater concentration of bullets than can be obtained by following through.

II. **THE FOLLOW-THROUGH METHOD.**--The alternative is to endeavor to follow the enemy, making throughout the correct allowance. If this can be done, the bullet group remains on him for the whole duration of fire and very much greater concentration on the target is, of course, obtained.

The difficulties of this method are of two kinds. In the first place it is necessary to have a much clearer idea of what the allowance should be, for if it is wrongly estimaged the bullets may miss all the time. In the second place the act of following him requires you to fly on a curve, the curvature of which may be greater than can be conveniently applied, owing to the effects of G and limited field of vision in a steep bank due to the length of the nose of certain fighter aircraft.

Now the allowance or deflection required to hit him is dependent upon his speed and either the angle between you and his direction of flight or the range. That is to say, the deflection can be judged either by estimating that he will have moved a certain distance during the time of flight of the bullet.

(a) THE ANGLE-OFF METHOD.--Estimation of the deflection by angle-off from the target is that recommended because it is nearly independent of range. If the bullet flew at a constant speed the deflection would be exactly independent of range, for if the range were doubled the time of flight would be doubled and the distance travelled by the target in this time would be doubled, leaving the deflection angle unchanged.

Actually the bullet slows up a bit at the longer ranges so that the allowance is slightly bigger than at short ranges, but this difference can be safely neglected in comparison with the much larger errors which you are likely to make in judging the angle from astern.

Estimation of the angle off the target can only be done by constant practice against model aircraft, by studying photographs, by use of the various characteristics of the aircraft in order to obtain this angle, e.g. tail aligned with wing tip.

Estimation of speed requires appreciation of the performance of the aircraft being attacked, and also of your own aircraft, under varying conditions.

The allowance required is obtained by multiplying the speed of the target by the sine of the angle-off. Obviously such a sum cannot be done in the air and pictures should be prepared showing the appearance of various targets for 1/2-ring, 3/4-ring, 1-ring allowance, etc.

(b) THE LENGTHS-AHEAD METHOD.--Some pilots prefer to use the lengths-ahead method of aiming. They decide to hold their aim at a point which is some chosen number of times the fuselage lengths ahead of the target, the number of lengths depending on the mean range at which they expect to fire. The more usual method of using the ring, described above, gives better results, but as the lengths-ahead method has some points in its favor it is worth consideration.

The idea behind this method is that at a given range the time of flight of the bullet, and therefore the the distance flown by the target in this time, is roughly the same for all angles. If therefore, the number of lengths ahead can be correctly chosen to suit the range and target speed, the aim will be correct for all angles.

The defects of this method are:

(i) The numbers of lengths ahead depends on the length of the target fuselage.

(ii) It gives the wrong answer when the range is different from that supposed and, futhermore, it depends on the range remaining constant during an attack.

AIWAYS REMEMBER: FEW PIIOTS EVER TAKE TOO MUCH LEAD, NEARLY AIL TAKE TOO LITTLE. BEGINNERS: TRY AND TAKE TOO MUCH, AND YOU'LL BE ABOUT RIGHT.

RANGE.--when a bullet is fired from a fixed-gun fighter flying at 400 m.p.h. it has a very high velocity (something of the order of 3,000 ft. per sec. or over 2,000 m.p.h.). This velocity, however, is very rapidly lost due to air resistance and half is lost when the bullet has traveled about 600 yards. This means a considerable decrease in hitting power at long ranges and your bullets would fail to penetrate the thinnest armor plating. It follows then that it is a waste of time and energy to open fire at excessive ranges.

As the range of the bullet increases so does the 'gravity drop'. A bullet takes more than twice as long to travel 600 yards as it does to travel the first 300 yards because it is slowing up at an increasing rate. This means that the pull of gravity has more than twice as long to act over 600 yards than over 300 yards, and thus the gravity drop at 600 yards is more than four times that at 300 yards because the gravity has an acceleration of 32 feet per sec., per sec. Now your sight and guns are not harmonized to allow for gravity drop at 600 yards, so if you do open fire at 600 yards you must make an additional allowance for this greater gravity drop by an amount which, at best, you can only guess.

When four guns are harmonized they are so arranged as to give some pre-arranged pattern at a definite range (usually 250 yards). This pattern is designed to to give the best chance of effective shooting from point-blank range up to some optimum range outside of which your chance of success rapidly deteriorates. With any type of gun the bullet pattern spreads out as the range increases. This means that the area of the pattern produced at 400 yards, say, is four times larger than that produced at 200 yards. This may at first sight appear a good thing, but it is necessary in addition to remember that the pattern area will contain practically every bullet fired. So, in terms of bullet density, the pattern at 400 yards contains only 1/4 of the number of bullets per square foot contained in the pattern at 200 yards. For example let us suppose that certain fighter in 1 sec. burst fires 200 rounds, his gives us approximately a bullet density at 200 ards of 12 bullets per square foot, at 400 yards the ensity is reduced to 3 bullets per square foot.

Correct deflection allowance is also bound up with correct range estimation especially if you use the lengths-ahead method described in Part II on deflection shooting. If you allow, say, three lengths for opening fire between 400 and 300 yards and then, by an error in range estimation, open fire at 600 yards, your deflection allowance will be insufficient and your bullets will pass behind your target.

From the foregoing it will be seen that shooting at excessive ranges produces:

(a) Loss in penetrating power of bullets, and thus loss in effectiveness of shots (even though your aim is correct).

(b) Increase in gravity drop which leads to an additional allowance which you must guess.

(c) A very thinly distributed bullet pattern and this means you have to fire a much longer burst to have the same effect as at short ranges.

(d) Errors in deflection allowances.

It follows from all this that successful air combat might well hinge on your ability to estimate range correctly. In fact it is not an overstatement to say that range estimation is one of the most important aspects of air fighting. It has this disadvantage, however, in that you must teach yourself, and to that end continuous practices on the ground with scale models must be carried out in addition to regular air-practices--at least one a week of both cine camera gun practices and air firing against towed targets.

AIR EXERCISES
AIR FIRING AGAINST GROUND TARGETS

TARGETS.--10 feet square (white) lying at an angle of about 50° to the ground. (Aluminum sea markers, or smoke floats, just thrown into the sea make very good targets). It is preferable to have the 10 foot targets located on soft sand or in shallow water in order that the pilot firing may see the results of his firing at the time.

This firing at ground targets is very useful work and must be conscientiously carried out as follows. If on fixed targets, fly to a position at right angles to the target, at a height of 2,000 ft. and so that a dive at an angle of 30° would take you into the target; throttle back, turn on to target and commence shallow dive. Get sights on immediately and open fire. Continue to fire, until at 700 feet. Cease fire. Then open up the engine and climb up and round into position to repeat. Check carefully any rough movements of the controls, paying particular attention to rudder. Do not fire with aircraft skidding.

When flying with dual control the effect of correcting errors in aim by using rudder alone, and the effect of wind on firing results are demonstrated.

QUARTER ATTACK (Carried out on A-B Target lines along airfiring danger area).--This is carried out with towed target over a course of approximately 1½ miles. Approach the target aircraft head on but about 400 feet higher up and the radius of an easy turn to one side; when approximately 500 yards ahead of drogue, start turn towards line of path of target. As early as possible sights should be got 'on' allowing correct deflection, fire open at 250 yards and held until angle decreases to 20 degrees. Break away downwards, turning in opposite direction to that of target and get into position at other end of two line so that exercise is repeated in the opposite direction.

The instructor will demonstrate: (i) How to keep (with bank and rudder) the line of sight dead in line with the path of the target. (To assist beginners the towing cable can be used as a rough check on this, although he must try to accomplish it without this artificial aid. It is a very bad habit to make use of such aids). (ii) The correct deflection and how this is gradually decreased as the angle of attack decreases and attacker falls astern of target. (iii) Minimum angle of attack so that pupil will know when he has reached the dangerous angle and bullets might prejudice the safety of towing aircraft. (iv) Check any tendency to keep sights 'on' by use of rudder alone. (v) Check roughness on controls.

ASTERN ATTACK (C.D. line).--This is possibly the easiest of all attacks and is carried out against a three-foot cone target towed so as to fly below and to one side of the towing aircraft. Never go lower than the cone. This rules out any possibility of the towing aircraft being hit.

You will be shown a three-foot cone target on the ground before taking off, and what it looks like from various ranges. Approach to the cone target is made from a position dead astern of the actual towing aircraft. This means that the target cone lies some 300 feet below, 300 feet to one side, and the attacker is approximately 500 yards astern. Throttle is eased back as soon as nose of aircraft is depressed, sights 'on' at once and open fire at 350 yards. Fire is opened as soon as target crosses danger area and firing only takes place in one direction, that is, into the danger area. If pupil flying aircraft with dual control, the instructor will demonstrate ranges. Watch bullet drop if using tracer. This is important and is one of the few practices which demonstrate effectively the amount that bullets drop over ranges of more than 200 yards. Any rough corrections with rudder should be checked and sights always kept 'on' by application of bank and rudder together.

The attacks should be repeated at various overtaking speeds.

During astern attacks, there is a danger of the attacking aircraft flying into the cone target if the towing cable breaks. For this reason a minimum range to which attacking aircraft may approach is laid down. Broadly speaking, this minimum distance is 200 yards when approaching at 160 m.p.h., 250 yards at 200 m.p.h., and 300 yards at 240 m.p.h.

HEAD ON ATTACKS (Camera Gun Only).--These are most important attacks because in spite of the very short length of the time in which one has to get the sights 'on' and fire, the enemy presents a fairly easy no deflection target, and every bullet that hits goes into the unprotected fuselage of the enemy with usually disastrous results.

When practicing these attacks strict orders must be laid down, and one aircraft must always be TARGET and whatever happens he must never alter course. If he does so he might easily alter it to the same place as the attacker had decided to pass; in which case a head-on collision results. Fire must be opened at a slightly greater range, otherwise one is inclined to leave it too late so that it is not possible to open fire at all. This attack invariably meets with little opposition and often one can carry out such an attack without even being fired at. If enemy turns, the attack can immediately be developed into a '¼' attack or an 'astern' attack.

EMPLOYMENT OF FIGHTER SQUADRONS
STRATEGICAL AND TACTICAL CONSIDERATIONS OF THE TASKS WHICH MAY BE ASSIGNED TO FIGHTER UNITS

In the order of importance, the tasks which may be assigned to a fighter unit are as follows:

1. Home Defence.
2. The offensive sweep patrols over enemy country.
3. The maintenance of air superiority over a given position at a given time in order to allow Naval, Military, or Air Operations to take place without interference of enemy force. This is sometimes referred to as forming a mushroom of fighters, a good example of this would be the British evacuation from Dunkirk.
4. Escort for bombers.
5. Ground straffing.

1. HOME DEFENCE.--Home defense is a very wide and varied task. It includes individual day fights, mass dog fights, individual attacks against bombers and synchronized and carefully planned squadron attacks. It is obviously impossible under this heading to discuss details of all the tasks mentioned above. However, certain principles do remain constant without going into detail of how the actual attacks take place. The principles I shall endeavor to outline below:

When working in a country with such a highly specialized defense system such as Great Britain, one is inclined to become careless regarding the presence of the enemy as normally one receives so much warning of the exact position of enemy aircraft. This is entirely wrong. One must always expect the enemy. Pilots taking off from English aerodromes have been shot down by German fighters. Keep your eyes open the whole while, as a matter of habit, looking for enemy. It is essential that the squadron sticks together from the moment it takes off until it returns to the aerodrome again. The squadron must work as a squadron and not as individuals. Pilots are only to attack when told by their squadron commander to do so. They must not break formation for any reason whatsoever, unless told to do so by their squadron commander. The squadron commander must always place his squadron in an advantageous position with regard to the enemy before he orders any attack. He must insure that he:

a. Has the advantage of the direction of the sun.

b. Has altitude over the enemy.

c. Notes carefully cloud formations and makes the best use of them.

d. Makes up his plan of action at once without any loss of time, gives his orders to his squadron as clearly and concisely as possible.

e. Launches and presses home the attack with determination. A timid attack is useless.

After attacking, if possible without too much hanging about, the squadron should reform or at least get together, but under no circumstances hang around trying to get into formation with each other in the vicinity the attack was made. Escort fighters will deal very severely with you if you so do.

2. OFFENSIVE SWEEPS.--The aim of these sweeps is to destroy enemy aircraft in the security of their own country. Obviously it is a fairly hazardous procedure unless properly carried out. The danger lies in being surprised and attacked by overwhelmingly superior enemy forces. In deciding in what formation one must fly, one has to consider these points. You are supposedly in offensive action, therefore, your formation must be one which can instantly be developed into any form of attack you might wish to make. The men who are in constant danger are the men who are at the back of the formation. So from this point of view, one would get the impression that the ideal formation would be a flat one so that everyone is well up and there are no 'back' persons. However, a formation of this sort is entirely unwieldy, as in the slightest turns, you get stragglers, owing to the difference in speeds between the persons on the outside and those on the inside. Once one crosses enemy territory, one automatically comes under fire from antiaircraft batteries; so you cannot fly straight with safety.

The most important point in the type of formation, must be its maneuverability. There are many types of formations used but I think the best is a squadron of 12 ships divided into flights of 4, each flight in line astern formation. These flights move out when passing through enemy antiaircraft fire and weave independently, they don't need to move out any great distance but just enough to break down the mass target effect. When over enemy territory, they must weave continuously and at no time fly straight for more than 30 seconds. Defensive and offensive tactics must be practiced continuously. In case of defensive tactics some maneuver must be executed in which the whole squadron supports each other. In the offensive tactics, always leave 1/3 of your strength up over you as a guard when you go down to attack.

Whatever occurs while over enemy territory, one essential is that you stick together. If the squadron is attacked and the formation broken, the pilots must remain in the same piece of air. Do not run away and leave your squadron for your own safety as well as theirs. There must be no straggling of any sort, any straggling is dearly paid for as the straggler is bound to be destroyed.

Owing to the fact that the serious danger lies in the squadron being surprised, possibly by a larger formation of enemy fighters, it is best to adopt this system:

The squadron commander searches for enemy targets to attack and also concentrates on his navigation.

The leaders of his other flights concentrate on maintaining positions and do what searching they can.

All the remainder of the squadron keep the sky above and behind and especially up sun carefully searched.

Radio silence must be strictly maintained. The squadron commander should be the only person to use the radio and he only uses it to give orders regarding attacks. If, however, the squadron is surprised, any person in the squadron who sights enemy fighters which might appear to constitute a menace, he is to warn the squadron on the radio at once.

3. MUSHROOM COVERING.--The strength of the mushroom covering is dependent on the strength of the opposition expected. It is obvious that the strength of the fighters must be considerably greater than the maximum strength that the enemy are able to muster in that area.

The fighter squadrons should be allotted to certain areas and altitudes and must strictly adhere to their allotted positions. Squadrons should be evenly spaced in their definite altitude between 5,000 feet and the ceiling of their particular aircraft.

The squadrons should patrol to the 'up sun' side of the locality. In this manner enemy aircraft are more easily seen should they enter the zone, and also it gives one the advantage should attack be necessary. Great care should be taken that you are not drawn off the zone. One must always bear in mind the area one wishes to guard; and when enemy aircraft enter, ATTACK but in no circumstances allow yourself, through over-keeness, to be drawn off in an extended pursuit. Radio silence must be maintained and only broken by the issue of necessary orders. The officer commanding the mushroom covering should be in the squadron at the lowest altitude.

Always detail the minimum number of aircraft to attack so that always the greatest number possible are ready to most further attacks. No one must attack without Commanding Officer's orders. The lowest squadron should look after the immediate air over the zone; the other three squadrons should be solely responsible for their own safety. This is most important, as the feeling of doing a job of work at 5,000 feet and not being certain that at any moment a horde of enemy fighters will descend upon you, seriously impairs the ability of the low squadron to carry out its task.

The high squadrons must not allow themselves to be drawn off in pursuit of the enemy. They must only attack enemy aircraft which attempt to interfere, and not rush after enemy aircraft away from the zone.

If could covering is 10/10 it is not necessary to patrol above, as it is impossible to maintain one's position and this covering to a great extent precludes enemy surprise attack as they are seen so easily the moment they break cloud cover and are not difficult to see as aircraft are at great heights up sun.

4. ESCORT OF BOMBERS.--The strategy of escorting bombers remains the same whatever the strength of the fighters available or the strength of the bombers to be escorted.

The bombers' should fly in a fairly compact formation, I think spread out in depth rather than width. The escort should divide itself as follows: One squadron for close escort, these should fly half a mile astern and a 1,000 feet or so above the bombers. The next squadron, if available, flies some 5,000 feet above and to the side of the first squadron. If other squadrons are available, they take up their positions besides and above the bombers until the air all around the sides, behind, and above the bombers are filled with friendly fighters.

The bombers' whole safety lies in whether or not the fighters are able to maintain these positions. As soon as the escort are engaged, they almost invariably have to turn and fight leaving the bombers unguarded. They must endeavor to ignore all enemy aircraft except the ones that actually attack or those obviously just about to attack and even then only engage them long enough to drive them off and on no account should leave the vicinity of the bombers. The control of the fighters must be rigid and the commanding officer must be careful, if he thinks it necessary for the bombers' safety, to order the minimum of the escort to engage the enemy at once, always holding the maximum in reserve.

One must bear in mind that there are always many more aircraft about than one can see. The escort wing must discuss a comprehensive scheme on the ground before taking off so that the minimum number of words need be issued on the radio.

When the target is reached, fighters should circle above the bombers to keep the air clear while the bombers go about their dangerous task of running up and bombing the target. As the bombers start for home, so the fighters take up position again and the same procedure is adopted. The fighters should remember that the bombers will be flying several miles per hour faster than on the outward journey owing to the fact that they have got rid of their loads of bombs. They must anticipate this and not allow themselves to get behind and become ineffective as escort. Another fatal mistake is to allow oneself to lose vigilance towards the end of an uninterrupted flight. One must remember that there is 70 percent more chance in being intercepted on the way home than there is on the way out. Once the bombers have started to stir up trouble you can expect the sky to be filled with enemy.

5. GROUND STRAFING.--The term 'Ground Strafing' is more commonly applied to attacks by fighters from a very low level delivered against enemy infantry or motor transport concentrated along roads or in camps. During these sorts of attacks there is only one rule which must be rigidly adhered to, and that is to keep as low and as fast as possible. Try and place between yourself and the enemy as much of the countryside as possible, that is take advantage of all trees, buildings and hills by keeping down below them if possible. One must climb a little at times in order to check one's whereabouts and to be able to make some sort of shallow dive on the targets you select; however, this climbing should be cut down to the barest minimum.

On the other hand, one might be assigned to the task of shooting up one definite target and after shooting it up to return home. I think if this be the case one should approach the target at some 15,000 feet and actually pass some five miles beyond it so that the attack may be delivered from a more unexpected direction and the get-a-way made easier. After passing some five miles beyond the aerodrome the squadron should be echeloned to one side or other and on the order to attack should peel off in turn, following within, but not at a greater distance than 600 yards. Actually this distance should not be less than 500 yards as it might not give the aircraf ahead full powers of maneuvering. For this approach the throttles are shut back and altitude is lost so that one makes contact with the ground some two miles from the target. These two miles are passed in very quick time owing to the extra speed gathered in the dive. As one approaches the target, one should climb slightly to three or four hundred feet in order to get a good view and be able to select profitable targets. Attack them as fiercely as possible opening fire at about 400 yards and continuing to fire to point blank range, turn immediately you pass the target so as to present a more difficult target yourself. By turns to each side shoot at as many targets as you can possibly find, but waste no time in circling or going back on your tracks. If you do this, you will only embarrass the aircraft following you. Make your get-a-way at ground level. Throughout the whole of this approach, attack, and get-a-way, watch carefully behind, and see thet the aircraft following you is indeed a friend.

FORMATION FLYING IN CLOUD.--A pursuit squadron commander in leading his squadron into combat must make use of all the elements to achieve his aim (which is the destruction of the enemy) and only in so doing can can he hope to be successful. In air warfare surprise is the greatest of all weapons. It is very difficult to achieve complete surprise, but in certain weather conditions it is possible to attain certain important advantages by judicious use of cloud. Of course when cloud is non-existent the only possible way to attain surprise is to maneuver to attack from the direction of the sun, but when certain cloud conditions prevail, it is very important that a squadron be able to maneuver through the cloud into such a position that an attack can immediately be launched without any loss of time thereby a degree of surprise can be attained. On the other hand, if in so maneuvering through cloud the squadron becomes detached and on coming out of the cloud the squadron commander finds that he is on his own and that his squadron has disappeared, he is naturally in a very embarrassing position. To be able to maneuver through cloud requires a great deal of practice and the more polished the squadron becomes in the art of formation in cloud flying, the more maneuvering the squadron commander may do.

The most successful formation to fly through clouds is the three aircraft in "Vic" and if the four aircraft section is favored the fourth aircraft takes up station close astern of No. 1. The other two or three sections, as the case may be, follow the section ahead. It is important that the leader of the squadron flies extremely accurately and it is better that he throttles his engine down considerable so as to give the pilots following a greater chance of catching up should they get behind. Of course cloud flying in squadron formation should not be attempted until pilots are proficient in maintaining station on their leader in section formation. To attain this proficiency the leader takes off with the two pupils, one on each side. He flies around with them at 4,000 feet carrying out steep turns from one side to the other, smoothly and without a break. When this is done successfully, these turns can be combined with dives and zooms until the two pupils can keep stationed accurately in any of these maneuvers. This "warming up" stage should last approximately ten to fifteen minutes. It is an important stage and it is certainly not advisable to take new pilots straight off the ground into cloud without first carrying out some form of practice flying such as I have outlined above. The selection of cloud for formation practice is important; it is realized that in America the opportunities for this practice are not so good as they are in countries which are naturally nine-tenths covered in various types of cloud. However, I think advantage can be taken of any of the other types of cloud except thunder cumulus cloud which should be avoided. Do not keep the pupils in the cloud too long to start with. They should be made to fly at not more than half a span distance from the leader; anything closer then this is dangerous and anything more distant the leader would be invisible. They should be informed that if they lose sight of the leader, they are to break away outwards and under no circumstances are they to attempt to reform in the cloud. Straight and level flying should be carried out until the pupils become proficient--after this slight turns may be attempted and then climbing and gliding. Of course for gliding the leader must take care not to completely close down his engine as the pupils will shoot ahead.

AIR FIGHTING AT OPERATIONAL ALTITUDES.--Nowadays very few combats are ever fought at altitudes of less than 17,000 feet. Many combats take place up to 38,000 feet so it is essential (since conditions at altitudes above 17,000 feet are so dissimilar from those at lower altitudes) that as much practice as possible should take place at operational altitudes--that is above 17,000 feet.

Firstly, it is absolutely essential that a serviceable oxygen mask be used. The best form of oxygen mask is one which fits tightly over the nostrils and mouth and under the helmet straps so that all the rarified atmosphere is excluded, the oxygen pipe flowing into the mask directly besides the mouth and flowing out directly opposite. This mask can also contain the microphone for the radio. Flying at oxygen height, if care is not taken to guarantee adequate supply of oxygen, is extremely dangerous. As everyone knows too well the danger of the shortage of oxygen lies in the fact that the pilot so suffering is completely unaware of the fact, as one minute he feels perfectly all right and the next second without any warning he can pass out. It might take many thousand feet before he recovers consciousness. In fact, it is seldom that such an incident doesn't end in the pilot striking the ground before he does recover.

Following are a few points which might help pursuit pilots who are to carry out exercises at above oxygen heights:

1. Before taking off.--Check the pressure gauge and see that sufficient oxygen is in the bottle. Check the flow meter to insure that oxygen is passing from the high pressure to the high pressure systems; this can be done by placing one's thumb on the outlet pipe and seeing that there is sufficient pressure behind the flow. Turn off the flow and listen carefully when the engine is not running for any leaks. Normally any leak of consequence can easily be heard as it makes an audible hissing noise. Plug in your oxygen lead and see that the flow passes into the mask--this is done in the same way and can actually be done at the same time as the item mentioned before. Make absolutely certain that your oxygen mask fits correctly.

2. Just after taking off turn on oxygen flow to 5,000 feet. Keep the flow meter well in advance of the height at which you are. Breathe quite normally the whole time.

3. At altitudes above 17,000 feet the pilot will notice that everything he does is more of an effort than it is when he is on the ground. Constantly check the flow meter and pressure gauge. See that the pressure gauge readings do not drop too fast; this will indicate that the system is leaking and the pilot must return to his aerodrome at once. It is imperative that one must not remain above 17,000 feet when the bottle pressure falls below the 'red line' minimum.

4. The pilot will notice that formation flying station keeping is more difficult as the aircraft has lost considerable amount of the sensitiveness of the controls, the control column and the rudder have to be used more violently as they are less effective and the throttle must be opened and closed more violently as the aircraft accelerates and deaccelerates very sluggishly. This is all due to the rarified air, and of course the higher one goes, the worse the conditions become.

5. Great care has to be taken to avoid collisions, both whilst maneuvering and during attacks because of the delayed action of firstly your mental ability and secondly because of the insensibility of the controls. One has the impression that one is thinking just as quickly as one does normally on the ground; this is a dangerous delusion because in actual fact one's mental power has deteriorated and one's brain functions a fraction of a second slower.

6. The stalling speed of the aircraft goes up. Care should be taken not to carry out maneuvers of too violent a nature or at too slow a speed. As a matter of interest and for quick reckoning one's true speed can easily be worked out from one's indicated speed at altitude by a very simple formula which is: add to indicated speed one mile per hour per 60 miles per hour for every thousand feet of altitude so that an indicated speed of 120 m.p.h. at 30,000 feet would in actual fact be a true speed of 120 + (2x30) which equals 180 m.p.h.

7. When diving to attack an enemy aircraft flying along straight some distance below, pull out of the dive in good time or you will sink a great deal farther below than you intended. Also one must start one's break away slightly earlier for the same reason.

8. Always remember that one cannot have too much oxygen and that it is fatal to have too little, so whenever in doubt about the amount you are receiving being adequate always turn on a little more for safety's sake.

9. Do not get flustered or make any physical effort in the cockpit as this will make you very short of breath. Take everything easily but think quickly.

GETTING OFF THE GROUND QUICKLY

QUICK-GET-AWAYS.--The importance of pursuit pilots being able to get off the ground in the shortest possible time is too great for me to have to emphasize. The reasons also, for having to leave the ground in such drastic hurry are so obvious that I think I can leave them unsaid. Suffice to say that cutting seconds off the time taken from the signal to take off and the actual time the aircraft leaves the ground may easily mean the difference between a successful interception or a complete failure, and I go so far as to say in certain circumstances where the enemy attack is directed against the pursuit aerodrome, it might end in disaster. To get off the ground quickly requires very careful planning. A set drill must be enforced both for the starting of the airplane engines and also for the quick dressing and seating of pilots in cockpits and the taxiing out and take off. It is impossible to keep pilots at an advanced state of preparedness for any length of time, to do so would put an unnecessary strain on them and severe fatigue would result. One has to remember that wars go on for years and so one must set a standard of alertness which can be carried on throughout the period of the war. In order to relieve pilots of unnecessary strain due to being kept in a high degree of alertness for long periods, the following states of preparedness have been arranged, and in practice have proved most satisfactory. It is a squadron commander's constant task to practice and practice in order to cut out seconds in the time to get off the ground after the order to do so is given.

1. "RELEASED". Pilots in this state are permitted to go wherever they choose and will not be required under any circumstances until the time the "released" period expires. Squadrons are always released until a definitely stated time. After this time they automatically revert to the next stage which is "AVAILABLE".

2. "AVAILABLE". Pilots in this state are required to be able to leave the ground within fifteen minutes from the time they are ordered into the air. This means that they must remain near a telephone or loud speaker system somewhere on the post reasonably near

their dispersal areas where their aircraft are parked, so that on the word "take off" they can rush to their aircraft and be in the air in the required time. From this state pilots may be required to come to the next state which is "READINESS"--ten minutes is allowed for this.

3. "READINESS". Pilots in this state are required to be able to leave the ground within five minutes. They must remain in the vicinity of the aircraft and be dressed in their flying clothing. They may be required to come to the next state which is "STAND-BY"; for this three minutes is allowed.

4. "STAND-BY". Pilots in this state are required to be able to leave the ground within two minutes. They must remain in their cockpits with the engines running. It is obvious that this high state of preparedness is governed by the length of time an aircraft engine can stay running on the ground without over heating. Of course pilots remaining for any length of time in this state become most fatigued. Quite normally this state is usually dispensed with as nearly always pilots are ordered into the air from the state of "readiness".

Of course these times stated above against states of preparedness are the absolute maximum times permitted. With practice the squadron should be able to cut them all down by about 75 percent. No squadron should be satisfied with the time they take off the ground from the word "go" and should constantly strive to improve this time.

I intend not to go through these states of preparedness and try to give some detail as to the points one ought to watch. Starting with the state of "RELEASED". The squadron is released say until 14:00 hours. At 13:45 hours all pilots and mechanics should report to their dispersal areas. The squadron commander should check his pilots to see that they know which is their allotted aircraft and it is their responsibility to see that everything is in order. The mechanics, assuming that the airplanes have had their daily inspections, etc., give the aircraft a quick check over and then start up the engines. The engines are warmed thoroughly, run-up and checked and then switched off.

The squadron can then report that they are now available. It is important that this be done before the time that the released period expires.

During the next state, "AVAILABLE", the aircraft crews should remain resting somewhere in the vicinity of the aircraft. The pilots are permitted to leave the immediate vicinity but must always remain in hearing of the loud speaker zone so as that they may return to their aircraft in the matter of a minute or two. All pilots' flying clothing must be laid out carefully so that the pilots can put them on in the least possible time without any trouble.

The next state, "READINESS", is the most important of all the states of preparedness and it is from this state that the most practice is required. Aircraft crews must remain handy. A definite starting drill must be enforced so that every man knows exactly what is required of him and the aircraft engine is started at once when the order to do so is given. The pilots must don their flying clothing and remain in the vicinity of the squadron operations room. When the order "take off" is given the pilots must run at their greatest speed to their aircraft, the engine of which should have been started by the time they reach there, strap themselves in, check all the instruments and other gadgets in the cockpit, make certain that the bulb in the reflector sight is functioning; if this is not functioning, it should be changed at once with one of the set of spares. (Many pilots have taken off and have even entered combat and then have switched their reflector sight on only to find that the bulb was fused.) The aircraft are then taxied out in such a way as to leave the aerodrome always clear for the leading aircraft to take off at once. Whilst it is the aim to take off in squadron formation, the squadron commander and flight commanders should not wait around for the squadron to form up on the ground, but take off immediately and by keeping their enginee throttled back allow the squadron to form up in the air. It is important though that the squadron should take off in a definite order, otherwise considerable maneuvering and shunting results. A sharp lookout must be maintained when taking off in case an enemy aircraft is ready to attack. It is vitally important that the squadron gets into its correct formation with the least possible delay.

The next stage, "STAND-BY", is very seldom used. The reason it is included in the "take off" itinerary is that sometimes one is not certain what the enemy is going to do and therefore it might be necessary to have a number of squadrons standing by in different parts of the country rather than have one squadron carrying out an extended stern chase. From "STAND-BY" to "TAKE OFF" is really the latter part of the "READINESS" to "TAKE OFF" drill, so needs no further enlarging.

QUICK LANDINGS.--It is very important that a squadron returning from a patrol or combat on reaching the aerodrome should be able to get out of the air on to the ground, taxi to the dispersal areas where the aircraft crews are waiting to refuel and to rearm, in the shortest possible time for these reasons:

1. Any number of aircraft seen circling a point on the ground by enemy aircraft would at once give the enemy aircraft an exact indication as to the whereabouts of the aerodrome. The enemy quite obviously must be kept in doubt as to which aerodrome the fighter aircraft are operating from; this can only be done in forward areas by cutting down this circling to the minimum.

2. The aircraft should remain non-operational for the shortest possible time, and quite obviously after combat or patrol duties a squadron returning without gas and perhaps without ammunition it is very definitely non-operational.

To get a squadron on to the ground and to the allotted positions for rearming and refueling in haste requires some definite drill for the approach, breaking up, landing and taxiing in. The most successful drill for carrying this into effect I have found is as follows:

When about three miles from the aerodrome, leader notices which direction the wind is blowing and knowing which side of the field his dispersal area is situated he plans to land so that he ends his run as near as possible to this dispersal area. With this aim in view he orders his squadron to echelon to a side so that on landing he does not have to taxi across the path of the remainder of his squadron coming into land. For instance, if during the final run into wind the dispersal area should lie on the right, the squadron would have ordered echelon to port; this allows aircraft to land in very quick succession and taxi straight to their dispersal areas without any delay or danger. So during this final three miles the leader makes a long sweep around the aerodrome gradually losing height with wheels and flaps down coming into land on the area he has selected as near to his dispersal point as possible. The squadron follows in quick succession. The taxiing to the dispersal area is done before the landing run is completed, pilots merely watching that the aircraft immediately ahead is clear; they do not worry at all about the aircraft following. At the dispersal areas the crews of the aircraft a e standing by with ammunition and gas all ready. Pilots taxi straight to their allotted positions and switch off the engines, the crews immediately getting to work. I cannot describe in detail the refueling and rearming operations as each type of aircraft has a different best way to be refueled and rearmed.

THE GUN SIGHT

BRITISH TYPE

TYPES.--One may say now that the old types of ring and bead, and aldis sights are obsolete. Anyway their construction is so simple as to need no special notes. The latest type of sight is the reflector sight. Instruction on this is amply covered in the manual dealing with the sight, but perhaps a few extra notes on the sight from the practical experience point of view might be appropriate. One of the snags about the sight is that it is lighted by an electric bulb and this bulb burns in a very small compartment in the sight and consequently is inclined to get very hot. I am not trying to say that the sight is in any way unreliable because of this point, but it is of the utmost importance that before taking off on patrol duties, the pilot does switch the bulb on to see that it does light. If it does not do so, it must be changed at once. Spare bulbs must always be carried and pilots should see that the spare bulb holder is carrying the two spare bulbs it should. The other snag is the very small base anchorage of the sight. I don't suppose the base anchorage is more than some 1 1/2 inches in diameter. You can see that the very smallest fraction of an inch movement on this small base would throw the sight some feet off the target at 200 yards, so it is of the greatest importance that the lining or harmonization of the sight with the guns is checked frequently. For some reason or other the sight makes a very attractive article at which to clutch in order to help one get out of the cockpit; all the mechanics invariably do this and one does find oneself reaching for the sight to help one out. Of course the sight must not be touched at all once it is correctly lined. Pilots should refrain from hanging their helmets or any other articles of clothing over the sights bearing in mind that the sight was not designed as a hook for such articles. After each flight the windshield of the aircraft should be wiped off; if this is not done it seems to hinder the effectiveness of the reflection.

OPERATION.--The reflector sight is absolutely fool proof and all that a pilot is concerned with in the air is the switching on of the bulb and the setting of the range bar. Personally, in combat I have never used the range bar as a range finder, but in practice I find it invaluable as a check of the range that I am opening fire at and I find with this practice in combat I am able to judge the range very accurately. However, I do recommend that a range be set on the sight and I think that range should be for a 60 foot target on 300 yards, this being the size of the average bomber target. I say 300 yards because one is inclined to watch the enemy until it fills the range gap and then open fire so that in actual fact one is always very much closer when the trigger is pressed than the range one has set on the sight. This means that one opens fire at the best possible range which is 250 yards.

I think also it advisable to leave the reflector sight light switched off when not in use. It has a very intensely bright bulb and if left on for any length of time will run the battery down if the generator is not functioning correctly. I have known generators to fail in the air and because the sight is left on the battery becomes quickly discharged and the sight useless.

HARMONIZATION.--There is no question that the careful and correct harmonization of the sight and guns is the most important of all the points in air fighting. It would be a pathetic state of affairs for a pilot to enter a combat and fight his hardest, firing his guns and yet achieve nothing because his guns are not pointing where his sight is aiming. The pilot himself should make it his personal responsibility to harmonize the sights and guns on his own aircraft; under no circumstances whatever should he delegate this responsibility to anyone else.

The procedure for the correct harmonization of sights is laid down in the appropriate manuals and should be strictly adhered to.

In this connection I should like to mention, not how to harmonize the guns, but at what ranges for the most effective fire one should set the harmonization point, that is the point at which the guns' bullets should meet. The greatest difficulty a fighter pilot has to contend with when firing wing-mounted guns is range, therefore anything which gives him more latitude in judging of range is bound to be helpful.

I have found it most effective to harmonize the two inboard guns to say 200 yards, the next pair at 225 yards, the next pair at 250, and so on according to the number of guns carried. If one draws a plan of the paths of the bullets from each gun, one will see that with a five foot target you have practically covered with a maximum density of bullets all ranges from 175 yards to, if using twelve guns, 325 yards.

NIGHT OPERATIONS.--I am not certain that I am qualified to voice any opinions on this subject, never having been successful at night. However, perhaps a few notes on the subject in general might at any rate be interesting.

Firstly, I am certain that fighter aircraft are most effective at night when used individually and not in formations. I cannot see any advantage of using more than one aircraft, but there are many disadvantages in so doing. The main disadvantage is that it is so easy to become detached from one another in the dark and this invariably ends in one fighter launching an attack on the other, or at any rate wasting valuable time in chasing each other. All the fighters should have definite zones to work in and should rigidly stick to them. The areas should be divided into zones for altitude as well.

I think recognition at night is still one of the most difficult and yet important tasks - great care should be taken to recognize what you are about to fire on - remember it is infinitely more desirable to let one enemy bomber escape than to shoot down one of your friends.

Fly with ALL lights off. This of course includes all interior lighting. This will facilitate search and also prevent the enemy seeing you first.

The new British device (which of course cannot be mentioned here) will bring you well into attacking range. However, do not open fire until you have placed yourself in a very favorable position to insure the enemy is destroyed in your first burst. Remember if you miss, in all probability that will be the last you will see of the enemy, who will not wait around and allow you another shot. So MAKE CERTAIN that FIRST burst is a good one.

Always place yourself in the best position with regard to the light available. Get the enemy silhouetted against some light patch - the moon or clouds; sometimes it is possible to pick them out against a moonlit sea. Fighter pilots have had great success in cruising over a large fire. The Germans invariably, once they have set something on fire, empty all their bombs into the fire. So if you remain over a fire you are certain to get a target. They show up well silhouetted against the flames.

On returning to the airfield waste no time circling--get down at once. Keep a careful watch behind the whole time. After landing get off the flare path at once, you may have been followed home by the enemy and if you remain in the flare path you might get hurt.

The lighting of flying fields is very much in the throes of redesigning. The Drem electrical system seems to be coming in, although I personally think that this is too much of a good thing for war time. Roughly, the system is as follows: All the lights are hooded so as to be invisible above 1,500 feet. There is an outer ring of lights about 3 miles from the perimeter of the airfield and then a funnel of lights leading you into the first touch down light. During the approach in your altitude is guided by lighted totem poles about 15 feet high, the procedure being that after permission to land is given, the lights are switched on and the pilot makes a circle of the outer ring until he comes to the lighted funnel and turns in, approaching into the funnel, checking his altitude on the totem poles touching down on first flare light. The whole system is then switched off immediately.

There are other systems, not so elaborate. Up to now we have used a flare path of ordinary hooded goose necked flares laid out in the form of a Tee. There are five flares one hundred yards apart and a sixth fifty yards, forming the long arm of the Tee (450 yards) and two flares 100 yards and at right angles to the last one in the long arm forming the cross of the Tee. A flood light is placed 75 yards to leaward of the first flare and is only used in an emergency. Beside the flood light is placed an important device called the "Angle of Glide Indicator". This only shows to a pilot coming into land if he is dead right in this angle of approach and shows a green light. If, however, he is too high an amber light appears, and if he is too low a red light appears. If he is too far to one side or other of the flare path the lights are invisible. Marking the extreme boundary of the safe landing point are two amber glim lamps of ordinary indirect flashlamp brilliance. Likewise marking the limits of the runway each end are placed two red glim lamps. No. 3 flare is a double one, so that if a pilot is not running along the ground as he passes this flare he must open up his engine and go around again. The whole lighting system is invisible from above 1500 feet. Sufficient crews must be standing by to douse all lights should an emergency arise.

Of course on moonlight nights no lighting is required other than perhaps two white glim lamps placed into wind some 600 yards apart on the best landing area.

Homing of returning fighter of course is highly secret and cannot be mentioned in these notes, but suffice to say that the procedure adopted is absolutely infallible and always 100% effective and brings one always back dead over the airfield.

There are many strategical methods of employing fighters at night, but as these are highly secret it is impossible for me to go into them in this manual. A night fighting pilot is usually specially selected and trained for the task.

It is hoped, however, that these few notes may be of use in a tactical sense.

ANTI-AIRCRAFT GUNNERY

I do not intend to go into any of the technical details of anti-aircraft gunnery, or even into the principles of the control or location of guns, in these notes, but rather into the question of the effect of this gunnery on you as pursuit pilots.

Firstly I might mention that I consider anti-aircraft gunnery entirely useless, unless used on the barrage principle. The direct firing of guns at aircraft at whatever altitude is, in my opinion, the question of good or bad luck as to whether a hit is obtained. Whether this will remain so in view of improvements of gun laying, etc., remains to be seen. Personally I think that anti-aircraft gun fire will always remain ineffective from pursuit pilot's point of view. During the last year of the war I believe that I flew many more than 100 hours over German territory and was continually under fire from the ground during the whole of that period and was always accompanied by at least 11 other fighter aircraft, yet I only lost one airplane during the whole of this time.

The most dangerous of all anti-aircraft fire is the quick firing light guns from 20 mm. to 37 mm. cal. Sometimes as many as eight 37 mm. guns are mounted as one gun, aimed and fired by one man. However I believe the effective ceiling of these guns is at the most, 10,000 feet. I also say that as they are rather on the heavy side for quick swinging around that they become ineffective at targets overhead at low altitude. I do not recommend flying under 10,000 feet over enemy territory unless it cannot be avoided. This is exaggerated if the base of the cloud is below 10,000 feet, as aircraft show up in bold relief and make such excellent aiming marks. So avoid flying over these types of gun under those conditions. Take the squadron over them in cover of the clouds or if this be impossible, owing to the mission you are on, fly at as high a speed as possible and as crooked a course as possible. If I couldn't cross the battery at above 10,000 feet I should, unless as I said before, the type of mission prevents it, fly at ground level. Below 3,000 feet small arms fire, such as 300 cal. machine guns and rifles, becomes reasonably effective - so do not wait around more than necessary and if possible, fly at ground level rather than at 3,000 feet, and as fast as possible.

From 11,000 feet to 15,000 feet is the most dangerous altitude for heavy anti-aircraft fire. However, changes in course or altitude will get you out of trouble. If it is imperative that you do not fly any straight and level course when flying between these altitudes, but I do say that the fire is ineffective if course and altitude are altered every 30 seconds or so. Above 15,000 feet one can afford to be reasonably slack. A shell takes quite a few seconds to reach this altitude so that a direct hit is most unlikely unless you have been kind enough to give them a real sitting target. Alter course continuously but one can afford to be much less violent.

The barrage system of firing does not really concern pursuit pilots because it is usually only encountered over important targets which it would never be a pursuit pilot's task to attack. However, on escort missions a pursuit pilot will get a wonderful view of this type of anti-aircraft firing in action, for as soon as the bombers near their objective this terrific gun fire will break out, but there is no need for a pursuit pilot to actually enter the zone. If enemy fighters are present, the gun fire will cease so if the bombers are attacked one will be quite immune to go into the zone, for whilst enemy fighters are in the vicinity, anti-aircraft fire ceases. In fact, the ceasing of gun fire often gives you an indication, if you have not already seen them, that enemy fighters are about. You will notice when on escort task that practically all the anti-aircraft gun fire is directed against the bombers and that almost invariably the fighters are left entirely alone.

So to sum up, one can say that

1. The most dangerous altitudes are from 1,000 feet to 10,000 feet because of quick firing light cannon. Counter this by speed and erratic flying, or preferably take cover in cloud or fly out of these altitudes.

2. Below 3,000 feet one encounters severe small arms fire, so make a difficult target by flying really low and fast.

3. About 10,000 feet and up to 15,000 feet one encounters accurate heavy anti-aircraft fire, counter by changes in course or altitude.

4. Above 15,000 feet one is reasonably safe if one changes course or altitude.

5. Sudden ceasing of anti-aircraft fire usually indicated a strong force of enemy fighters.

6. Fly at over 15,000 feet or at zero feet altitude unless mission prevents it.

On home defense it is essential that all pursuit pilots do know the abouts of the defended area so as not to embarrass anti-aircraft gunners in the defrnse of these areas. However, the control of the guns is so highly organized that this is an unimportant worry, as I consider that a pursuit pilot has more than one hundred percent chance of bringing down enemy aircraft than have the guns, and the guns come under the direct control of the same controller as the fighters so are always given the order to quit in good time. It is just as well to inform the controller by radio telephony of your intention of entering the gun zone to make doubly sure.

Finally I say that the only effective use of antiaircraft gunnery is when it is effectively controlled and laid and fires on the barrage principle. In order to deny the essential bit of air for accurate bombing to the enemy bomber. On a small target the bombers have to fly over certain small areas to release their bombs and this area should be alive with bursting shells, making it impossible for the enemy to enter. Direct firing at enemy aircraft is in my opinion almost a waste of time.

AIR COMBAT

The subject of air combat, that is the actual fighting in the air, I have avoided purposely so far because practically everyone who has to do the actual fighting differ in their opinion as to the best methods of combating in the air. Obviously there is an aim to be achieved and no one can differ on this point; the aim is the certain destruction of the enemy aircraft in as short a time as possible without getting yourself hurt in so doing. I propose now to detail my version of how I endeavored to achieve this aim. I have listened to many discussions on the subject and I do say a great majority of fighting men agree with me and so I place these opinions on record with the idea that even if you do not accept them, you will at any rate in condemning them, perhaps discuss the merits further with your friends, and in the discussion you may learn your version of the answer. I always look on myself as a good advertisement for my method as I am still alive to tell you about it.

One of the interesting points of this war is that there are no outstanding Aces. There are however many "Ace" Squadrons and Stations. The reason is that this war is a war, not of the individual, but of teams. The Squadron being the team. The Squadrons that work well together are always successful in achieving the aim I have outlined above. Their casualties are practically non-existent, and their victories are innumerable. If a Squadron does not work as a Squadron, the results are disastrous. After quoting as above, it seems a little strange to go straight into a discussion on individual combat (this however is what this preamble is working up to) especially if I follow to say individual combats are a thing of the past. You must understand that even if you do meet an enemy on your own, you must always expect him to have his whole Squadron "just around the corner", and you must go into your combat with this in mind.

By the term individual combat, I really mean a combat by a Squadron which has broken formation and is "mixing it", and even when this occurs you are still a team and are all fighting together and must always remain in the same piece of sky, so you can always support each other and not allow yourself to be drawn away, where you are bound to be dealt with severely. If you do so, you are letting your Squadron down. The foremost thing to remember as a pursuit pilot is that your one and only task is really the destruction of ENEMY BOMBERS. Your fights against Pursuit Aircraft are really only to allow you to achieve this aim of the destruction of the bombers. Combats against pursuit should in the normal circumstances be avoided if in so doing you are allowing a free passage to enemy bombers to reach your target areas. It may be so that your Squadron be given the task of dispersing and by liquidating the enemy fighter escort of the bombers, in this case, of course the combats would be fighter against fighter. You must keep in your mind your assigned task so that if you are detailed to attack the bombers, even though they be escorted, you must attack them and if possible not become involved in a fight with the escort. If you are detailed to deal with the escort, remember that you must get at them as soon as you can because it might be that another Squadron has been detailed to attack the bombers which would be hazardous if the escort had not been dispersed. To disperse the escort is the easiest thing in the world to do, and it might be just as well if you remember when your task is escorting bombers, just how easily you drew the fighter escort from the enemy bombers and not allow yourself to be drawn away from your charges. Any sort of attack or the mere fact that you appear in the sky in the vicinity of the bombers is usually enough to get the whole lot of enemy fighters after you at once. Of course this has achieved your task, although to make a good job of it, it would be as well to be able to deal effectively with as many fighters as possible to teach them a lesson as to what to expect in the future.

This is what I mean by individual combat and it usually means that the whole Squadron becomes involved and there are no spare aircraft to act as guards. Another cause of this type of circumstances would be a surprise attack by enemy fighters while you are carrying out an offensive sweep over their country. The question of bomber escort is dealt with in my booklet so I do not propose to go into any details on that score except to again impress on the student that if he is escorting bombers, he must stay with the bombers and not be drawn away. Merely attack and disperse any immediate menace but never follow them away. So individual combat should not develop under those circumstances.

It has taken me a rather lengthy preamble to come to the point, but, I do feel a detailed explanation is required to define individual combat as I see it and the circumstances generally leading up to it. Otherwise, beginners are inclined to get the wrong impression of modern war and have dreams of making "Aces" of themselves after the style of Ball, McCudden and Bishop. These illusions are dangerous, not only from your point of view, but from the safety of your Squadron as well. So to individual combat.

Altitude and speed are the only important points in combat. Of course altitude can always be converted into speed merely by depressing the nose of your aircraft. I am convinced it is suicidal to place any importance on maneuverability. Maneuverability is only a form of defense which is not required if you have sufficient speed to get you out of the trouble. You do not require any kind of exceptional maneuverability to attack and if you have not got the speed, the enemy can always avoid combat without relying on his powers of maneuverability to do so.

Realize that circumstances for every combat are different and it is impossible to lay down any hard and fast rule what one is to do and what one is not to do in certain predicaments. It is not my intention to do so. For instance, if you have an enemy pursuit ship on your tail, you don't need any advice from me as to how to get rid of him (just one big kicking scrambling turn will take care of that and the enemy would be stupid, in my opinion, to attempt to stay behind you). However, if he were to start climbing the moment you started your "ham fisted" maneuvers, he can then open the attack whenever it pleases him, as you will be in a very much worse position when you have finished. The initiative is his and by the law of averages he must always win on these tactics. At any rate, one thing is certain, and that is, you will not. You cannot win a dog fight on maneuverability, because it is not a form of attack but merely a method of giving a momentarily respite which will only last while the maneuver is being carried out. It must eventually stop, and if you have lost a lot of altitude in your "ham fisted" flying, you will be in a very dangerous predicament. So the essence of successful dog fighting is not to sit on a man's tail indefinitely whatever the tactics or maneuvers he carries out, but to come in behind him, open fire with your sights on and just stay long enough to get a really good burst in, or until his "ham fisted" maneuverability makes firing impracticable, then break away and climb at your best climbing angle watching him and positioning yourself the whole while and as soon as he stops, renew your attack. Of course, you must take special care to see that someone else is not trying the same tactics on you. That is one of the main good points of these tactics, you always have sufficient time for thinking and careful watching. If you are attacked and some one settles on your tail, a hard steep turn with messes of rudder will always get you out of trouble. However, don't go on any longer than it is sufficient to make him break off his attack. Fight with your eyes wide open, making sure your every movement improves your tactical position. Always remain in the same piece of sky as your Squadron. Keep together. Matters are considerably simplified if you have sufficient fighters to allow about half to remain above you to keep guard; you can then allow yourself a little more latitude for "ham fisted" maneuvering and you may be more successful in "sitting" on some enemy fighter's tail until he is destroyed. Frankly, I am against even this. My method I have found really successful, which to put it simply is that if at any time your enemy does his "ham fisted" maneuvering you take advantage of it by gaining altitude, at the same time maintaining a good position aloft. When you dive to attack, you do not close your throttle, but use your extra speed to take you aloft again. Come in behind your foe, open fire at 300 yards, to any minimum range you wish, then break away zooming up so that you always maintain your tactical advantage of altitude. Fly hard, fast, and with determination. Of course, if the enemy is flying two place fighters or anything that is armed aft, you must not zoom directly up, but break away downwards until you are out of range with your engine at full power using every scrap of gained speed to carry you aloft again. If he is armed astern you do not get any closer than 150 yards.

The Squadron Commander must take great care in positioning his Squadron before he attacks the bombers. The sun, clouds and every possible aid must be used to achieve advantage in positioning and surprise.

All opening attacks should be synchronized. I shall describe in detail how I think these attacks should be carried out. In my opinion you need only three types of attacks. All these attacks can be launched from any direction. That is, from ahead, from either beam, or from astern, and if you wish (but not recommended) from above or underneath.

It is essential to leave a certain amount of initiative to the members of your Squadron because if you lay down, and practice, attacks in any rigid sequence, when the actual thing comes along, some detail is bound to be different, and if, as I said, you have laid down the law too much the attack will become chaotic.

I will go into details as to the merits of launching the attacks from the various angles later.

When the Squadron Commander has decided that the best thing is to attack with one aircraft at a time he orders a number one attack. This, of course, is a very seldom used attack as even when attacking a solitary enemy aircraft, it is still better to attack with two or three others in order to lessen the effectiveness of the fire coming from the rear of the enemy. Anyway, the point is, if the Squadron Commander decides that an attack by one aircraft in succession is the best tactics, he orders a number one attack. The direction in which it is launched does not matter. What does matter is that only one aircraft attacks at a time in succession. If a leader finds himself confronted by a formation of enemy bombers flying in a flat V, that is in almost line abreast formation and he has not sufficient fighters to engage them simultaneously. This attack can prove most useful. It is launched from the beam on the flank enemy bombers, care being taken to hide yourself from the defensive fire of the other bombers by keeping the target you have selected between you and his friends. This will mean that you only have the defensive fire of one enemy to contend with.

If the Squadron Commander decides that the attack should be carried out by two aircraft simultaneously, in succession he orders a number two attack. The circumstances leading up to this attack would be if the enemy only presented two targets by flying in sharp V formation so that it would be impossible to get at any of the other of the aircraft except the two tails of the V. This, therefore only allows two attackers at a time to get a shot. This attack may be carried out against single aircraft. Again the attack may be launched from any direction.

Lastly the No.3 Attack. The Squadron Commander decides that three or more aircraft can attack successfully at the same time. This may be against one bomber or any number. If it is against one bomber, of course, it would be impracticable to attack with more than three. However, the aim of the attack is that as many aircraft as possible attack at once. The number attacking is limited by the C.O. over the radio. There are serious snags against this attack on one bomber, the main one being that the sections have to split if you intended that attacks be delivered from both flanks.

You may however all attack from the same flank, No.1 doing a beam attack, No.2 doing a quarter attack, and No.3 doing an astern attack. No.3 is really the man that counts; it is he that is in the position to do the real accurate shooting. Nos.1 and 2 are merely there to distract the enemy's rear gun fire. These attacks have been very successful in England, but in my own mind I am not certain that if you attempt it with inexperienced pilots you are losing more than you gain by the distraction from accurate aiming due to one's attention being almost wholly occupied in avoiding collision. If you are using the four ship element, No.4 can act as a guard, getting a shot in if he possibly can. When more than three attack at the same time, the Squadron is echeloned to one side of each other so that they are flying almost in abreast formation. The leader picks out the flank enemy his side of the echelon, and goes into the attack, his No.2 taking the next target, No.3 the next and so on.

An important point is this - do not attempt to watch more than one of your friends; forget the rest of the Squadron. I mean No.2 should only watch and position himself on No.1, and No.3 should only watch and position himself on No.2 and so on. Do not attempt to watch the whole Squadron. The attacks should arrive in range as near together as possible, open fire together, and break away downwards and to the side of the leader in very quick succession; in fact as nearly together as possible. A good way to launch this attack from ahead of the bombers intending to pass some 600 yards to the flank and turn in behind and from a flank, in this the leader echelons the Squadron so that he has the longest path to make good, that is from the outside of his Squadron to the outside of the bombers; this will ensure that he has no stragglers, as all his Squadron has a shorter distance to travel than he. Of course, should the attack be launched from a flank in this manner the turn should be done in almost line astern formation, the Squadron coming into a flat echelon as the turn completes and the run on the target commences.

The Squadron Commander always informs his Squadron over the radio which ships are to attack with him by saying, "One section, number three attacks go" or "Flight number three attack go" or "Squadron: number three attack go". The ones not detailed, remain as guards. These attacks are simple and allow tremendous variations and altitude and I have found them very successful. Remember too, it is advisable to take only half your strength into the attack leaving the other half to look after you so that you can give your undivided attention on the attack and aiming instead of having to always keep such a sharp look around for surprise attacks.

In defense, I recommend the defensive circle. A great deal of practice should be given in forming this circle from the search formation in as short a time as possible. Half seconds count.

If the enemy are encountered in this circle, a section (that is a pair, or three aircraft), may be dispatched; the Squadron stands by. They enter inside of the enemy circle and turn in the opposite direction firing at each enemy as they appear in range. This invariably breaks up any enemy defensive circle then the Squadron pitches into the debris. This is possible owing to the better maneuvering qualities of American and British pursuit ships.

Not too much altitude should be lost on the breakaways because the attacks might be in need of repetition, or they may be escorted and you might place yourself badly with them. On the other hand, if a complete get-a-way is intended, you can continue to ground level. If you have ammunition left, I do not favor this.

My ideas have been to try and outline the general principles of these three attacks, and I do realize that there are so many "ifs" and "whens" that one could never discuss them in the bounds of these few notes.

I do not favor an attack in V formation because of the difficulties of breaking away.

Whatever attacks you may conceive after reading these notes, I earnestly repeat, must be simple and most easy to execute, otherwise complete chaos will result. Always unrehearsed incidents take place, so a great deal of latitude must be invested in each member of the Squadron to act as he thinks best.

SUMMARY

So to sum up the important points a pilot should remember in combat, they are:

1. That you are not an individual ace but rather a member of a team working and fighting in the organized and synchronized attacking of enemy formations. Always work and fight together.

2. That your primary aim is the destruction of enemy bombers and combat with enemy pursuit aircraft should normally be avoided unless circumstances are very much in your favor and there are definitely no enemy bombers to engaged or the enemy pursuits are actually preventing your achieving your primary aim, which is the destruction of the enemy bombers.

3. Whenever possible gain altitude. This can always be converted into speed and always allows you the initiative.

4. Maneuverability is only a form of defense and should only be reverted to when the enemy is definitely flying a faster ship than you are. If you are flying a faster ship, do not resort to maneuverability in defense. Get in, shoot, and get out.

5. When surprised, under any circumstances, always turn TOWARDS your foe. NEVER turn away. Even when surprised, still try and be the attacker. Aggressiveness is an important point.

6. Once you commence a turn to one side or the other with an enemy on your tail, you must continue to turn as steeply as you are able and not, under any circumstances whatsoever, slacken this turn or reverse it. Keep an eye on your foe and only continue this defense maneuver so long as he is actually on your tail, he will then be unable to aim sufficiently far ahead of you to hit you. Easing off the turn or better still reversing it, is exactly what he would wish you to do as this would allow him immediately to be able to lead you sufficiently to blast you out of the sky.

7. When diving to attack an enemy, whether in formation or individually, do not dive at a slight decline all the way towards him, but dive steeply to his level then flatten out, using your excessive speed gained in the dive to make a swift approach from dead astern.

8. When it becomes imperative to break off combat with enemy pursuit, do not dive away in a straight dive but dive in as crooked a course as possible. Downward rolls are ideal but make them straight down.

WHAT THE EXPERTS SAY
ADVICE ON TACTICS AND AIR FIGHTING

I am sure that Wing Commander Malan and other of our successful fighter pilots will forgive me if I enclosed in this manual his very sound advice on the subject so I have taken the liberty of enclosing some very sound notes written by them on this subject.

A FEW IMPORTANT DON'TS

DON'T dive away from a Hun in a straight dive.

DON'T alter your direction of turn in a dogfight--each time you do, you are a sitting target and your opponent can catch up on you. If you're being chased and you can't turn and face your enemy--for example, if you are limping home with a damaged engine--try kicking on rudder and doing "ham" flat turns. That puts his aim out.

DON'T do stall turns and copy-book aerobatics as evasive action. When your speed drops you are a sitter. Remember, skid and slip are good evasive tactics--but of course they ruin your own shooting, so use them properly and at the right time.

DON'T lose a little height--always try to gain height in a dogfight; unless it is "time to go home" and then lose all the height you've got and beat it.

DON'T forget to LOOK.

DON'T neglect your shooting--regular and correct practices with cine camera or with P.P. gear may easily mean--

(a) "This pilot already has x confirmed victories and y probables--"

(b) You get the swine who thought he could get you.

DON'T let him get away--the only decent Hun is a (confirmed) dead Hun.

DON'T LOSE YOUR HEAD.

NOTES ON TACTICS AND AIR FIGHTING

By Wing Commander A. G. Malan, D.S.O., D.F.C.

Generally speaking, tactics in air fighting are largely a matter of quick action and ordinary common-sense flying. The easiest way to sum it up in a few words is to state that, apart from keeping your eyes wide open and remaining fully alive and awake it is very largely governed by the compatibilities of your own aircraft in comparison with that flown by your opponent. For example, in the case of the Spitfire versus the ME. 109F, the former has superior maneuverability, whereas the latter has a faster rate of climb. The result is that the Spitfire can afford to "mix it" when attacking, whereas the ME. 109F, although it tends to retain the initiative because it can remain on top, cannot afford to press the attack home for long if the Spitfire goes into a turn. Obviously there are a lot of factors involved which must govern your action in combat--such as the height at which you are flying, the type of operation on which you are engaged, the size of your formation, etc.

There are however, certain golden rules which should always be observed. Some are quite obvious whereas others require amplification. Here they are:

(1) Wait till you see the "whites of his eyes" before opening fire. Fire bursts of about one to two seconds and only when your sights are definitely "on".

(2) Whilst shooting think of nothing else. Brace the whole body with feet firmly on the rudder pedals having both hands on the stick. Concentrate on your ring sight (note Rule 3).

(3) Always keep a sharp look-out even when maneuvering for and executing an attack and in particular immediately after breakaway. Many pilots are shot down during these three phases as a result of becoming too absorbed in their attack. Don't watch your "Flamer" go down except out of the corner of your eye.

(4) If you have the advantage of height you automatically have the initiative.

(5) Always turn and face an attack. If attacked from a superior height wait until your opponent is well committed to his dive and within about 1,500 yards of you. Then turn suddenly toward him.

(6) Make your decisions promptly. It is better to act quickly even if your tactics may not be the best.

(7) Never fly straight and level for more than 30 seconds at any time whilst in the combat area.

(8) When diving to attack always leave a proportion of your formation above to act as top guard.

(9) INITIATIVE: AGGRESSION: AIR DISCIPLINE: TEAM WORK, are words that mean something in air fighting.

(10) Get in quickly--punch hard--get out!

FORMATION FLYING.--When adopting a type of formation certain points must be borne in mind. The main point is whether you are on defensive operations, or on the offensive over enemy territory. For defensive work, formations should be maneuverable and compact. When flying on an offensive operation the formation should be stepped up and back from the given patrol height and should be divided into attacking and defensive units.

Fighter formations must maintain extreme maneuverability, while guarding the dreaded "blind spot" behind. You'll soon find that if you try to find the answer to the blind spot by simply spreading your machines over a broad front, you'll have lost the first essential, i.e. maneuverability. If you choose line astern, which is very maneuverable, you'll be blind behind.

At a very early stage of the war I discovered that the only satisfactory answer was to fly in line astern and have the leader change the course of the whole formation at regular intervals.

SQUADRON TACTICS.--At this point it would be a good thing to take you on three main types of operation.

First we'll put you into a squadron at "readiness" on a station in SE England, with bomber raids coming over. If fighters are expected it is always advisable to climb for your height outside the combat area. Your raids are reported at 20,000 ft., therefore enemy fighters may be stepped up to at least 25,000 ft. If you have no other squadrons supporting you, you should aim to intercept, if possible, from the sun--from about 23,000 ft., unless you have time to get higher. You intercept and, if there are not fighters present, you must first destroy the bombers' main method of defence, i.e., formation flying. A good maneuver would be to attack with a section of four, with the object of breaking up the formation--obviously the most effective method of achieving this is to attack from ahead. But this is generally difficult. The section should go in singly from different angles and attempt to fly through the bomber formation--with plenty of speed, and firing at the same time. With any luck the bombers should break, particularly if one or two of the leading machines get badly hit. The next thing is for the remaining eight machines to work in pairs and attack--two to one bomber. We found that formation attacks did not work in practice, for many reasons which I will not discuss here. Deflection shooting on the whole is a difficult operation, and the most effective form of attack is a diving attack approaching originally from the flank and developing into a curve which brings the attacker, with about 100 miles per hour overtaking speed, 2,000 yards behind and below. At this stage throttle back and, at about 800 yards, come up to the level position and give a short burst to put the rear defense off as you are closing in; at about 250 yards open fire, first at the fuselage and then concentrate on each engine in turn. This was found very effective with eight machine guns--the result with cannon should be quite devastating.

Should the bomber formation have fighter escort, about one-third of your formation should be detailed to engage the attention of the fighters without actually going into combat, whilst the remainder go in in two waves, with the same object as before. In the case of the squadron one section of four would maintain height and fly on the flank in such manner as to menace any enemy fighters who attempt to engage the attackers.

1. Operating from same Station during raids by bomb-carrying fighters at 23,000 ft. with escort.

If the Hun approaches from the Dover area it is best to climb well towards the flank in a southerly direction, in three sections of four in line astern on a narrow front, and climbing on a zig-zag course, keeping in a look-out, until a height of 27,000 or 28,000 ft. has been reached. Having attained your height out of harm's way, the course from now on is shaped according to the raid information. If there is any possibility of intercepting before the enemy reaches his objective every attempt should be made to meet him from the sun and with superior height of 2,000 to 4,000 ft. If, on the other hand, it is not possible to meet him on the way in it is best to curl round and attempt to meet him head-on on his way out. It is well to remember that the enemy must come home sometime and usually he has not sufficient petrol to play around. Therefore it is best to to get between him and his home with superior height because, if he dives away, as is usually the case, you can start your half-roll and dive in sufficient time to prevent the fight developing into a long, stern chase. The basic rule applies here as elsewhere, i.e., one section of four will remain up and guard against surprise attacks on the attacking eight.

(NOTE.--Had it been possible to gain height in time to await the enemy on his inward journey a good method would be to patrol about two miles up sun from his predicted course in line astern and with the sun on either one beam or the other. A useful hint when patrolling in the rarefied atmosphere at height, and when attempting to search in the direction of the sun, is to raise a wing tip until it covers the sun. It will be found that the area both sides of the wing will be quite free from glare.)

2. An offensive sweep over enemy territory.

When deciding upon a formation for offensive work the aim should be to spread the units loosely, and stepped up and back, or up and to the flanks, having the major proportion on the lower level, and smaller and looser units acting as a top guard. Owing to the clean lines and high speed of the modern fighter an engagement usually develops from an empty sky in a matter of seconds. If the enemy sights and decides to engage, the tendency will be for him to spot your lower and more obvious formations, and miss seeing your light top screen in the heat of the moment.

In most cases the patrol height is decided upon before departure. One of the important points in patrolling the other side is conservation of fuel, so climb and cruise at an economical speed with weak mixture. If the patrol height decided upon were 27,000 ft., I would climb the formation to about 31,000, and with the units stepped behind and down until crossing the lines. From then on I would proceed on a very gentle dive to 27,000 ft. and leave my rear units above and stepped up as arranged, when the lower units would be primarily for attack, whereas the upper screen would always remain up, and act purely as a defensive screen.

Rigid air discipline is essential, and idle chatter on the R/T should be almost a courtsmartial offense. It is impossible to lay down rigid rules. The two main rules, however, are that each unit must know the role it has to play--and that a whole unit should never go down to attack--always leave a top guard. If you dive, pull up again after your attack. Don't give away height.

CHARACTERISTICS OF THE HUN.--In his training the Hun fighter pilot appears to pay a great deal of attention to tactics. This is a good fault but, unfortunately for Hitler, the German fighter seems to lack initiative and "guts". His fighting is very stereotyped, and he is easily bluffed. Another factor is that his fighter aircraft in this war has been less maneuverable than ours. There are certain things which it is well to remember when fighting him.

His tactics, as I have stated before, although basically sound, are generally executed without a great deal of imagination, and he repeats the same old tricks with monotonous regularity. There was a saying in the last war: "Beware the Hun in the sun". In this war it seems to be truer than ever for three reasons:

(a) The Hun seldom attacks from any direction but from the sun.

(b) The modern machine, with its clean lines and good camouflage, is more difficult than ever to spot against the sun.

(c) With the fast speed achieved by the modern fighter little warning will be given before he gets within range and, furthermore, it is a well-known fact that the man who knocks you down in aerial combat is usually the one you did not see.

For some reason or other the Hun prefers to resort to what he considers a clever trick to catch the unwary, rather than make full use of his initial advantage and go in with a solid punch. For instance, a common trick is to detach a pair of decoys, who will dive past and in front of a British formation, hoping that someone will be fool enough to follow them, when the rest will immediately do a surprise attack from above. I am sorry to admit that some British pilots have been caught by this oft-repeated ruse. I deplore this as a tactical maneuver. The obvious, and most effective, action in this case would be for the Hun to make full use of his initial advantage in height and surprise by immediately attacking the formation below him.

NOTES

By Wing Commander A. G. Malan, D. S. O., D. F. C.

DON'T LOOK NOW!

........But I think you're being followed.

How many times have we been asked the same question--"Please sir, what do I do to get a 109 off my tail?" As if we knew. The answer really is: "Why did you let it get there, anyway?"

ATTACK.--The essence of Dogfighting is always to be the attacker--if you find yourself at the receiving end, well, we hardly like to say so, but you weren't really looking hard enough, were you? Or if you and a Hun have met suddenly, your reactions were a bit slow, perhaps. Anyhow, you're up the creek.

Well, we'll try and paddle you out of it. But remember--it's quite hard to turn defense into attack--so don't start on the defensive. First, when you are practicing dogfighting don't continue going round and round in ever decreasing circles. That's O.K. for a while--at least, if you turn hard enough. But you are unlikely to be able to get on the Hun's tail that way, so think up something more clever.

DODGE.--For example, a 109 dives on you--he's got superior speed, so you can't hope to fly away from him. Try foxing him then by closing the throttle and tightening up the turn. He's going too fast to out-turn you, so he over-shoots. Give him a moment to get by you, then--stick forward a bit, get behind him and shoot him down. That trick has worked many times.

FACE THE MUSIC.--Next, if you are about to be attacked, always turn and face your attacker once he is committed to his attack, even if you haven't any ammunition left. Look aggressive--that'll immediately cut down his self-confidence by half. As he comes up, turn in behind him. Whether you have any rounds left or not, it'll make him worried. If you have, why, go in and shoot him down. If not (say you're coming back from a sweep), choose a moment when you're pointing the right way, go straight down in a bit of a spiral, pull out, and streak for home. It'll take him probably ten seconds to realize you're no longer on his tail--then he has to turn and spot you--by which time you're well on your way. If he comes at you again, try the same trick, or pull another out of the hat...

FEINT (DON'T FAINT).--Such as doing a head-on attack and going down in a vertical spiral directly you pass him. He's fairly sure to lose you. That doesn't mean you don't have to weave though! Keep weaving till you are home--and remember, a good look out in time is worth any amount of evasive action.

CLOSE RANGE

Notes by a Polish Pilot

Firing at close range is the only way to be sure of getting your man. This has been proved by pilots of all nations in every war since flying started.

If you want confirmation, just read this:--Captain Albert Ball, V.C., D.S.O., M.C., By R.H. Kiernan.

Time and again this book states that Ball closed into extremely close range, so close in fact that even taking into account the slow aircraft of those days it leaves one gasping. On page 94 there is a paragraph: " . . . . .Ball would then fasten on below the nearest machine, so close that other enemy aeroplanes could not shoot him off without risk of hitting their own man."

(Page 96.) "Ball was too close to miss, after five or ten shots the German toll . . . ."

(Page 104.) "Ball followed, firing another drum at twenty yards range . . . . the German crashed."

(Page 105.) "Ball closed to fifteen yards range beneath the nearest machine . . . ."

(Page 113.) "Ball had found that you must carry the flight as closely and relentlessly as possible to the enemy machines to be sure of success . . . ."

Flying Fury. James B. McCudden, V.C., D.S.O., M.C., M.M.

(Page 170.) "I closed to thirty yards on the second Hun . . . .Caught up with the Hun at the top of his zoom, opened fire, and continued doing so until I nearly crashed into his tail . . ."

Richthofan also used to stress the necessity of holding fire until extremely close range.

In this war we have Fighter Command Combat Films, Intelligence Bulletins, and the experience of pilots who have been fighting throughout the war, and one and all bear out the necessity for close-range firing, The The Air Fighting Committee Paper (A.F.C. III) states:

"The primary factors in the destruction of bombers are aim and range. It has been proved by night fighters recently that the eight-gun Hurricane, with a four-second burst, is quite capable of destroying any of the armoured German bombers, and this is probably due to the fact that the night fighter closes to a range of 100 yards or less. During daylight, it is more difficult to hold aim and to obtain close range, because of the evasive tactics adopted by the enemy. Nevertheless, the importance of closing to short range before opening fire cannot be too strongly stressed."

All the above illustrates that conclusion of different kinds of experience gained in air fighting in different times is the same: Generally speaking a short range, when shooting, is a factor of primary importance. It gives you incomparably greater chances of success than a relatively long range. Research workers who work on air firing calculations and tests say:

(a) Probability of hitting generally can be assumed as inversely proportional to the square of the range.

(That means that, for example, if you are shooting from 150 yards you will probably hit the enemy aircraft with about nine times greater number of bullets than when firing the same number of rounds from 450 yards. Remember, of course, to aim a bit high at a short range, if your guns are in the wings.

(b) The velocity of a bullet drops when range increases. Therefore, there is more certainty of piercing armour plating when the range is short.

(c) A certain Squadron during special trials was partic larly asked to open fire at 300 yards, and break off at 100 yards. Believe it or not, the result (proved by camera) showed that the pilots had opened fire at distances from 800 yards to 1,200 yards.

That should have convinced you that short-range firing is the only way to get a good score sheet. Now, how to be sure you get close enough.

Firing at close range is not simply a thing that can just be done; no matter how courageous the pilot, nor how determined, he will not as a rule be able to execute close-range firing without studying it carefully and practising. The main trouble in judging distances in the air is the lack of other objects, in particular, the ground, with which to compare the objective. Speed of approach makes judgement difficult, and a subconscious fear of collision keeps telling a pilot that he is much closer than he is. General excitement is also inclined to make a pilot open fire too soon, unless he is close range conscious. At altitude the air is generally much clearer, and although the objective does not look bigger, details of it are more apparent. All this, however, can be overcome if some trouble is taken.

Here are some pointers:

COMPARISON OF THE SPAN OF AN AIRCRAFT WITH DIAMETER OF YOUR GUNSIGHT.--Try to retain general mental impressions of the attached diagram. Look through it and try to remember some easy points, as for example: If a single-engined fighter just fills the ring, the distance is of the order of 100 yards. If the same happens with a large twin-engined bomber, the distance is of the order of 250 yards. If those aircraft only half fill the ring the distances are about 200 yards and 500 yards respectively. Even quite a small bomber must appear about twice the size of the ring if you are really 100 yards from it. Try that in flight when you have an opportunity. If you know beforehand which type of aircraft is concerned in your training attacks, use the figures for that type from the diagram.

FREQUENT STUDYING OF AIRCRAFT AT KNOWN DISTANCES is essential. A good way to do this would be to put up a post at a definite distance, say 100 yards, from one aircraft dispersal point, 300 yards from another, and say 500 yards from another. By this method it would be possible to obtain a rough idea of ranges, especially if different aircraft were occasionally put in the dispersal points chosen. When doing this, an idea of detail should be established: For example, a wireless mast may be just visible at a certain distance, but not visible at any greater distance; while some colours may lose definition at certain distances. There are plenty of other such details to be found. It must be remembered, however, that generally altitude lends clearness to details.

THE CAMERA GUN is a great help in judging distances and should be more commonly used than it is. Most pilots will receive quite a shock when they realize just how far away they actually were from their target. (See Squadron results mentioned above.) Camera results are accurate and should be relied upon; they teach a lot. A general indication to know if you have really fired at close range is whether you were really impressed at the surprising closeness and size of your target. If you were not, you were probably too far off.

In conclusion, it may be said that any pilot, with practice and thought, can learn to fire at close range, and fear of collision soon goes when it has been done once or twice. The first time is the worst--but it must be close.

QUICK JUDGMENT OF RANGE BY MENTAL IMPRESSIONS OF THE WAYS IN WHICH VARIOUS TYPES APPEAR IN YOUR GUNSIGHT AT DIFFERENT DISTANCES

1. When the Aeroplanes just fill the Ring of the Gunsight they are at the following distances (to the nearest 10 yards).

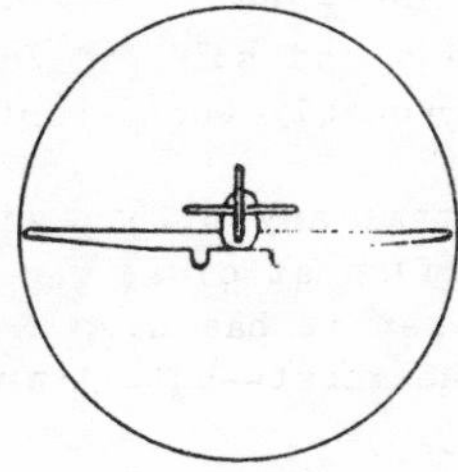

SPITFIRE
110 Yards

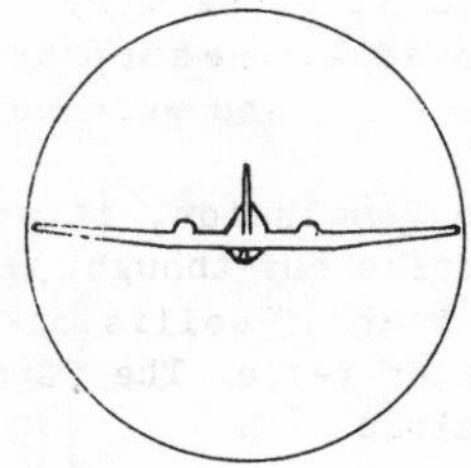

WELLINGTON
250 Yards

Corresponding Distances for other types are given below (to the nearest 10 yards).

SMALL AIRCRAFT Distances below 150 yds. (e.g.One-Engine Fighters)		MEDIUM AIRCRAFT Distances between 150 & 200 yds.	
He. 113		Me. 110	150 yds.
Me. 109	90 yds.	Battle	160 yds.
Spitfire	110 yds.	Ju. 88	160,170, or 190 yds.
Hurricane	120 yds.	Anson	160 yds.
Ju. 87	130 yds.	Blenheim	160 yds.
		Beaufort	170 yds.
		Hudson	190 yds.

LARGE AIRCRAFT Distances between 200 & 250 yds.		VERY LARGE AIRCRAFT Distances over 300 yds.	
Hampden	200 yds.	Condor	310 yds.
He. III Mk V	210 yds.	Sunderland	330 yds.
Whitley IV	240 yds.	Ju. 90	330 yds.
Wellington	250 yds.		

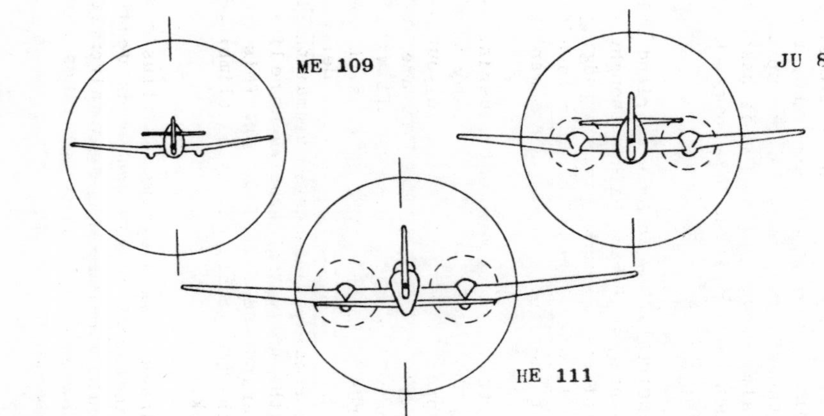

2. Your best chance of success is to Fire at Close Range. From 100 yards you get the following views in your sight

THE TIZZY ANGLE

An Interview with 'Zura' (F/O Zurakowski)

When discussing air fighting or even air firing we are always told to close to point blank range, but many pilots lament that they have been involved in a long, stern chase and have had the utmost difficulty in getting into range because when they first saw the enemy they thought they would close up quickly. The fact is that almost every pilot in his haste to get into close touch turns towards his enemy, the moment he sees him (Fig. 1).

ZURA'S PRINCIPLE.--Now we have a friend called Zura, and Zura is a practical man. He has thought this matter out and now offers a simple tip for judging correctly the distance to steer ahead in order to effect an interception at the earliest possible moment.

Zura says that if you are not steering at a point sufficiently far in front of the enemy then his aircraft will appear to move forwards in your windscreen. (Fig. 2.) If, on the other hand, you are steering too far in front of him then the aircraft will appear to move backwards (Fig. 3), and he goes on to say that only if you have allowed the correct deflection will the aircraft remain stationary, thus maintaining a constant angle (the Tizzy Angle) between the line of flight of your aircraft and his (Fig. 4). This rule is not altered by the fact that you may be climbing or diving to the attack.

We have drawn some diagrams to illustrate Zura's principle, and here are his own words describing the action he would take on sighting an aircraft to starboard, which curiously enough he wishes to intercept in the minimum time:

"Fly towards him in what you believe to be the correct direction. Fly steadily for a moment--hold your head stationary and note in which direction he appears to travel along your windscreen. If he appears to move forward steer further ahead and hold that course. Check again and continue to steer further ahead until he appears stationary.

If he appears to move backward in your windscreen then turn more towards him and repeat this process until he appears stationary. You will then be flying on the shortest route to intercept him. Check from time to time as you fly along this line for he may increase or decrease his speed".

Some of you may wonder if this tip is worth worrying about. The answer is given in Fig. 5 of our diagrams. It will be seen that the distance between the two aircraft is more than halved by keeping the angle of approach constant.

P.S.--You may say "Won't the aircraft get bigger in the windscreen as you get nearer, making it difficult to tell which way it is going?"

Zura says "this is the time to avoid a collision."

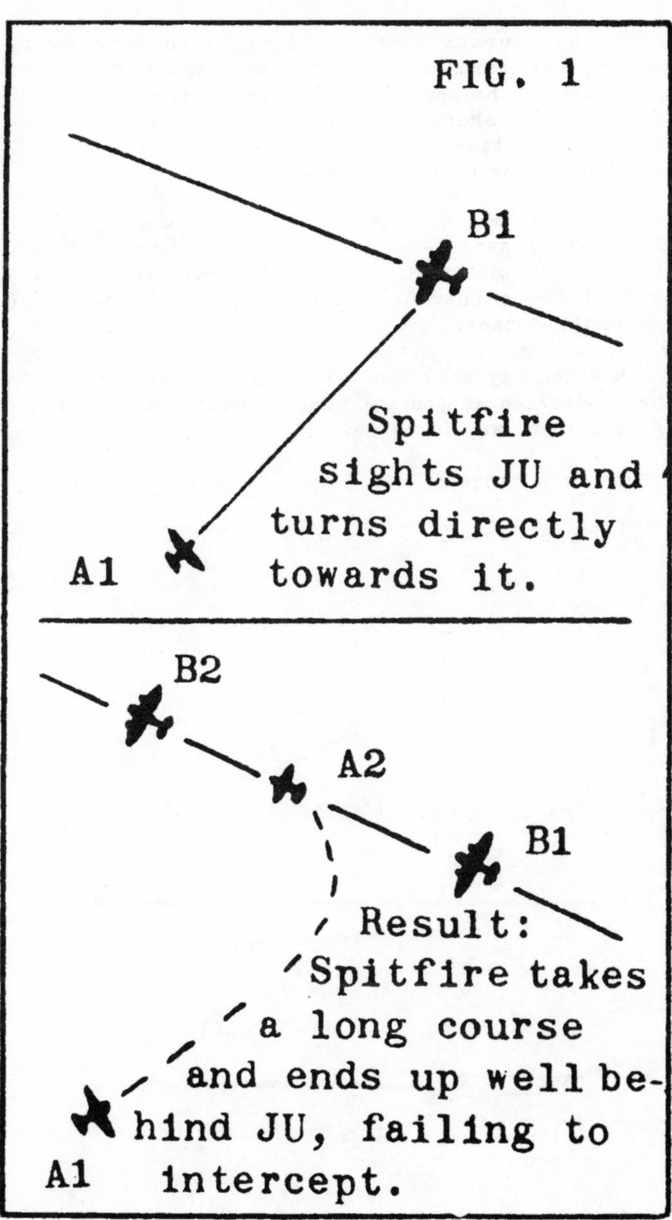
FIG. 1
B1
Spitfire sights JU and turns directly towards it.
A1
B2
A2
B1
Result: Spitfire takes a long course and ends up well behind JU, failing to intercept.
A1

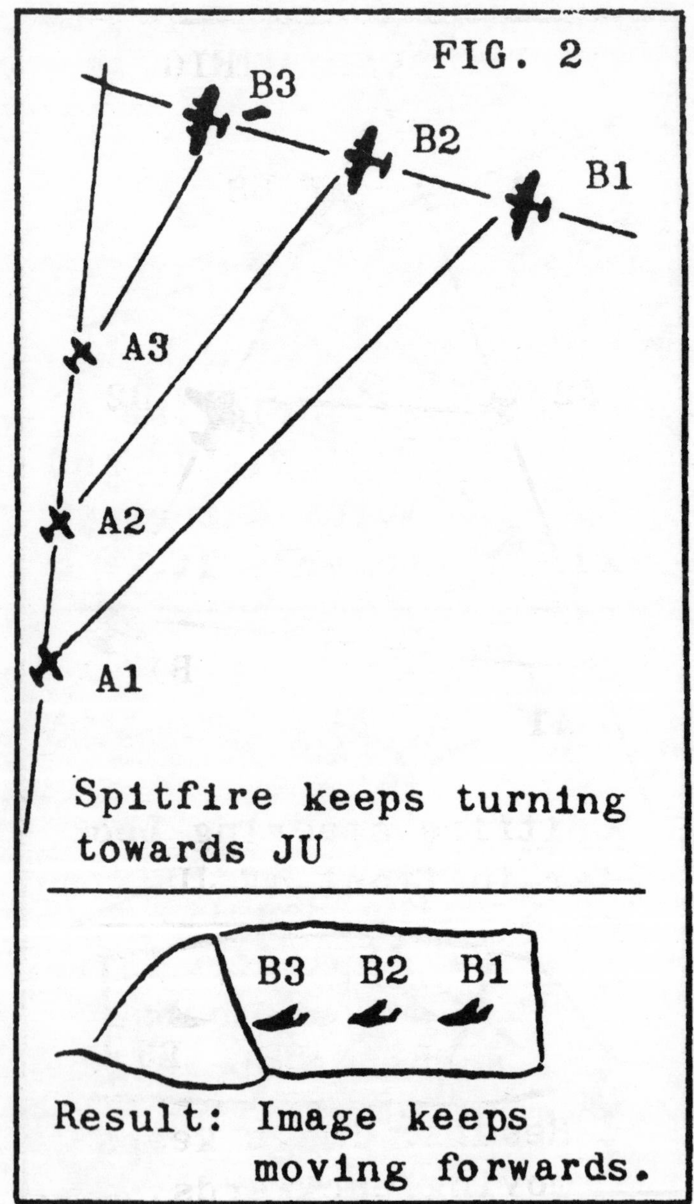
FIG. 2
B3
B2
B1
A3
A2
A1
Spitfire keeps turning towards JU
B3 B2 B1
Result: Image keeps moving forwards.

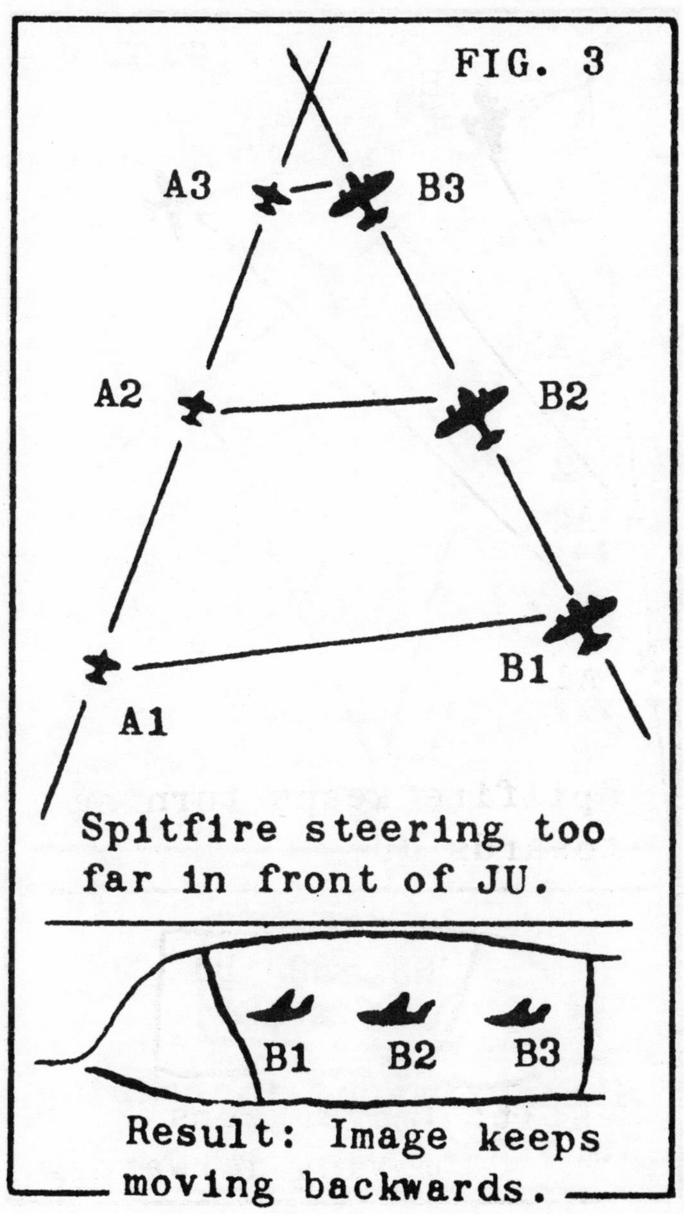
FIG. 3
A3
B3
A2
B2
B1
A1
Spitfire steering too far in front of JU.
B1
B2
B3
Result: Image keeps moving backwards.

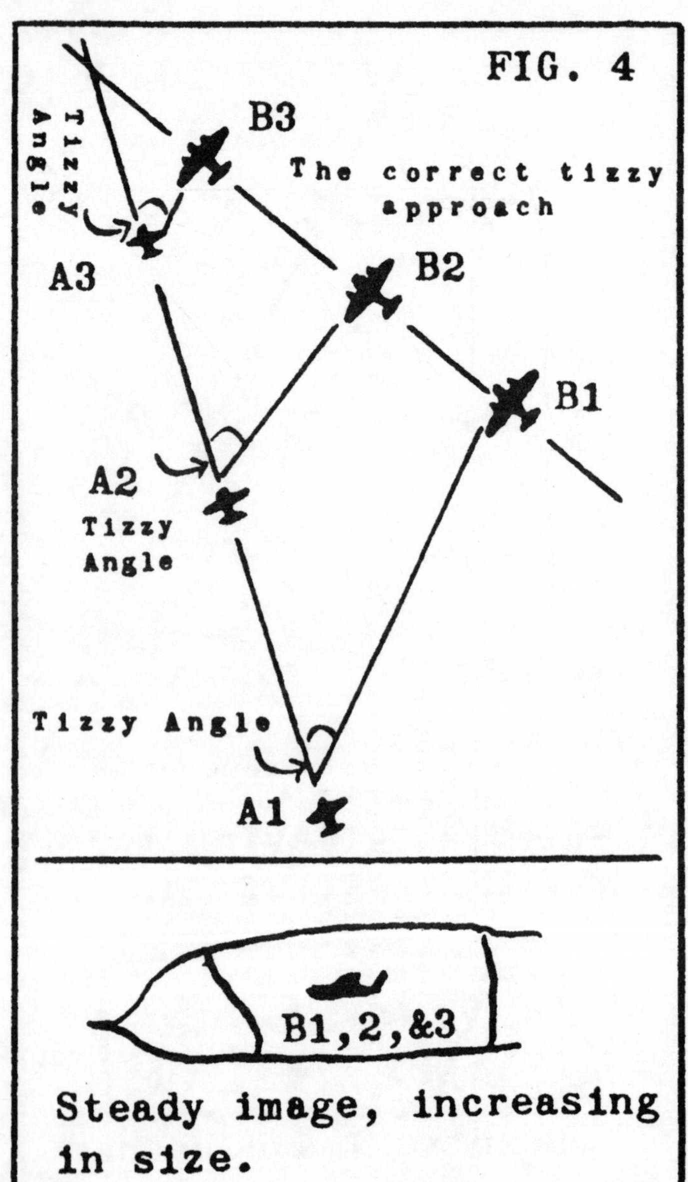

Steady image, increasing in size.

FIGURE 5.

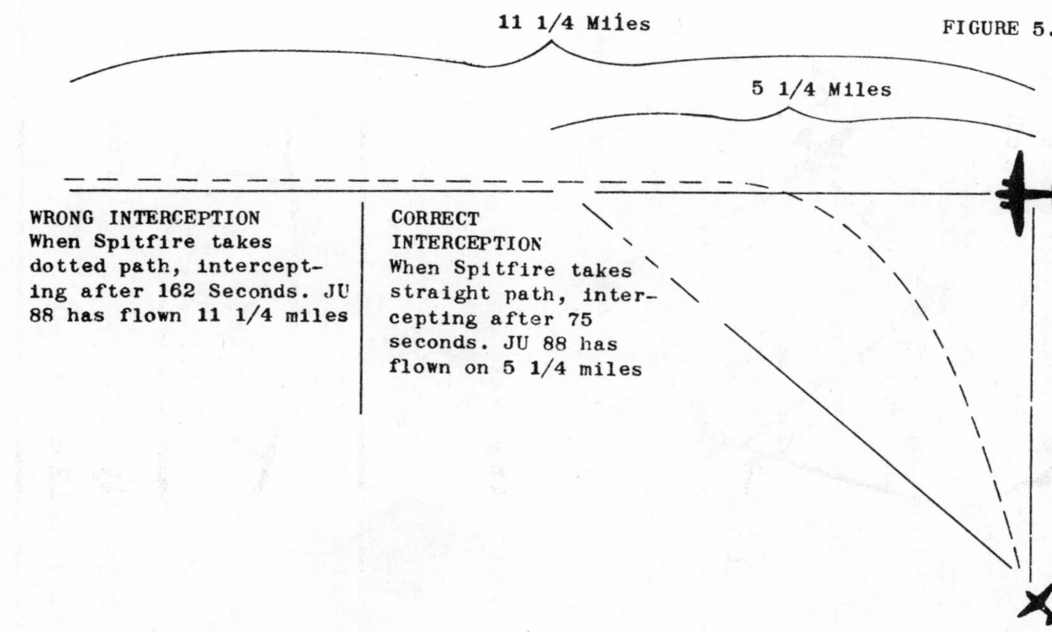
11 1/4 Miles
5 1/4 Miles
WRONG INTERCEPTION
When Spitfire takes dotted path, intercepting after 162 Seconds. JU 88 has flown 11 1/4 miles
CORRECT INTERCEPTION
When Spitfire takes straight path, intercepting after 75 seconds. JU 88 has flown on 5 1/4 miles

LECTURE OF DEVELOPMENT OF THE AIR DEFENSE OF GREAT BRITAIN AND ALSO ON AIR FIGHTING

I am going to try to describe to you tonight, very, very simply, indeed, the air defense of Great Britain. In order to do this, I go back to 1936 when this defense was practically non-existent. In 1936 we had approximately twelve squadrons of fighters defending Great Britain. These fighters were grouped around the southeast side of London, London being considered the only military target in Great Britain. The reason for this is the fact that 11,000,000 people live in greater London and in order to feed 11,000,000 people three times a day, it is necessary to have a very specialized docking system in order to get the food off the ships into the mouths of the people three times a day before it goes bad. A docking system of this nature was considered to be very vulnerable to their attacks and any sort determined bombing it was thought would disorganize the entire system. The people would then get hungry and the war would be lost. These fighters then grouped around the southeast side of London were concerned only in the defense of the Capitol. However, these few fighter squadrons were the nucleus of the tremendous defense scheme of the present day.

The quipment of these squadrons were Bristol Bulldog Aircraft. Their speed was approximately 125 m.p.h. (it is interesting to note that the slowest Italian bomber at this time did over 200 m.p.h.). The Bulldogs were armed with two vickers machine guns each. These guns were most unreliable and when they did fire, fired approximately 600 bullets a minute. When one took off in a Bulldog to carry out air firing practice, one took with one a large tool kit consisting of hammers and spanners with which to beat the guns when they stopped in the hopes that one could make them fire again. Actually, when the guns were not in use we removed them as the aircraft flew rather better without them. Fighting a war at this time certainly never entered our heads. The ground organization and control of the fighters from the ground was practically non-existent. I am not sure what the procedure would have been; I should imagine that some form of standing patrols would have been the order of the day.

In 1937 (I am speaking entirely as a person who was serving as a comparatively junior officer in the R.A.F. and was not really aware of what the powers that be had in mind) I was acting as squadron commandor of a squadron on the south coast. I was suddenly informed that one of the flights in the squadron should in the future be called No. 73 Squadron. That made things rather confusing for us as the personnel and aircraft remained the same. This was done to all the other fighter squadrons. Then some politician got up in parliament and said, "I double the air force". This state of affairs, I am glad to say, didn't last very long. Through this year and the next, we made these squadrons up to strength in personnel and aircraft. New squadrons were also formed and a new defense scheme whereby the fighters were controlled from the ground was started. I shall describe this scheme presently. In 1938 when Chamberlin went to Munich, the poor fellow didn't have much to argue with and had to accept peace at any price. The country was in a very bad state with regard to all her armaments. There were tremendous shortages in A.A. guns and such like. I had actually heard tell at the time that our main aircraft factory at Bristol was protected by four obsolete A.A. guns which had no breeches. The situation was serious everywhere. Munich gave us a shock, and it started to dawn on us the possibility of war, so we decided that something very, very drastic had to be done at once to try to put this situation right. All our factories worked in double shifts and in a year a wonderful change came about. All the squadrons were re-equipped with Hurricanes and Spitfires and dozens of new squadrons had been formed.

You can imagine now that this huge defense material needed very careful organizing to insure its best effect. The fighters were now grouped around the entire British Isles in considerable force. This, of course, meant that the command of the fighters had become too large to be handled by one headquarters, so the British Isles were divided into fighter groups, each group commanded by an Air Vice Marshal. These groups were divided into sectors commanded by group captains and in the sectors were the fighter stations and squadrons situated. Now we know the exact position, the exact number, the exact height of every enemy aircraft over or near our coast.

This information is plotted by means of small discs on operations room maps of which the headquarters fighter command, the group headquarters, the sector, commanders and the station commanders all have. All these plots appear simulteneously on all the maps throughout the country so thateverybody concerned with the control of the fighters knows the position of the enemy aircraft. As each enemy raid appears on these plotting tables the Commander-in-Chief of the fighters decides whichgroup those raiders are going to enter. He then details that group to take care of that raid. giving the raid a serial number. The Air Vice Marshal then decides which sector in this group the raid is going to enter, and details that sector commander to take care of the raid. The sector commander then orders the squadrons into the air. These squadrons come under the sector commander's direct control and are in touch with him the whole time they are in the air by R/T*. You see that as we know the exact position of the enemy raid, all we have to do is to tell the fighters where to go. We could tell them to proceed to a certain locality at a certain height, but in certain weather conditions it would be impossible for the fighter squadron commander to know when he was over the locality ordered because the ground would possibly be obscured. So we have to have a system which will work whatever the weather conditions. We accomplish this by fitting in every fighter aircraft a little device called a pip-squeak set. This set sends out a signal automatically, and this signal is picked up by Direction Finding Stations who report the exact positions of the fighters. These positions are plotted on the operations room maps throughout the country in the same way as the enemy raider plots, so that the sector commanders know the exact position of both friendly fighters and enemy bombers All he has to do is to order the fighters to steer certain courses which will bring them into contact with the enemy. The whole system is childishly simple, and is 100 percent effective, because there is nothing that can go wrong. One can see the importance we place on efficient R/T communication and I can tell you that we have developed a radio set which takes care of this important point. Of course, when the enemy is sighted by the fighters, it is up to the squadron commander to deal with them in the way he thinks fit. He takes over the control

*R/T Radio Telegraph

and orders what attack he thinks best to suit the circumstances existing.

I should now like to just mention what sort of aircraft we are employing. It is impossible for me to go into any detail as details are secret. Suffice to say that anything that will not do over 400 m.p.h. and be able to climb to 40,000 feet is no good. I am glad to say that we have very large numbers of such aircraft. Our latest new fighter, that is not counting the latest marks of Spitfires and Hurricanes, is the Tornado and this really is a tremendous airplane. It is very heavily armed and I can tell you altogether, it is a very lethal weapon. The armament of these fighters are cannons and machine guns. Last year, of course, we only had eight Browning machine guns in each airplane. This is an interesting point to Americans because the Browning gun is an American gun; I am sure you will be proud of the fact that in my squadron alone during about five months of active warfare, we fired some 3,000,000 rounds of ammunition and you could count the number of stoppages these guns had during this time on the fingers of one hand. It really is a remarkably reliable gun. Some of you might question the effectiveness of machine gun fire against heavily armored enemy aircraft. If you do question this, I should like to tell you an incident which convinced me how effective this concentration of machine gun fire is. You must remember each gun fires 1,200 bullets a minute which makes a total of 9,600 bullets a minute coming from one airplane. This particular incident took place in France last year when we were endeavoring to back up our army which was fighting over there. I came across one German soldier and took a careful aim and pressed the trigger--I was amazed to see the man disintegrate. There is no question that the bullets just drilled him; they literally blew him apart. And so when firing against aircraft, however heavily armored, this concentration is sufficient to blow off some quite important parts to the embarrassment of the German pilots concerned. It is quite obvious that if one were to blow the tail unit off an airplane, it doesn't really matter how heavily armored he is. The cannon has tremendous power and there is no doubt as to its value in air fighting. A cannon shell can penetrate practically any thickness of armor, but of course has a slow rate of fire, and one has to be more careful in one's aim.

We picked up a German M.E. 109 fighter which had been shot by a cannon shell. This shell had penetrated through the rudder, sternpost, through various members of the fuselage, the wireless set, two thicknesses of armor plate, both sides of the gas tank, the back of the pilot's seat, through the pilot's chest removing various ribs and passed out through the dashboard and out the front of the airplane. This was a most effective demonstration of the power of penetration of the cannon shell.

The Americans, I think, are of the opinion that the English are rather slow, but I should like to say that in most of the important points, we have led the Germans. For instance, all British aircraft were heavily armored before the outbreak of war. The value of this has been demonstrated to us a thousand times in the saving of pilot's lives. No German aircraft at the outbreak of war were armored, and it was an easy thing to destroy them with a very small burst of fire. After the fall of France the Germans decided that they would have to armor heavily their aircraft for that reason. All our fighters were so armored fore and aft including the fitting of bullet proof windshields. The German fighters were not so armored until a year later. The German bomber had no protective armament except one machine gun which we ignored as the rear gunner stood in the slipstream of the propellers and couldn't really aim carefully. Compare this with our heavily armored bombers with carefully protected power operated turrets.

I should like todiscuss next in very simple language some of the difficulties a fighter pilot has in air firing. I should like to do this because most of you think that all one has to do is to point at the German and press the trigger and down goes the German, but it is not like this. In order to hit a German aircraft traveling at 240 m.p.h. at a range of 400 yards, one has to aim 180 feet ahead of that aircraft in order to hit it. Mind you, 240 m.p.h. is a very slow speed for modern fighting as I have said before. Modern fighters now go at more than 400 m.p.h. so these distances are considerably increased. In other words, one has to anticipate the position your target will be in a fraction of a second later. This is the point you must aim at because the bullets take a certain length of time to travel 400 yards. Unfortunately, it is not even as easy as this because by application of rudder and holding off bank, one can make an airplane go along like a crab--that is, it doesn't travel in the direction that it is pointing. The difficulty is, of course, to tell what direction it is actually traveling in order to be able to aim the required amount ahead. Another difficult problem is that the fighter pilot is inclined to to bring his sights to bear by pulling the nose of his aircraft around by use of the rudder only; this, although actually bringing his sights to bear, causes the fighter to skid sideways thereby imparting a sideways velocity to the bullets which is enough to take them quite clear of what he is aiming at.

Now the next important thing in air fighting is the identification of the enemy aircraft. It is obviously no good if you are going up to fight the enemy if you cannot at once recognize an aircraft to be friend or foe. I should like to tell you two incidences in which this mistaken identity proved an important point. The first concerns a sergeant pilot in my squadron who one day became detached during an offensive patrol over enemy territory. These offense patrols last. year were very hazardous, indeed, and unless a squadron stuck rigidly together it was liable to get into very serious trouble from attack by overwhelming numbers of enemy fighters. So to become detached was an unforgivable sin. This pilot became detached during a maneuver we were carrying out after some member of the squadron had shouted the alarm on the radio. After this maneuver we straightered up and continued our patrol and it was then that I noticed that I only had eleven airplanes instead of twelve. I thought the poor chap had been picked off during this maneuver. We returned to England and were refueling when this sergeant pilot arrived back. Of course, I was livid with him for breaking formation and demanded an explanation, informing him that if it were not a good explanation, I should have him courts martialed. His explanation was that after straightening up from the maneuver in question, he had continued on at the back end of the squadron until he became seriously worried regarding the amount of gas he had left. He then looked ahead at the aircraft that he had been following some twenty yards astern of and noticed that it had bracing struts from the tailplane to the fuselage. He said he then opened his cockpit hood and looked behind at his own tail unit; to his horror he saw that he had no struts. He then moved out slightly to one side and saw black crosses painted all over this airplane he had been following. He said he he thought the German squadron commander would be just I was patrolling the beaches and had notification that didn't know what to do as he was following a squadron of twelve M.E. 109's. He eventually got fed up with following and took a careful aim at the last M.E. 109 and pressed the trigger. This M.E. blew up so he rolled on to his back and dived to ground level. As he was beating this hasty retreat, he looked back and saw that the enemy squadron were continuing their patrol. The other incident occurred when we were defending Dunkirk. I was patrolling the beaches and had notification that some British bombers would be returning through my area and would I keep a friendly eye on them. After a while seven Bristol Blenhiems appeared out of the smoke of Dunkirk. To my horror, I noticed they were closely followed by seven twin-engine German fighters, M.E. 110's. So I detailed seven of my fighters to accompany me and we went in behind the M.E.'s. I was about to open fire on the leading M.E. when the rear gunner started to wave at me. I immediately thought that the M.E.'s were in fact British Hampdens bombers which are quite similar in appearance having the double rudders which the M.E. has. I ordered my squadron to break away at once without firing and we were in the process of reforming when the M.E. decided that we were enemy. A terrific fight ensued in which we only were able to shoot down three of them--this was a disappointment to us as we should have got the lot. Now you see what had happened. The M.E.'s had obviously got orders to escort seven of their Junkers 88 which were to bomb the shipping off the coast and had by accident formed up on our Bristol Blenheims (which are not dissimilar in appearance) and were actually escorting their enemy. When we arrived they must have mistaken us for M.E. 109's which had probably been detailed to escort them. So there were the Blenheims being escorted by M.E.'s who were being escorted by Hurricanes, so you can see that these mistakes in identity do happen and are a very serious point.

I should like now to discuss the German and the British fighter pilots. If an English fighter pilot comes across half a dozen M.E. fighters and runs away, he is considered by Englishmen to, perhaps, have a cowardly streak in him. The German fighter that runs away from any English fighter is considered by the Germans to be a shrewd person, and not a coward in any sense of the word. One time I can remember having to escort thirty-three Blenheim bombers on a raid to France to try and disperse tank concentrations. Before we reached the coast, I noticed smoke pouring from one of his engines and I expected him to immediately turn for home. However, he appeared to ignore it and after a little while the engine stopped solid. Although he couldn't maintain height, he still continued on his course. It then became difficult for me owing to the fact that he was getting so far behind, to effectively look after both him and the other Blenheims. I decided that he was too good a man to lose and that I should look after him myself and told my No. 2 to carry on the close escort of the other thirty-two Blenheims. This man was unable to maintain altitude and passed over the gun positions on the enemy coast at a very dangerous altitude and at times was almost invisible from the bursts of the A.A. shells; but still he continued. He reached the first concentration of tanks, shut off his good engine, dived down and dropped two perfect bombs which blew a tank well into the air. He then went to the next target and did the same thing again. I knew that he only carried four such bombs and expected him to make for home now. But he didn't. He went down to ground level flying like a huge crab on one engine whilst his rear gunner machine gunned German infantry which were moving up in support of their tanks. He appeared in no hurry to start for home and it was not until he had completely finished all his ammunition that he eventually started across the seventy miles of water back to England. Now the important part of this story lies here. On arriving home I got in contact with this pilot's squadron commander intending to have him commended on his very brave action. I was almost disappointed when talking to the C. O. to find that he thought nothing of the incident at all; he thought the pilot had done his job and that was merely what was expected of him. I found that act a tremendous inspiration and I certainly never have seen a German pilot do anything but make for home on the very slightest pretext of engine failure. Another incident occurred when my squadron was ordered up to dispose of some 250 enemy fighters over a south coast port. We had been in a lot of action around about that time and were reduced to eight airplanes. We had a ninth, but unfortunately because of damage by enemy bullets, I didn't consider it safe to fly. So I proceeded to this port with the eight serviceable airplanes. We arrived at the port at about eight thousand feet and we could see the Germans, masses of them, from about thirteen thousand feet right out of sight. We started to climb to engage them which appeared to me to be almost a forlorn task. However, after climbing for a while, I saw that we were not gaining on the Germans--they were climbing too. I cannot understand why they did this. At this moment, two M.E. 109's with yellow noses broke formation and started to come down. I thought that this was the beginning of the lot, but I was glad to see that only two came. I then noticed that those two M.E. 109's were not coming down on me at all but to a point about three miles astern of us. Looking carefully, I saw that they were diving on the ninth Hurricane that I had forbidden to come. I shouted a warning over the radio which he purposely ignored. The leading M.E. went in behind him and opened fire. This he appeared to ignore, merely dodging very slightly from one side to the other. He kept the M.E. this way engrossed and I was able to settle in behind the M.E. and shoot it down. My No. 2 got the other M.E. which was a beautiful flamer and exploded after burning for a short while. I thought that would start the fight as I anticipated the Germans would be very cross to see two of their number dealt with in this fashion, but on looking back I saw that they were all returning home. They had obviously been recalled by their home base, but I cannot imagine any English squadron allowing eight enemy aircraft to get away with such cold-blooded murder. The other point in that story is the typical spirit which prompted this English pilot to take a bullet-riddled airplane into combat knowing that he was to fight 250 of the enemy when he had a perfectly good excuse to stay on the ground. I am sure you will admit that this spirit is unbeatable--especially as these incidences I have related are every day occurrences. Compare this to the way I saw some German fighters, flying M.E. 109's, amusing themselves. These pilots were diving on milk cows and firing at them with their cannon. One cow I saw had a hind hoof blown off and was rushing around making the most awful noises in agony. The German pilots didn't fire any more, but merely dived on the cow to make it run on its three legs. I must say I cannot see any point in this brutality at all. Another incident I had the misfortune of witnessing occured in France when a number of women and children were walking along the roads from a town with all their belongings on some old carts, etc. A German pilot in a Henchle 126 (a slow airplane used for army cooperation purposes) descended to within about twenty feet of them and opened fire on them with his rear gun. He went up and down the road a number of times until not a living thing appeared to remain. I saw a little child sitting on a woman's chest trying to bring the woman back to life. After awhile this little child discovered the bullet holes which had completely pierced the woman's bosom, and he was sitting there sticking its little fingers into the bullet holes. I am sure that these things should not be.

Now everybody the world over knows that the Germans are the most wonderful organizers. They work out the most complicated schemes to the minutest details, yet often one small, but very important, detail is overlooked, consequently spoiling all their carefully laid scheme. There are many instances of this, but two come to my memory now. The first one concerns the placing of hospital buoys which are moored some ten miles off their coast. These buoys were placed in these positions all around the coast with the object that aircraft which was severely damaged and would obviously not be able to reach the shore would be able to land in the water beside one of these buoys and the crew could swim to the buoy where they would find everything with which to make themselves comfortable. The buoys were visited by a patrol boat sometime during the night to pick off any visitors. They have the most luxurious equipment, four comfortable beds, a special heater for drying clothes, another for heating water, first-aid outfits, brandy, whiskey, beer, and some choice wines, cigars, cigarettes, pipe tobacco and pipes are all provided. Yet, perhaps the most important item, seeing that to get any heat from their heating aparatus or to light any of these cigars, cigarettes and pipe tobacco would be the provision of matches or some such thing with which to light them. The importance of matches is accentuated when one bears in mind that to reach the buoys from the aircraft one has to swim through some distance of sea water. The second instance is rather of a different nature, but I think serves to illustrate how this cleverness on the part of the

Germans is a fallacy. When Germany was building her immense aircraft manufacturing organization, their experts traveled around the country selecting suitable sites to build the factories. Camouflage was the order of the day. Sites in one instance were selected in fir tree forests, and special railways were constructed for transportation purposes and the factory buildings were built to a special design so that they exactly reached the top of the trees and were suitably screened and were literally invisible from the air. Should, however, enemy air forces manage to locate one of those factories, which would have been an almost impossible task, the buildings were so situated in the forest that one bomb could not possibly damage more than one building, the factory being divided into the smallest working parts. On the face of it, one would despair of attempting any successful air action against such a layout. Yet if one remembers last autumn when these fir trees oozed their most inflammable resin the Royal Air Forces flew over these forests, dropping tons and tons of incendiary material and getting the forests well and truly on fire. The factories were burned with the forest. If one considers it in this light one realizes that perhaps the worst place in the world to construct a factory would be in such a highly inflammable position. Everyone knows that the most complete destroyer of material of any description is fire.

Other instances of Germany's so called cleverness comes most apparent in their propaganda broadcasting service. I don't suppose the person who talks on the radio from Germany almost hourly is so well known to you Americans as he is to us in England. We call this person Lord Haw Haw. He takes his task incredibly seriously and pours out the news in the most serious tone. He is English and the subjects he talks about are very cleverly thought out. To the uninformed they would be liable to make a very grave impression, making this propaganda service a very serious potential weapon. So you would think that the Germans would take a certain amount of trouble, not necessarily to speak the truth, but to tell clever lies, ones that would not readily be found out. However, they have completely spoiled any value this service could have by failing in this very point. For instance, Lord Haw Haw one night regretted in a most regretful tone of voice that he had to announce that H. M. S. KESTREL had been sunk. He even went into a fairly lengthy description of the sinking, presumably to lend his information more weight. It was a pity that H. M. S. KESTREL is in fact the Royal Air Force post at Worthy Down near Winchester, more than a hundred miles from the nearest sea. So you might say that through these trifling, though important, mistakes Germany has nullified any military value their radio propaganda service might have had. Of course it was obvious that in the instance I have described, Lord Haw Haw had gleaned the information regarding H. M. S. KESTREL from the Admiralty list published before the war, the navy calling all their shore bases a ship.

One doesn't have to look very far to discover other blunders that the Germans have made. For the first nine months of war the average Englishman hardly knew there was a war on. I suppose an Englishman with his placid nature might be termed lazy, seeming just to do enough work to keep things going. Perhaps even, there were some signs of discontent, people were getting bored with their neighbors' company, there being little else to talk about except a war which wasn't even being fought. From the English point of view something very drastic was required to be done to bind these neighbors together and to bring home to the English the seriousness of the war. The Germans have done both these most successfully for us. They have bound the nation together by their ruthless bombings of our oldest towns as it has never been bound together before. Everyone is now working their hardest with only one object in view and that is revenge. The Germans don't seem to understand that when one has a dear relative killed or maimed for life, one doesn't throw in the sponge and give in, but does everything in his power to get even. This would be obvious psychology to anyone except the Germans. Another blunder in my opinion and I think a serious blunder, was the attempted bombing of Buckingham palace, the home of our King in London, by a Nazi airplane in broad daylight. This attempted bombing did not make the nation cringe and cower as it was supposed to have done, but had the exactly opposite effect. It brought home to us English all the love and affection that an Englishman has for his King and Queen, in that here was a man whom all were extremely fond of, who is an idol to us all, in serious danger sharing with us all the perils of the war. It showed at once that our King had no more special protection or was any more exempt from the perils of war than the ordinary man on the street. This little incident did our country a world of good.

7

BAG THE HUN!

Another booklet for trainee fighter pilots, this example, published in 1943, once again relies upon diagrams and amusing cartoons to get the point across.

CHAPTER I

ESTIMATION OF RANGE

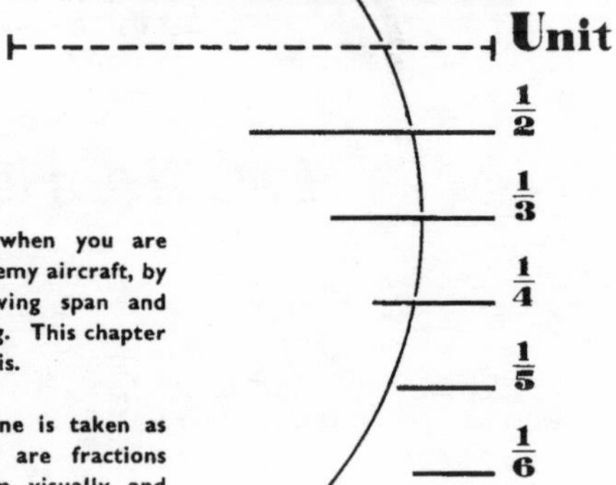

Unit

$\frac{1}{2}$

$\frac{1}{3}$

$\frac{1}{4}$

$\frac{1}{5}$

$\frac{1}{6}$

Range can be estimated, when you are almost dead astern of the enemy aircraft, by comparison between the wing span and the diameter of the sight ring. This chapter will show you how to do this.

On this page the dotted line is taken as a unit. The other lines are fractions of this unit. Check them visually and remember them — they are the basis of range estimation.

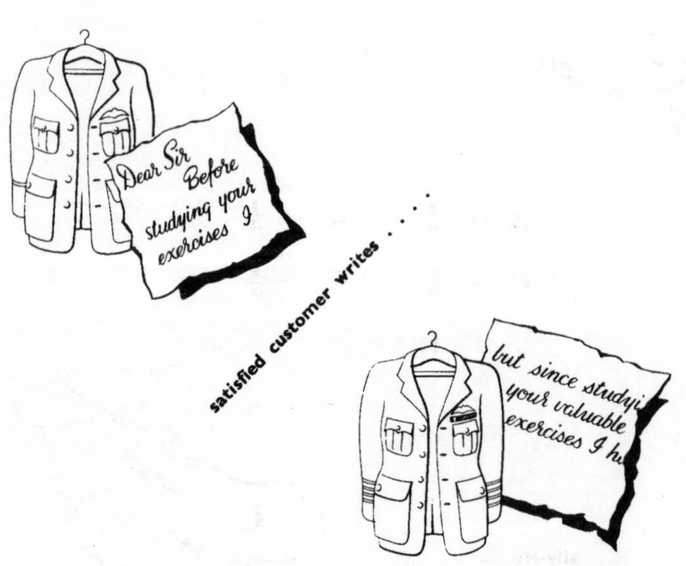

The dotted line is the unit. What fraction of this unit are the lines marked A, B, C, D, and E?

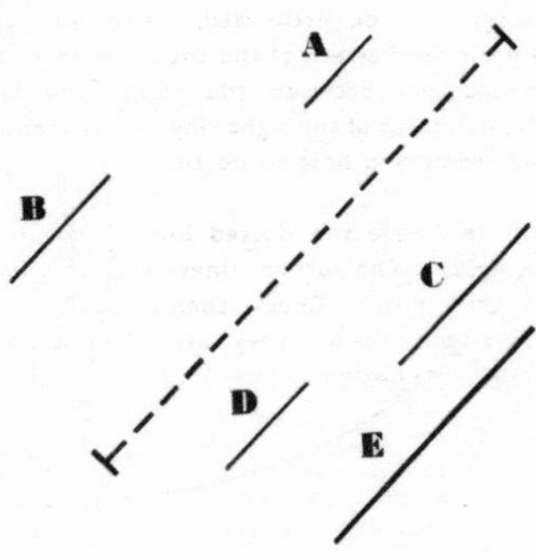

Solution

$A = \frac{1}{6}$ $B = \frac{1}{4}$

$C = \frac{1}{3}$ $D = \frac{1}{5}$

$E = \frac{1}{2}$

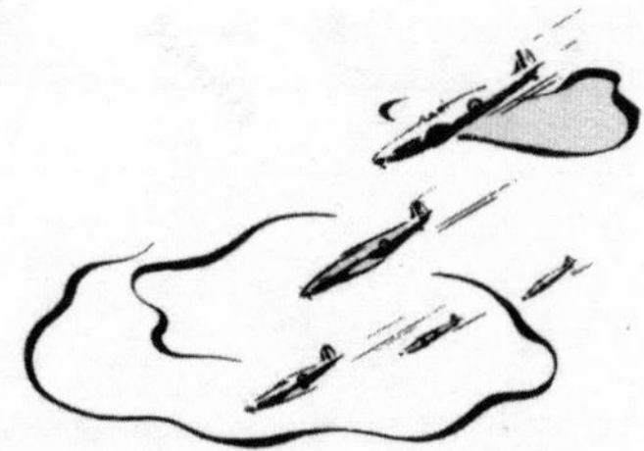

Tally-Ho——

The dotted line has now become the diameter of the red circle. What fractions of the diameter of the circle are the lines A, B, C, D, E, and F?

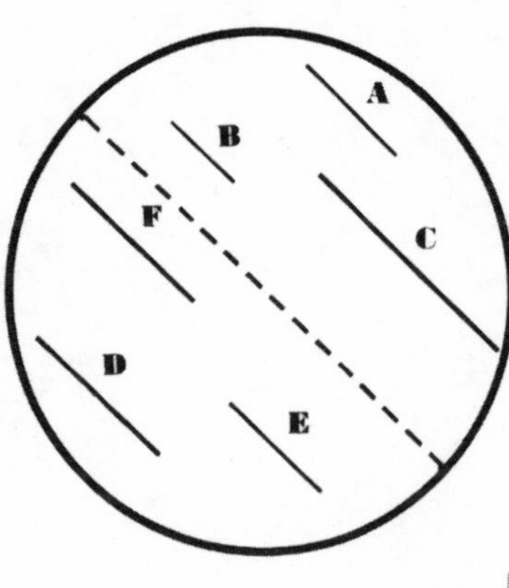

Solution

$A = \frac{1}{4}$ $B = \frac{1}{6}$

$C = \frac{1}{2}$ $D = \frac{1}{3}$

$E = \frac{1}{4}$ $F = \frac{1}{3}$

—and funnily enough, it worked . . . .

From this point onwards the dotted line, which was drawn in as the diameter of the ring, is omitted and can appear only in your imagination.

Now state what fractions of this diameter are represented by the lines A, B, C, D, and E.

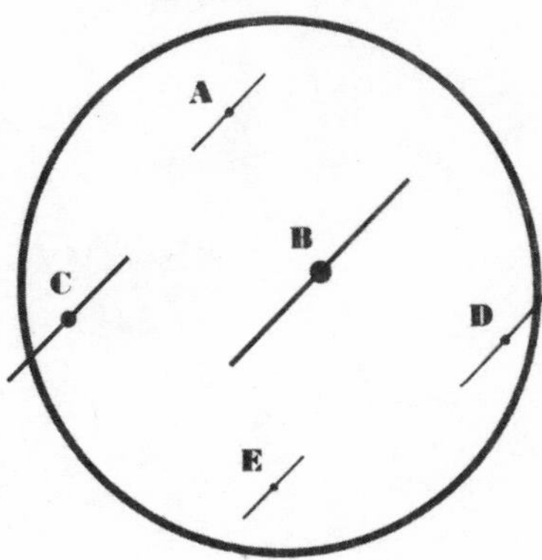

$A = \frac{1}{5}$ $B = \frac{1}{2}$

$C = \frac{1}{3}$ $D = \frac{1}{4}$

$E = \frac{1}{6}$

that's when I let him have it . . . .

The ring has now become the sight ring. The lines will shortly appear as Fw 190's. The span of a Fw 190 (and Me 109, too) is such that it appears equal to a diameter of a ring when it is 100 yds. away, half a diameter when it is 200 yds. away, and so on.

In future, then, instead of 1/2 state 200 yds.

1/3	300 yds.
1/4	400 yds.
1/5	500 yds.
1/6	600 yds.

You will then be giving the range of the Fw 190.

This method is definitely dated . . . .

Now the Hun has appeared. You ought to know what to do to estimate his range. Jot down your answers.

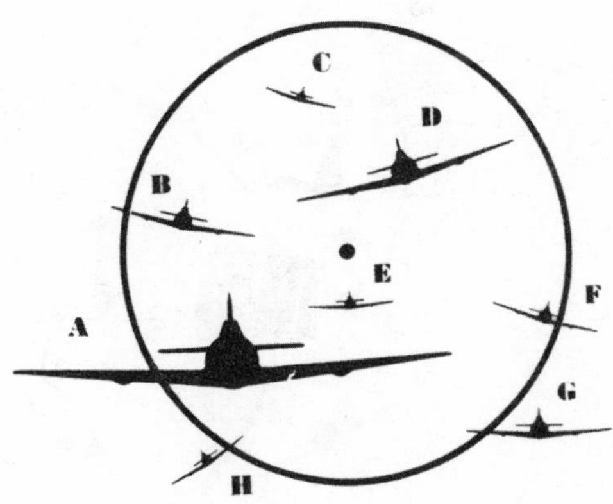

A = 100 yds. B = 300 yds. C = 600 yds.

D = 200 yds. E = 500 yds. F = 400 yds.

G = 300 yds. H = 500 yds.

The Hun knew his range

Try these too

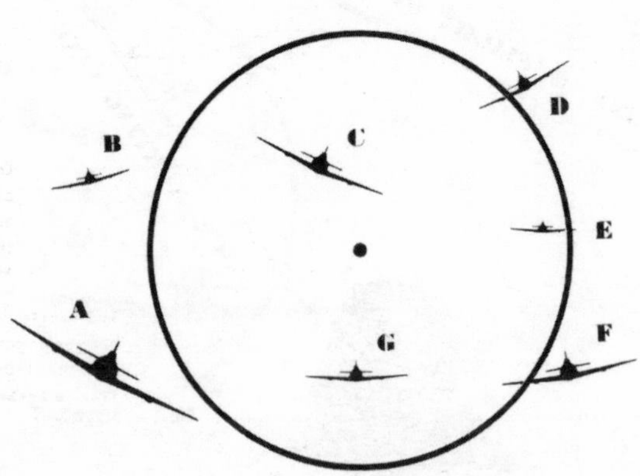

A=200 yds. B=500 yds.

C=300 yds. D=400 yds.

E=600 yds. F=300 yds.

G=400 yds.

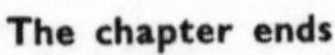

The chapter ends

CHAPTER 2

ESTIMATION of DEFLECTION

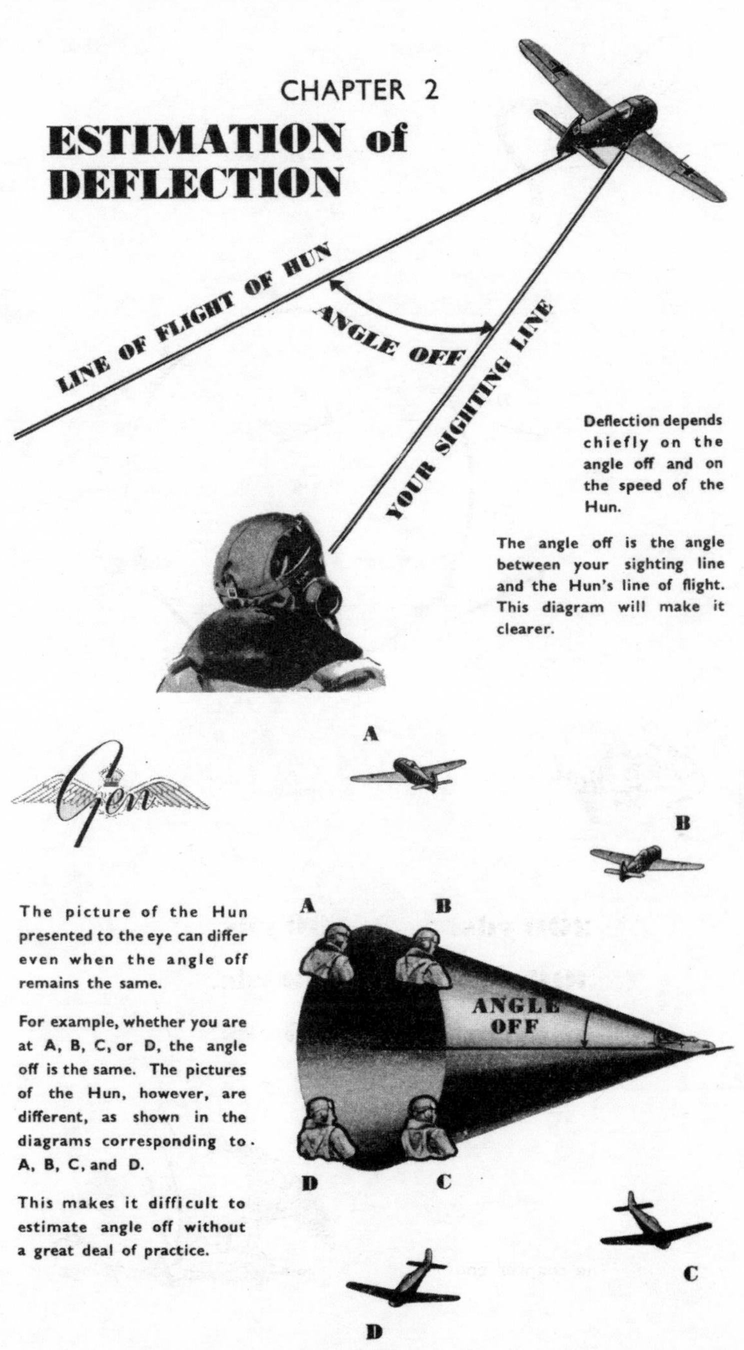

Deflection depends chiefly on the angle off and on the speed of the Hun.

The angle off is the angle between your sighting line and the Hun's line of flight. This diagram will make it clearer.

The picture of the Hun presented to the eye can differ even when the angle off remains the same.

For example, whether you are at A, B, C, or D, the angle off is the same. The pictures of the Hun, however, are different, as shown in the diagrams corresponding to A, B, C, and D.

This makes it difficult to estimate angle off without a great deal of practice.

ANGLE OFF

Make yourself familiar with these pictures

Jot down what you think are

C

D

E

G

F

the angles off for these planes

H

Solution

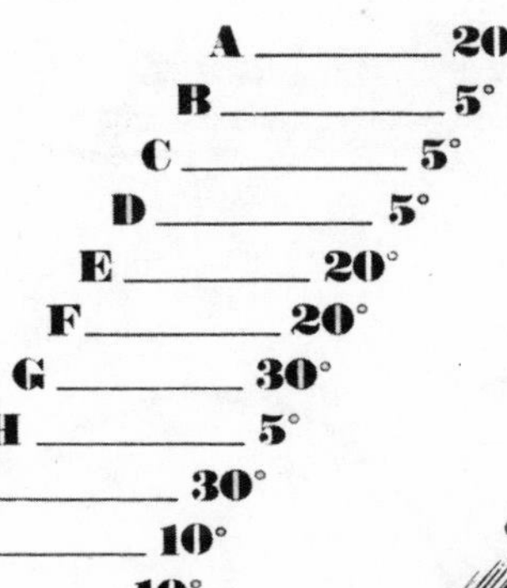

A ________ 20°
B ________ 5°
C ________ 5°
D ________ 5°
E ________ 20°
F ________ 20°
G ________ 30°
H ________ 5°
I ________ 30°
J ________ 10°
K ________ 10°
L ________ 30°

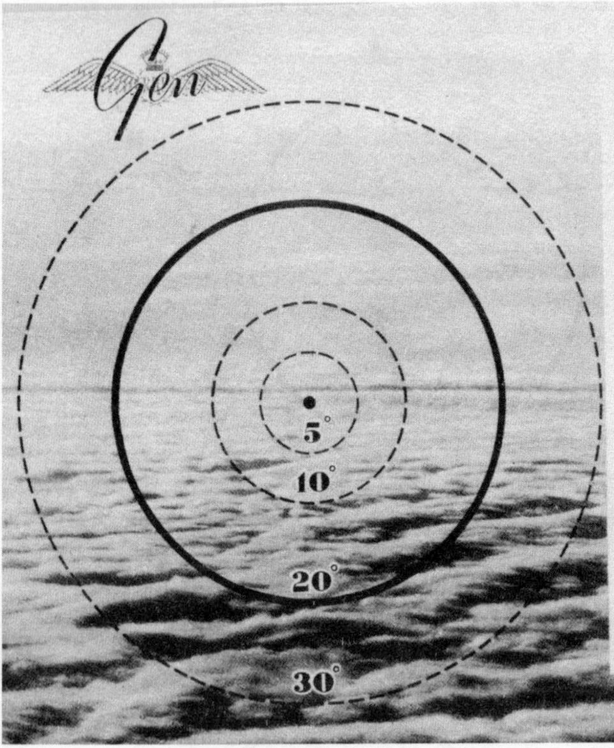

Gen

5°

10°

20°

30°

This diagram shows where the target ought to appear in the sight ring, according to the angle off. The nose of the target should touch the appropriate circle. (Notice that for 20° angle off, this circle is the sight ring).

Note—The diagram is almost exactly correct, under average combat conditions, for ·303 in. ammunition against a 300 m.p.h. target, or for 20 mm. ammunition against a 350 m.p.h. target. A change in target speed of 50 m.p.h. alters these allowances by only one-sixth, and deviations from the assumed combat conditions alter the allowances even less. Such variations are nearly always covered by the bullet pattern, and thus the scheme shown here covers a wide range of conditions.

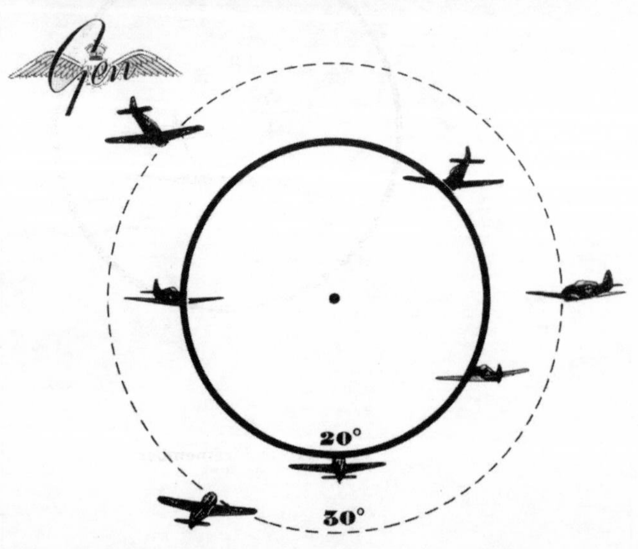

Diagrams on pp. 28, 29 and 30 show the Hun at various angles off, and with various appearances for the same angle off, positioned correctly. Study these carefully.

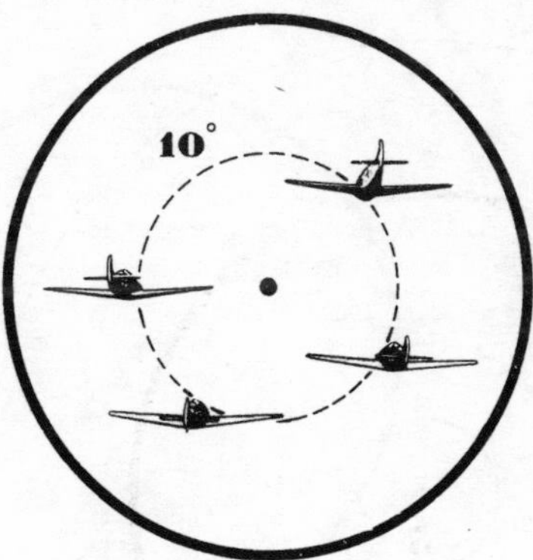

Combat films show that very often only half the correct allowance is made !

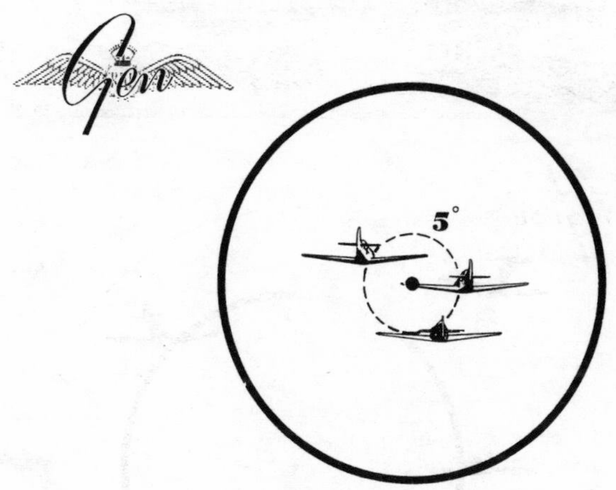

Study and remember

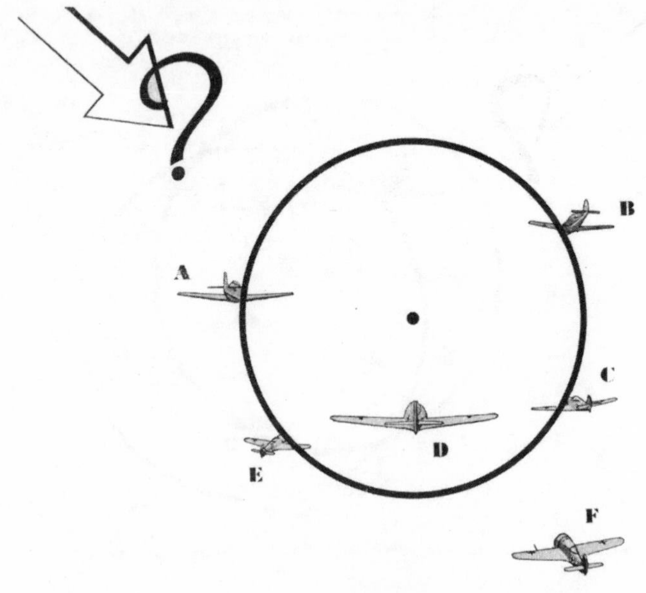

Some of these aircraft are positioned correctly: some are not. For each aircraft, estimate the angle off. Is correct deflection being made? If not, is it too great or too small?

Solution

	ANGLE OFF	DEFLECTION
A	10°	TOO GREAT
B	20°	O.K.
C	20°	O.K.
D	10°	O.K.
E	30°	TOO SMALL
F	30°	O.K.

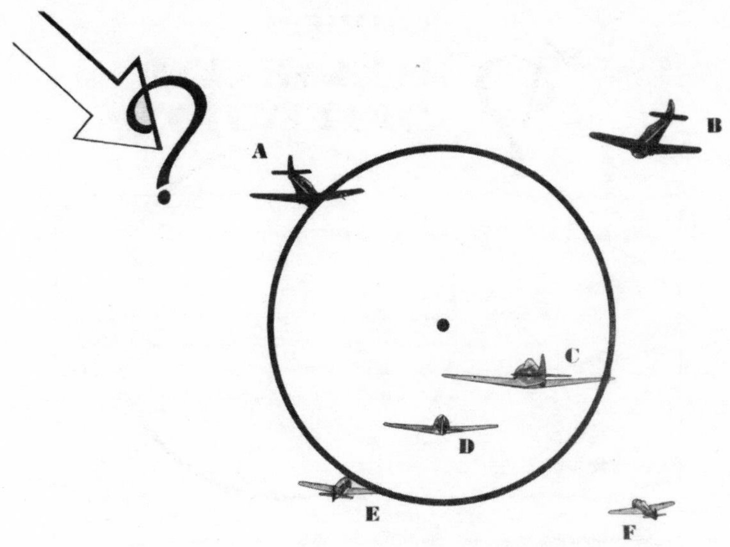

Try these exercises as well—you can't have too much practice!

	ANGLE OFF	DEFLECTION
A	20°	O.K.
B	30°	O.K.
C	10°	O.K.
D	10°	O.K.
E	20°	O.K.
F	30°	O.K.

CHAPTER 3

RANGE AND DEFLECTION

We now combine the work of the first two chapters.

1. Range

   Estimate the number of times the span of the Fw 190 goes into the diameter of the sight ring. The range is that number of hundreds of yards. This method holds even when the angle off is as large as 30°. Remember always to concentrate on the span of the aircraft.

2. Deflection.

   Estimate the angle off and position the enemy aircraft accordingly.

With practice these two operations should become one.

Look at these. You may not believe it, but the range, the angles off, and the deflections are correct.

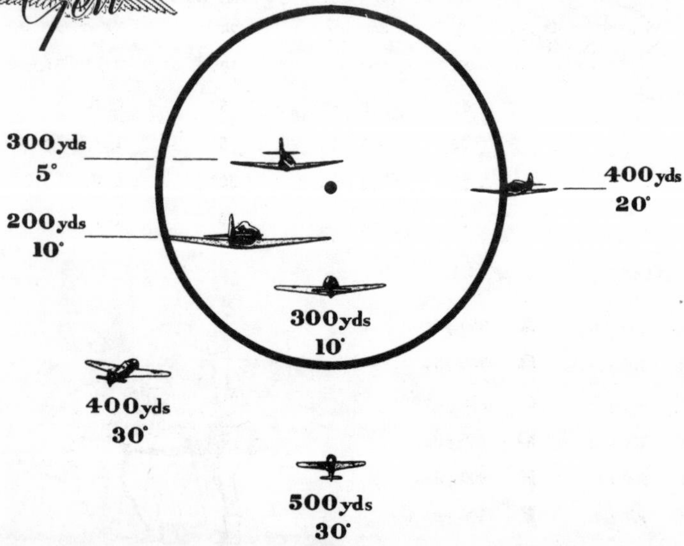

300 yds
5°

400 yds
20°

200 yds
10°

300 yds
10°

400 yds
30°

500 yds
30°

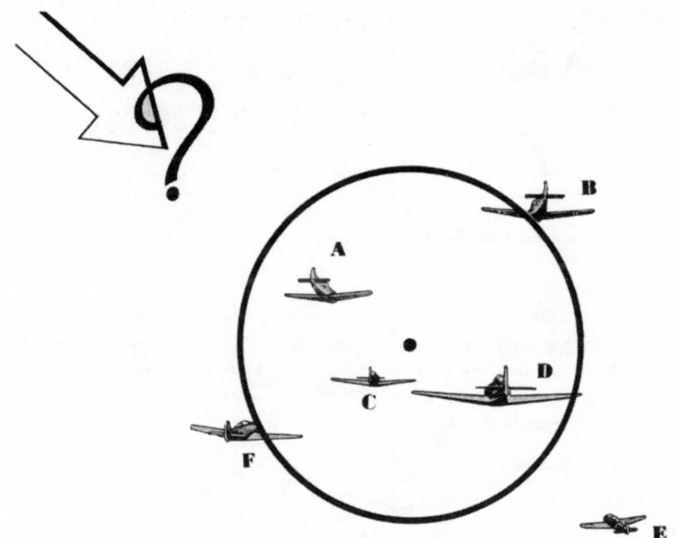

1. Estimate the ranges of the aircraft shown on pp. 31 and 33.
2. Try your hand now at estimating the ranges and the angles off in this diagram. Is the deflection correct, too great, or too small ?

Solution

	RANGE	ANGLE OFF	DEFLECTION
A	400 yds.	20°	TOO SMALL
B	300 yds.	10°	TOO GREAT
C	400 yds.	5°	O.K.
D	200 yds.	5°	TOO GREAT
E	500 yds.	30°	O.K.
F	300 yds.	20°	O.K.

PAGE 31		PAGE 33	
A	300 yds.	A	300 yds.
B	400 yds.	B	300 yds.
C	400 yds.	C	200 yds.
D	200 yds.	D	300 yds.
E	500 yds.	E	400 yds.
F	300 yds.	F	500 yds.

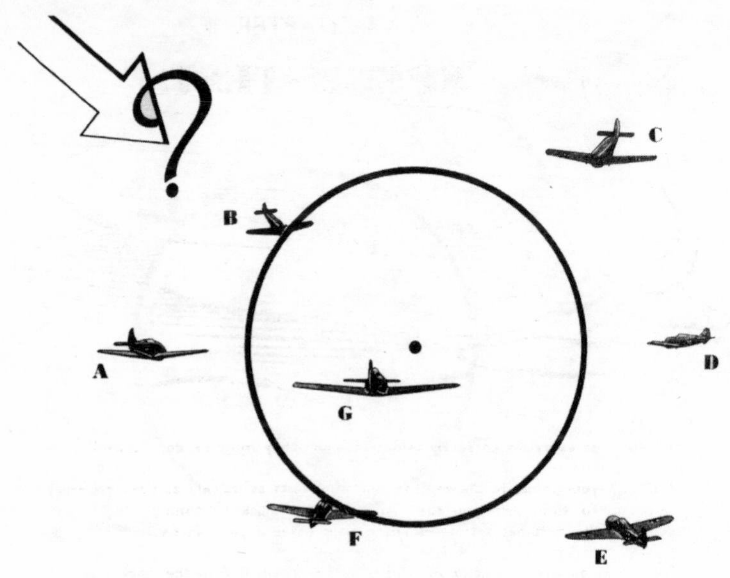

Now try these

Solution

	RANGE	ANGLE OFF	DEFLECTION
A	300 yds.	20°	TOO GREAT
B	500 yds.	30°	TOO SMALL
C	300 yds.	20°	TOO GREAT
D	500 yds.	45°	TOO SMALL
E	300 yds.	30°	O.K.
F	300 yds.	20°	O.K.
G	200 yds.	5°	O.K.

CHAPTER 4

SPEED TESTS

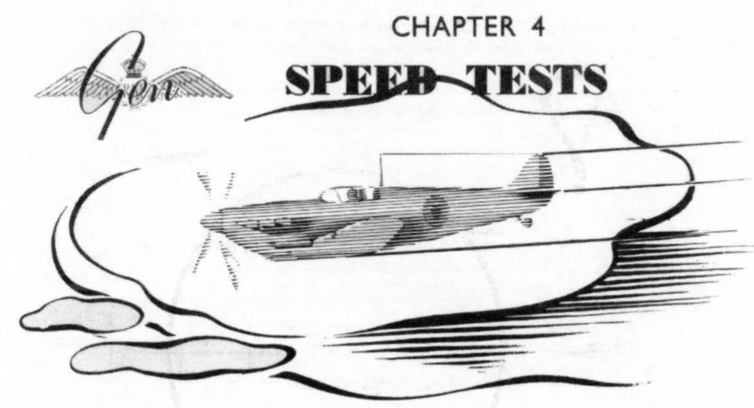

To do these exercises correctly is not enough; they must be done speedily.

Make up your mind to answer the following tests as quickly as possible. Get someone to time you—you can have your own back by timing him! Each test after the first has a time estimate given. See if you can beat it.

From now on use the celluloid ring which you will find in the pocket at the end of the book. Estimate the range of the aircraft shown, and the correct point of aim.

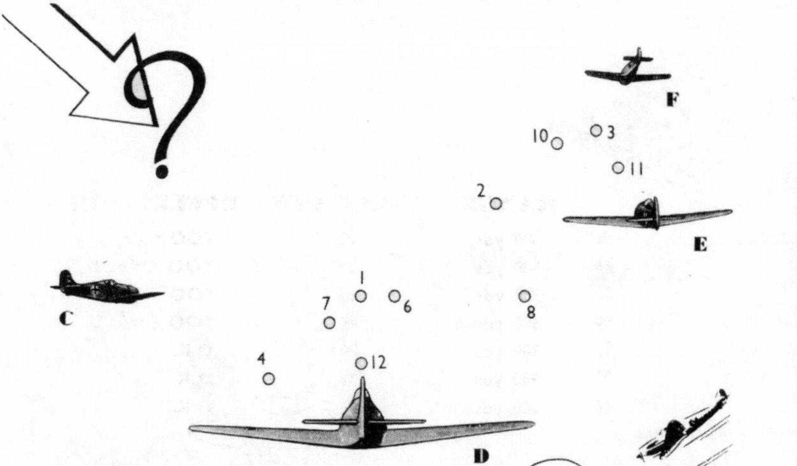

In the table below, fill in the range, and the number corresponding to what you think is the correct point of aim for each of the aircraft on the previous page. Although no time limit is set in this instance, bear in mind that, in the subsequent tests, you are fighting against time as well as the Hun.

Aircraft	A	B	C	D	E	F
Range						
Point of aim						

	RANGE	POINT OF AIM
A	200 yds.	5
B	300 yds.	7
C	300 yds.	8
D	100 yds.	12
E	200 yds.	3
F	400 yds.	2

<u>First speed test.</u> Complete the table as in previous exercise, but remember that you are being timed.

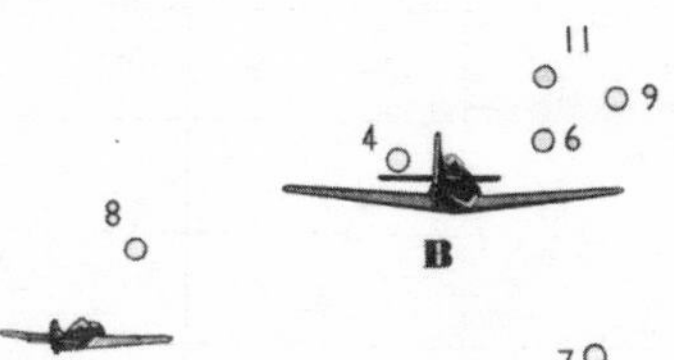

Aircraft	A	B	C	D	E	F
Range						
Point of aim						

	RANGE	POINT OF AIM
A	400 yds.	4
B	200 yds.	6
C	300 yds.	3
D	300 yds.	10
E	400 yds.	1
F	200 yds.	5

<u>IF</u> (a) you have less than 10 items correct, or
(b) you took more than 45 seconds, your performance is unsatisfactory.

<u>More practice is indicated.</u>

Beware the 'Waistammo' gremlins

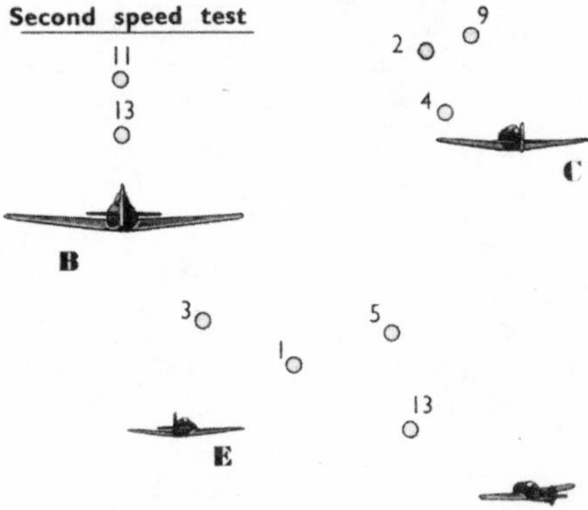

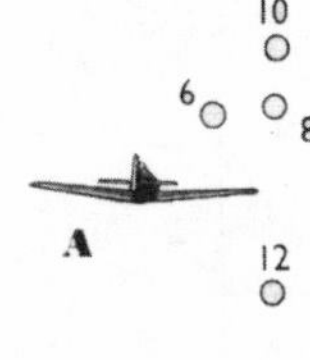

7

D

F

Aircraft	A	B	C	D	E	F
Range						
Point of aim						

	RANGE	POINT OF AIM
A	300 yds.	6
B	200 yds.	13
C	300 yds.	2
D	500 yds.	3
E	400 yds.	1
F	200 yds.	7

TIME 45 secs.

Fighter Pilots should—

BE MODEST

BE TOUGH

FLY LIKE ANGELS

AND SHOOT LIKE W/Cdr. W. TELL

FRONT GUN QUARTER ATTACK

a) FIRE BETWEEN 60° AND 20° ANGLE OFF

b) RED FIRES ON RED PORT ATTACK, GREEN ON GREEN STARBOARD ATTACK.

NOT TO SCALE

8

WARPLANES: A CARD GAME FOR AIRCRAFT SPOTTERS

From the outset, the skies over wartime England were full of aircraft engaged on various duties: defensive patrols, interceptions, engaging the enemy, training sorties, ferry flights, test flights, the list is endless. The aviation-minded craned their necks and strained their eyes skyward to catch a glimpse of Spitfires, Hurricanes, Flying Fortresses, Lancasters – and even enemy intruders like the He 111, Ju 88 and Stuka. A plethora of publications concerning aircraft recognition were produced, including these playing cards, issued early in the war, showing largely the silhouettes of popular service aircraft from various angles. The selection here illustrates those cards dealing with the Spitfire, Hurricane, Me 109 and 'He 113'. The latter was a propaganda spoof by the Germans, because although a very limited quantity of the type was built, none actually entered service. Nonetheless, this did not prevent numerous RAF fighter pilots reporting having fought them throughout the Battle of Britain! Clearly, therefore, there was a serious element to games involving aircraft recognition: research today indicates innumerable, often tragic, incidents of 'friendly fire' throughout the air war of 1939-45.

GERMAN AIRCRAFT

HEINKEL He 113

Single-seat Fighter (1,500 h.p. Daimler-Benz DB 601H motor). Estimated speed about 400 m.p.h. at 19,000 feet.

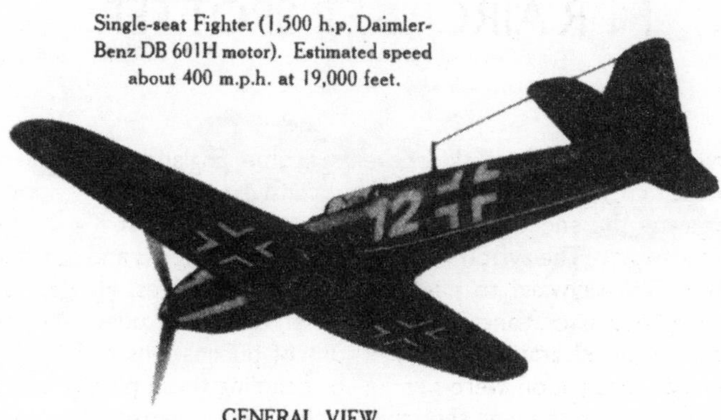

GENERAL VIEW

Recognised by straight-tapered wings with rounded tips. Cylindrical pointed nose.

ENDS

MESSERSCHMITT Me 109

Single-seat Fighter (1,150 h.p. Daimler-Benz DB 601 motor). Maximum speed 354 m.p.h. at 12,300 feet.

GENERAL VIEW

Recognised by square-cut low wings, broad nose, single fin and rudder.

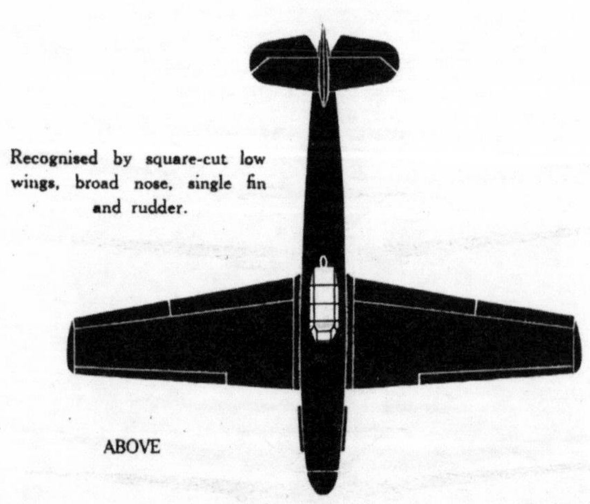

ABOVE

Recognised by square-cut low wings, broad nose, single fin and rudder.

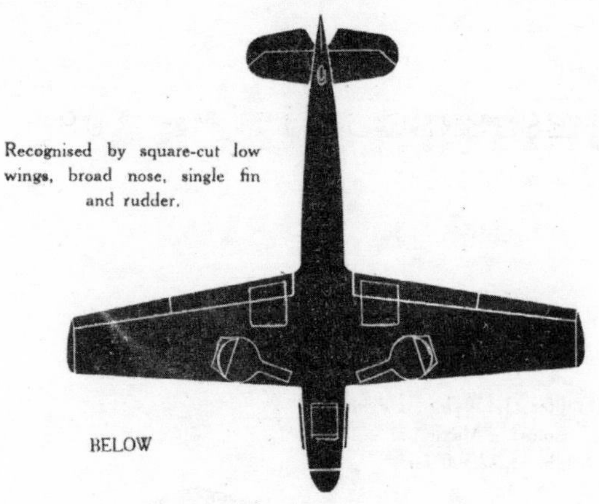

BELOW

Recognised by square-cut low wings, broad nose, single fin and rudder.

SIDE

Recognised by square-cut low wings, broad nose, single fin and rudder.

ENDS

BRITISH AIRCRAFT

Hawker HURRICANE

Single-seat 8-gun Fighter (1,030 h.p. Rolls-Royce Merlin II motor). Maximum speed 335 m.p.h. at 17,500 feet.

GENERAL VIEW

Recognised by straight tapered wings, radiator under centre section, rounded fin and rudder.

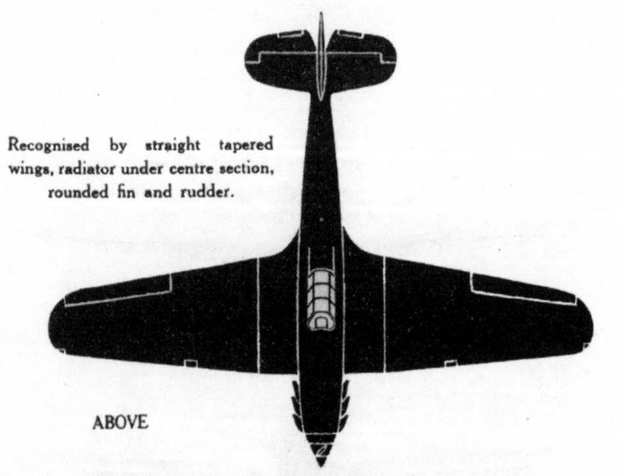

ABOVE

Recognised by straight tapered wings, radiator under centre section, rounded fin and rudder.

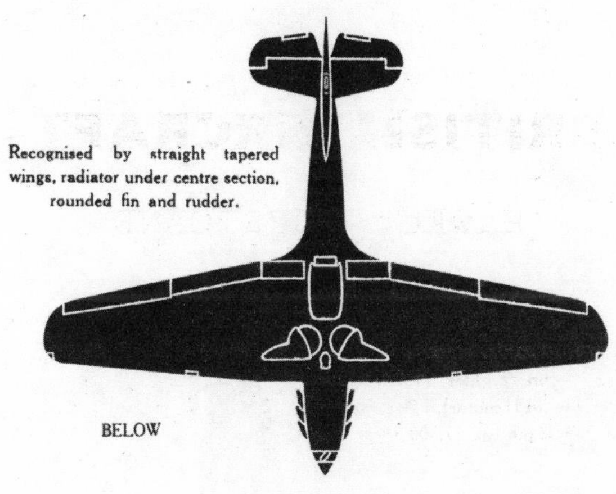

BELOW

Recognised by straight tapered wings, radiator under centre section, rounded fin and rudder.

SIDE

Recognised by straight tapered wings, radiator under centre section, rounded fin and rudder.

Supermarine SPITFIRE

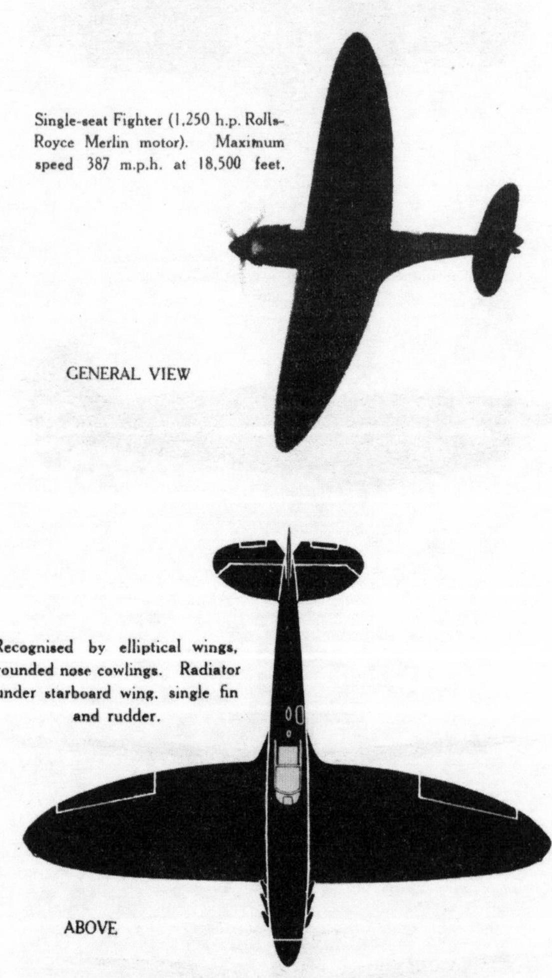

Single-seat Fighter (1,250 h.p. Rolls-Royce Merlin motor). Maximum speed 387 m.p.h. at 18,500 feet.

GENERAL VIEW

Recognised by elliptical wings, rounded nose cowlings. Radiator under starboard wing, single fin and rudder.

ABOVE

Recognised by elliptical wings, rounded nose cowlings. Radiator under starboard wing, single fin and rudder.

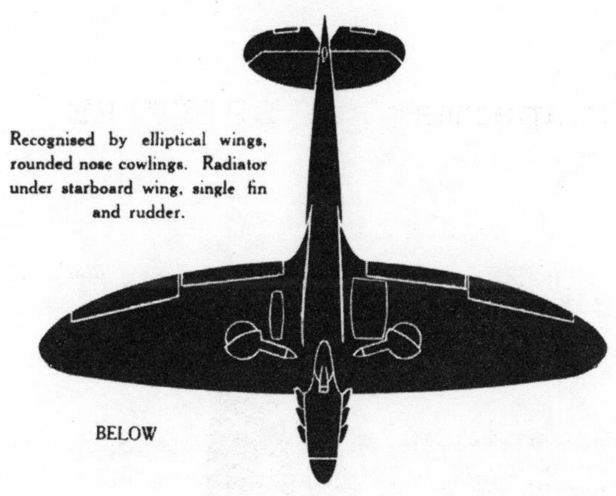

BELOW

Recognised by elliptical wings, rounded nose cowlings. Radiator under starboard wing, single fin and rudder

SIDE

Recognised by elliptical wings, rounded nose cowlings. Radiator under starboard wing, single fin and rudder.

ENDS

ACKNOWLEDGEMENTS

Firstly, this book was not my idea but that of my publisher, Jonathan Reeve, whose enthusiasm for such projects matches my own.

Secondly, my great friends, sadly the now late Air Vice-Marshal Johnnie Johnson, and his son, Chris, have always been extremely generous with documents and photographs concerning 'Greycap's' wartime service, and hence the inclusion of the extracts from the great man's log books here.

Thirdly, all of the Spitfire pilots quoted in this book are, or were when they were alive, friends of mine, always supporting my work with their time, patience and enthusiasm. The record compiled of their memories provides history with a rich primary source – and will be in use, I daresay, long after I too have departed to the great Sector Station in the sky.

Also available from Amberley Publishing

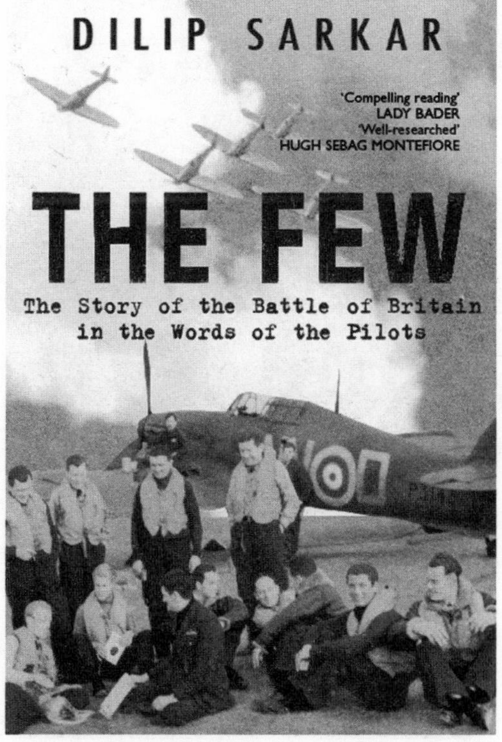

The history of the Battle of Britain in the words of the pilots

'Over the last 30 years Dilip Sarkar has sought out and interviewed or corresponded with numerous survivors worldwide. Many of these were not famous combatants, but those who formed the unsung backbone of Fighter Command in 1940. Without Dilip's patient recording and collation of their memories, these survivors would not have left behind a permanent record.' LADY BADER

'A well-researched detailed chronicle of the Battle of Britain'. HUGH SEBAG MONTEFIORE

£20 Hardback
100 photographs
336 pages
978-1-84868-215-3

Available from all good bookshops or to order direct
Please call **01285-760-030**
www.amberley-books.com